EMERGING HORIZONS IN INDIA-VIETNAM RELATIONS

EMERGING HORIZONS IN INDIA-VIETNAM RELATIONS

Editors

Shakti Sinha

Sonu Trivedi

PENTAGON PRESS

The book has been published with the partial support received from Indian Council of World Affairs.

Emerging Horizons in India-Vietnam Relations
Editors: Shakti Sinha and Sonu Trivedi

ISBN 978-93-86618-37-5

First Published in 2018

Published by
PENTAGON PRESS
206, Peacock Lane, ShahpurJat
New Delhi-110049
Phones: 011-64706243, 26491568
Telefax: 011-26490600
email: rajan@pentagonpress.in
website: www.pentagonpress.in

Printed at Aegean Offset Printers, Greater Noida

Contents

Acknowledgements

This book focuses on the emerging horizons of India-Vietnam relations in the backdrop of the enduring partnership between the two countries which has progressed and matured over the years. Such an analysis would not have been possible without the inputs from the experts in the field of government, academia, researchers and media persons. In such an endeavour, the July 2017 International Conference on 'Emerging Horizons in India-Vietnam Relations' provided a forum for such deliberations to take place. A few of the papers presented at the conference have been complied in this book to serve as a future source of references for the scholars studying the dynamics of relationship between the two countries of India and Vietnam.

We take this opportunity to thank all our partners, Indian Council of World Affairs (ICWA), Indian Council of Cultural Relations (ICCR), Indian Council of Social Science Research (ICSSR), and Embassy of the Socialist Republic of Vietnam for facilitating this event and providing the required financial support. The Conference was organized by the Southeast Asia Research Group (SEARG), University of Delhi in association with Nehru Memorial Museum and Library (NMML), New Delhi. Our volunteers (SEARG) and staff members (NMML) put in that extra effort that made the impossible, possible. A big thank you.

We are also thankful to all the contributors of this volume for their insights and well researched papers. Compilation and editing would not have been completed without the help of Dr. Debdatta Chatterjee and Suhasini Sinha, who worked tirelessly on the entire manuscript given the pressing deadlines. Our special appreciation goes to the efforts of our publisher Mr Rajan Arya and his entire team for publishing the book and making it available for the readers.

SHAKTI SINHA
SONU TRIVEDI

Abbreviations

ADIZ	Air Defence Identification Zone
ADMM+	ASEAN Defense Ministers Meeting Plus
AEC	ASEAN Economic Community
AEP	Act East Policy
AIFTA	ASEAN-India Free Trade Agreement
AIIB	Asia Infrastructure Investment Bank
AITIG	ASEAN-India Bilateral Trade in Goods Agreement
ALH	Advanced Light Helicopter
APEC	Asia Pacific Economic Cooperation
APSC	ASEAN Political-Security Community
ARF	ASEAN Regional Forum
ASCC	ASEAN Socio-Cultural Community
ASEAN	Association of Southeast Asian Nations
ASEM	Asia-Europe Meeting
BMISTEC	Bay of Bengal initiative for Multi-Sectoral Technical and Economic Cooperation
BRI	Belt Road Initiative
C4ISR	Command, Control, Command, Computers, Intelligence, Surveillance, Reconnaissance
CARC	Common Archival Resource Centre
CLCS	Commission on the Limits of the Continental Shelf
CLMV	Cambodia, Laos, Myanmar, Vietnam
CoC	Code of Conduct
CPV	Communist Party Vietnam
DoC	Declaration on the Conduct of Parties
DRDO	Defence Research and Development Organisation

DRV	Democratic Republic of Vietnam
EAMF	Expanded ASEAN Maritime Forum
EAS	East Asia Summit
EEP	Educational Exchange Programme
EEZ	Exclusive Economic Zone
ESCAP	Economic and Social Commission for Asia and Pacific
FDI	Foreign Direct Investment
FICCI	Federation of Indian Chambers of Commerce and Industry
FON	Freedom of Navigation
FTA	Free Trade Agreements
GCSS	General Cultural Scholarship Scheme
GoI	Government of India
HADR	Humanitarian Assistance and Disaster Relief
HPA	Hanoi Programme of Action
ICC	International Control Commission
IMF	International Monetary Fund
IPCC	Intergovernmental Panel on Climate Change
ISDR	International Strategy for Disaster Reduction
ITEC	India Technical and Economic Cooperation
JWG	Joint Working Group
LDCs	Least Developed Countries
LEP	Look East Policy
MDGS	Millennium Development Goals
MGC	Mekong Ganga Cooperation
MIDCOM	Malaysia-India Defence Cooperation Meeting
MoU	Memorandum of Understanding
MPAC	Master Plan on ASEAN Connectivity
MTCR	Missile Technology Control Regime
NAM	Non-Aligned Movement
NCNST	National Centre for Natural Science and Technology
NHIDCL	National Highway Infrastructure Development Corp. Ltd.
OECD	Organisation of Economic Cooperation and Development
ONGC	Oil and Natural Gas Corporation
ONVL	ONGC Videsh Ltd.
PRC	People's Republic of China
PTI	Press Trust of India
RCEP	Regional Comprehensive Economic Partnership

RTIA	ASEAN-India Regional Trade and Investment Area
SATI	State Agency for Technology Innovation
SCS	South China Sea
SLOCs	Sea Lines of Communications
TPP	Trans-Pacific Partnership
UAV	Unmanned Aerial Vehicles
UNCLOS	UN Convention on the International Law of the Sea
UNISDR	United Nations International Strategy for Disaster Reduction
UNSC	United Nations Security Council
USAID	United States Agency for International Development
VEFTA	Vietnam-European Union Free Trade Agreement
WSSD	World Summit on Sustainable Development
WTO	World Trade Organization

List of Tables and Figures/Maps

TABLES

FIGURES

MAPS

About the Contributors

Abira Bhattacharya, Assistant Curator, National Museum, New Delhi.

Athira Anand, Assistant Professor, School of Distance Education, University of Calicut.

Bharti Chhibber, Assistant Professor, Lakshmibai College, University of Delhi.

Dhrubajyoti Bhattacharjee, Research Fellow, Indian Council of World Affairs, New Delhi.

Do Thu Ha, Head, Faculty of Oriental Studies, Vietnam National University, Hanoi.

Huynh Thanh Loan, Deputy Head, Department of International Relations, Vietnam Institute for Indian and Southwest Asian Studies, Vietnam Academy of Social Sciences.

Munmun Majumdar, Associate Professor, Department of Political Science, North Eastern Hill University, Shillong.

Nguyen Phu Tan Huong, Vice Dean, Faculty of International Politics and Diplomacy Diplomatic Academy of Vietnam, Ministry of Foreign Affairs, Vietnam.

Nguyen Tran Tien, Deputy Dean - Faculty of Oriental Studies, University of Social Sciences and Humanities, Hanoi.

Nguyen Van Lich, Department of International Economics Diplomatic Academy of Vietnam.

Om Prakash Dahiya, Assistant Professor, Zakir Husain Delhi College (Evening), University of Delhi.

Ram Madhav, Director, India Foundation and National General Secretary, Bhartiya Janata Party.

Rashmi Singh, Associate Economist, PHD Chamber of Commerce and Industry, New Delhi.

Shubham Singh, Research Scholar, Department of English and Modern European Languages, University of Lucknow.

Subhadeep Bhattacharya, Research Assistant, Netaji Institute for Asian Studies, Kolkata.

Ton Sinh Thanh, Ambassador of the Socialist Republic of Vietnam to India.

Introduction

Shakti Sinha

Speaking in Washington DC in October 2017, the US Secretary of State, Rex Tillerson made very significant observations about the rise of two countries, China and India. The rise of China is, of course, far more impressive in terms of numbers. However, China is rising by increasingly violating the letter and spirit of international rules, the very same rules that have enabled China's rise. These rules of international law include the law of the seas as we have seen in the South China Sea, the island building, the blatant violation of national sovereignty of Philippines, of Vietnam, and of Malaysia. In 2016, following the seventh visit of His Holiness the Dalai Lama to Mongolia, China in retaliation effectively shut down Mongolia for one full week. It prevented its access to the world. It was a complete violation of international law because landlocked countries have an inherent right of access.

On the other hand, Tillerson praised the role of India as a responsible country. It is not that India has not had border disputes with its smaller neighbours. Take the case of the Indo-Bangladesh maritime boundary, which went to the international tribunal under the UN Convention on the Law of the Seas. The tribunal in June 2014 ruled 70 percent in Bangladesh's favour and 30 percent in India's favour. And the Indian government accepted that tribunal order, without any fuss. In fact, there was no public controversy or criticism on this issue. Being a responsible member of the international community, India follows the international norms. Unlike the China-Philippines case, India did not reject an unfavourable verdict, nor did it challenge the legality of the proceedings. So, in other words, India sees itself as a responsible country growing within the rules because it realises that if there were no commonly-accepted international rules, then the big will always get away with bullying the small. On the other hand, speaking at Hanoi in 2013, in the context of the disputes in the South China Sea, the Chinese State Councillor Yang Jiechi told at the ASEAN meeting that they should just accept that China was a big country and they were small and that was it.

India does not think that it is a right way to deal with inter-country disputes or relations. India feels that its emergence as a leading power is contingent on following certain acceptable rules. Though some of the rules of the game, made by the winners of World War II and the Cold War are stacked against countries like China, India and Vietnam, to give three examples, who wish to see themselves occupy their place in the sun, is a reality. This is a fair criticism of the international system. However, in order to avoid falling into the Thucydides Trap, the way forward lies in negotiations between stakeholders, if necessary by creating new platforms like BRICS, RCEP, etc., and by demonstrating yourself to be a strong economy. If a country's economy is strong and it seen as contributing to global growth, if not being a driver of global growth, then others listen to it much more. It is not just about having a strong military, because military power of a country can only bully a neighbour; but not a nation far away, very easily. But if a country has a strong economy and is recognised as a strong responsible member of the international community, then its voice is heard.

At the Paris climate change talks, India played a constructive and responsible role in bringing about consensus. It agreed to make considerable sacrifices to achieve a better future for the world despite the fact that its per capita income is only around US $2000, and despite the fact that on per capita basis, India's emissions are extremely low. It demonstrated the imperative to work with everybody and not seek special treatment, however, justified. The appropriate analogy is of asking a person eating less than two full meals a day to sacrifice some of her food so that somebody else wasting enormous amounts of food is persuaded to waste less. India's emergence must be seen in this context.

The trouble with marking the emergence of a new world order, identified as belonging to the 21st century, is that we really don't know when the new century started. Even though 1st of January 2000 is just a date on the calendar, but can one truly saw that it was anything more than that, other than it being the last day to have sorted out the Y2K problem? According to many, the 21st century started as early as 1979 when the rules of the game were changed with the Soviet Union sending its troops into Afghanistan. It led to many things, mostly unintended. Primarily, it marked the beginning of the end of the Cold War, which culminated in 1991 with the dissolution of the Soviet Union and America's unilateral moment. For too many, the 21st century is actually just beginning with the age of Artificial Intelligence and the Internet of Things. This is something the young generation should be really worried about on the one hand, and on the other, it is also a tremendous opportunity. To put it in context, Maruti's new factory with less than one-tenth of workforce of its earlier plants is able to manufacture more cars. That simply means that we can do more with less. Well, it gives human beings more leisure time, but where would employment come from? So, while modern technology does gives a way out, it also poses a very serious challenge in talk of demographic dividend.

But to go back to the story, when did the 21st century start? And I would argue that it started in September 2008 with the collapse of Lehman Brothers in the United States, and the financial crisis which hit the United States, and then Europe. It pulled the world down, world trade stopped growing and that was the moment which convinced China and the resurgent Russia that America's unilateral moment of control of the world was over. On what basis is this claim made? In 2008, Georgia faced with the problem of the emergence of two de facto independent states of North Ossetia and Abkhazia, supported by Russia within its territory, tried to reassume sovereignty over rebel areas. Russia intervened militarily, stopped it by overwhelming the miniscule Georgian army. However, the Russians operated under a legal fiction of being "peacekeepers." They did not say that the Russian Army was intervening, only maintaining peace. And in international affairs, nuances and legal fictions are very important. In 2013, when the Ukraine trouble started, the Russian Army walked into Crimea, held a referendum within three days and "incorporated" Crimea into Russia. Subsequently, Russia took over de facto control over East Ukraine, though here it continues to maintain a degree of deniability. However, unlike 2008, the Russians aggressively and unilaterally changed facts on the ground, and defended their actions vigorously. Similarly China, which had earlier agreed to move with ASEAN on the Code of Conduct for parties in the South China Sea, now not only refuse to talk about it, but has aggressively changed facts on the ground/seas by creating artificial islands in the disputed seas and militarising them.

Similarly in 2008, President Bush was able to pressurise China into agreeing to give India a permanent waiver at the Nuclear Suppliers Group (NSG), which would enable India to be an active partner in the international field of buying and selling nuclear technology. But in recent years, as India tried to become a member of the NSG, China has been successful in stalling it, and even in creating a "coalition of the willing" that has become a roadblock. In short, China and Russia in 2008 were willing to listen to the United States, work with consensus etc., but after a few years, have become less inclined to do so. These are the kind of changes happening in the world that one has to be conscious of. India's immediate neighbourhood and larger region are difficult and challenging, made more complicated for the simple reason that the weight of the global economy and, therefore, the global strategic forces has shifted towards the Indo-Pacific.

The economist Angus Maddison has arrived at GDP figures of earlier centuries. These are based on reasonable assumptions but should not be confused with rigorous statistical data that modern countries routinely collect, collate and disseminate. It is clear that India and China were very big, no doubt about it; the largest economies though the exact percentages are not available. But now we have the numbers, and shift happening can be seen. This is in itself, is a good thing that is happening, a natural correction. Look under per capita basis, China and India, particularly the latter are still very far behind the western countries. Among the emerging countries, China is considered an emerged country with its per capita income in excess of US $10,000. China's massive GDP of US $11 trillion and sustained growth rates has made it a big driver of global growth. India is comparatively speaking a smaller driver, but growing important each year. As the focus is shifting towards the Indo-Pacific, the challenges before countries in the region are growing.

The global shift in economic weight towards the Indo-Pacific and the general belief that the US is retrenching is made more complicated by the changes in China's profile, economically and strategically. Further, Xi Jinping's name and his thoughts are part of the constitution of the Communist Party of China (CCP), a rare happening; in fact, even the Belt and Road Initiative has been mentioned in the constitution. China, as Xi Jinping said in his marathon speech at the 19th Congress in Beijing on October 18, 2017, aims to be "a nation with pioneering global influence" by 2050. Clearly, this is a serious challenge for ASEAN, Vietnam, India and others as China is operating in their immediate neighbourhood; it has deep pockets, it is willing to invest in these countries, it is prepared to meddle in internal affairs and even subvert established groupings like ASEAN. It is another matter that the terms of its investments are very dodgy, but that would be mostly a problem for the next generation.

In these circumstances, India doubtlessly feels constrained and to give credit to the government, it has been acting within these constraints with tremendous amount of flexibility and far-sightedness without becoming belligerent. In Doklam, India acted with tremendous amount of restraint. The language being used against India on a daily basis by the Chinese government was absolutely objectionable, well beyond all diplomatic norms, but not once did India raise its voice. And yet at the end of the day, India made the point that China could not build a road on disputed territory and status quo was ensured. The Chinese stand was rigid - that India should first withdraw, and then there could be negotiation on the status quo. The Indian stand was clear – status quo should be restored. And ultimately that is what happened. The point was established that it made sense in such extenuating circumstances that a country must remain firm and that being confident was absolutely important. By not resorting to shouting, and matching the Chinese word to word was equally important. Most importantly that being seen as a responsible player, and not getting provoked into speaking and/or acting rashly was necessary because credibility is critical at the end of the day. A country, as much as an individual should be taken seriously because words and action must be consistent with each other. But if it says one thing and means something else, others would trust it less and be more suspicious. And, therefore, credibility should be established.

In these circumstances, India behaved itself in a mature manner and that is something for the others to learn. The second, of course, is that no country can exist in isolation, and try to sort out everything by itself. Hence, while many analysts say that India has entered into strategic alliances, this would not be correct. India does not enter into alliances, but what it does have strategic partnerships, or platforms of cooperation with a whole host of actors. India, Japan, and the USA carry out the annual Malabar exercises, which is in the field of the maritime operations. The experience of Malabar would be very useful if these partners were required to carry out Humanitarian Assistance and Disaster Relief (HADR) operations jointly, for example. There are other platforms of collaborations where on specific issues different countries can be co-opted in. In other words, each country retains its sovereignty; there is no question of surrender of sovereignty to either an institution like a military alliance or to a hegemon.

Joint or collaborative exercises like Malabar serve strategic purposes also. The Japanese Prime Minister, Shinzo Abe, made the point when he came to Delhi in 2007 and called for a Free and Open Indo-Pacific, joining the two oceans Indian and Pacific. And over the past years, he has talked about connectivity between the two continents, Asia and Africa, and in that, Tillerson also spoke up in favour of it. The fact is that countries of this region need large amounts of investment in infrastructure. That money is simply not available like in the past. Countries are desperately looking for money. The Chinese money looks very attractive but actually comes with very heavy terms. The Sri Lankans have found out how expensive the Hambantota Port project is going to be for them; they had to hand over control of the port to a Chinese government entity in addition to substantial land for setting up a Chinese industrial park. Pakistan has already found out how expensive the CPEC is going to be for them. They have pulled the US $14 billion Diamer-Bhasha Dam out of CPEC, though it was supposed to be its largest single component. The terms attached to CPEC projects were simply too onerous to make the project commercially viable. Similarly, three thermal power plants in Sindh (Tharpakar) are on hold for similar reasons. Guaranteeing rate of return of 14-20 percent on equity or debt rates hundreds of basis points above LIBOR cannot be paid out if the project is to be financially sustainable. This is where the Asia Pacific connectivity programme of India, Japan and now with the USA comes in. As its promoters have been at pains to point out, it would have been responsible financing. Further, it must follow the international norms on environment, it must be transparent, it must be with the participation of the communities concerned and it must respect national sovereignty. So, obviously these countries would not be writing cheques with hidden clauses and they won't be giving out suitcases of cash. But what it would do is accepting the host country as a sovereign equal, with whom they would work to move ahead. It would be slower to execute but would be environmentally and financially sustainable, carried out with the consent of the affected stakeholders.

This is the reason why India's rise is going be an incremental and not a sprint. It is not going to be an easy rise. One, it is a participative process, with lots of talks and dialogue which is a good thing. It would be full of disagreements and occasional roadblocks, which is also always not a bad thing.

But it would be able to generate consensus, which is not an easy job. Partisanship sometimes degenerates into outright hostility, which is something that certain democracies at different times have to cope up with. But a dispassionate look at the overall figures, at the trends in growth, the impact is strongly positive. There would be more disruptions to come because India since 2014 is trying to move from a system which was 70 percent informal to a system which becomes 90 percent formal. Circumstances that would lead to the universal payment of taxes have been created, courtesy the GST and the establishment of a unified market. And since cash is increasingly getting replaced by electronic money, there would be disruptions. At heart, people do not want to pay taxes, because they do not see the system delivering. People express abhorrence at corruption, but when something is held up, are prepared to pay a little bit of grease money to smoothen things. As the Nobel Prize winner in economics Richard Thaler says, governments and systems must nudge people on the right path. Behavioural change is never easy especially if led by the government, but it is absolutely essential to happen. India's emergence is happening slowly and unevenly with ups and downs, but is consistently on the move.

India is emerging as a serious player in the international field, and is seen as a player which is willing to engage with others, which does not look at size alone. In economies obviously size matters, but size alone cannot dictate nation-to-nation relationship. Vietnam has emerged as a natural partner since the two countries share similar world views. People has emphasised the ancient link between the two countries, shrouded in the misty past. They empathised with each other's anti-colonial struggle, and extended moral and diplomatic support, to the extent that India-ASEAN relations sunk to lows due to India's support to Vietnam's efforts to end mass killings in Cambodia, to give an example. These firm foundations needed to be built upon, and that has been done.

Essentially, these two countries' priorities are economic growth, abolition of poverty and improvement in the quality of lives of their citizens. They wish to live at peace with their neighbours and resolve disputes through negotiations and by increased understanding of the other side. Both recognise that successes should be built upon, areas of agreement enlarged and misunderstandings progressively reduced. That no dispute should hold up movement in other areas, since a zero-sum-game would hurt all. They do not look for disputes and do not indulge in provocative behaviour; rather they underplay it in the hope that a way forward could be arrived at without loss of face of any party. They do not wish to be part of any military alliance, Vietnam's "three nos" comes to mind, and would not like to be part of any group that is targeting a country. However, they are sensitive about national sovereignty, and are not frightened by disparity in sizes. They have stood their ground against vastly superior forces and honour those who have not surrendered despite all limitations, Vietnam's Trung sisters for example.

Significantly, they do not let the ghosts of the past bog them down; America's popularity in Vietnam is a case in point. They are realists driven by national goals, cited above, and sensitive to their autonomy, have not let their realism sink into cynicism. In fact, it is the opposite with hope and optimism in a better future driving their efforts.

Both have had very good working relations with China and have increased their economic links with that country. That should not be seen as their weakness, rather a desire to grow together and a realisation that war and hostility are obstacles to economic growth. They have no intention of either being part of any effort to encircle China, or even letting any desire to check China drive their bilateral relations. But if pushed, will not hesitate to work in concert with other powers to defend their interests.

This volume has fourteen detailed chapters looking at a whole range of issues plus a detailed conclusion by Sonu Trivedi and two short pieces by Ambassador Ton Sinh Tran and Shri Ram Madhav.

Huynh Thanh Loan's chapter *India in Vietnam's Foreign Policy in the New Context* analyses the changes and transitions in Vietnam's foreign policy, especially in relation to the changing equations with India and the growing role India plays in Vietnam's foreign policy. It concludes that Vietnam has increasingly put greater attention on India's rising role in the region and the world and a number of measures have been applied to strengthen the bilateral relations between the two countries. It primarily focuses on the core aspects and dimensions of Vietnam's foreign policy and India's role in it from the larger perspective of international relations.

Growing Significance of Vietnam in India's Act East Policy by Subhadeep Bhattacharya is in some manner a thematic continuation of the previous chapter. Bhattacharya emphasises on the element of revival on the part of the current Indian government in forging better relationship with the nations in the South-

Asian region including Vietnam. It examines this emerging relationship from the lens of the "Act East Policy" and argues that the necessity of balance of power in the region especially in relation to growing Chinese dominance is one of the primary triggering points behind the initiation of this historic step. Moving further, the paper talks about the various dimensions of this policy by the Indian government and the manner it has been implemented till date and the larger economic and geo-political ramifications and effects of the exercise.

Nguyen Phu Tan Huong's paper *Prominent Features of the Vietnam-India Comprehensive Strategic Partnership* centres on a prominent diplomatic development in India-Vietnam relations, namely the upgrading of relations between Vietnam and India from "strategic partnership" to "comprehensive strategic partnership" in September 2016 during Indian Prime Minister Narendra Modi's official visit to Vietnam. This has made India the third nation (after China and Russia) to enjoy this highest level in Vietnam's bilateral relations. Deploying the realist theory of international relations the author tries to comprehend the current scenario of the India-Vietnam relations. One of the central arguments of Huong is that since power is a relative concept, it requires continuous evolution and negotiation, and the tremendous development in the bilateral relations between India and Vietnam is a direct outcome of this where both countries are exploring mutually beneficial grounds in a completely volatile and competitive world.

In the paper titled India, *Vietnam and the South China Sea,* Munmun Majumdar chapter talks about the larger canvas of the India-Vietnam relations but her focal point is the growing maritime territorial disputes and the subsequent tensions in the South China Sea. This, the author argues, has been one of the strongest instigators between the tremendous growth in the relationship between India and Vietnam in the recent times as there are high stakes for both the nations in the region both from the perspective of security and economy. Majumdar argues that the present political regime in India has shown the maturity to identify this necessity and has been working in this direction especially from the perspective of developing cooperative and rule-based security architecture in the region that would in turn enhance regional and global security.

Dhrubajyoti Bhattacharjee's chapter *India and Vietnam: Defence and Strategic Cooperation* looks at the India-Vietnam relationship from the lenses of defence cooperation and strategic partnership between the two countries. Hinting at the shift in power positions both globally and especially in the

South China Sea, Bhattacharjee talks about the concept of systemic stability and the crucial importance of regional alliances in this regard and to which India-Vietnam relationship is not an exception. Moving on the paper discusses the various steps in this regard and especially the ones in the recent times like the US$500 million credit line which India has provided Vietnam for the purpose of developing its defence sector. The author argues that India-Vietnam relationship is a time-tested one and that the strategic cooperation between the two countries is both a continuation of the past in new forms and also a necessity of the present times.

Om Prakash Dahiya's chapter *India-Vietnam Maritime Cooperation: An Indian Perspective* seeks to identify the opportunities and challenges for India and Vietnam to strengthen and expand maritime cooperation. One of the crucial arguments of the author is that naval diplomacy is crucial to build and maintain trust and that it contributes towards conflict prevention and resolution. The paper also examines the convergences to promote cooperation in bilateral as well as multilateral forum like ASEAN. This paper looks at the subject in three sections. First it looks at the history of the decade of strategic cooperation between the two countries. Moving on it studies the template of India's various successful defence agreements to see what can be replicable in case of India-Vietnam relations and then concludes by suggesting areas for future cooperation. The effort here is also to bring out the possible areas of cooperation where the bilateral perspectives overlap.

India-Vietnam Bilateral Economic Ties: The Road Ahead by Rashmi Singh looks at the bilateral relations between India and Vietnam from the lens of the economy. The initial part of the paper looks at the macroeconomic performance of both the countries and highlights the major blocks of both the economy. Commenting on the current state of affairs the paper argues that though the relationship is based on a set of historical commonalities it has been moving towards addressing shared strategic concerns of energy security. And that both the countries can act as facilitators of economic growth for the other. While Vietnam can help in materialising India's Act East Policy, India can act as a great balancing in the larger aspect of Vietnam's relationship with nations like China especially keeping in mind the changing dynamics in the South China Sea. Using a number of economic tools the paper examines the various aspects (including the impending challenges) of this economic relationship between the two countries and suggests that a proactive approach on the part of both countries is mutually beneficial.

As the very title suggests *Solutions to Promote Economic Relations between Vietnam and India* by Nguyen Van Lich and Nguyen Minh Trang talks about the various means to further enhance and boost the already growing economic relations between India and Vietnam. At the beginning this chapter lists the primary efforts which have been taken in the direction of improving economic cooperation. It then moves on to discuss the persistent difficulties and limitations in the relationship in the present times such as high tax rates, corruption, poor infrastructure, etc., and comments that the economic cooperation between the two countries have grown in recent years. But the results have been modest compared to the potential and desires of both sides. As far as the solutions to these problems are concerned, the paper takes a multiple directional approach by talking about the economic-political solutions and also about the specific tasks to be undertaken by the states and also the business community of both the countries.

Nguyen Tran Tien's chapter *India and China: Vietnam's Neighbourhood Issues in the New Regional Context* is primarily concerned with understanding the balancing act by Vietnam while maintaining relationships with its powerful neighbours especially India and China. The paper presents a history of Vietnam's relation with its neighbours and tries to explain how it negotiates within this complex power corridor especially in a situation where the relationship between its powerful neighbours is strained at times. The paper looks at the various dimensions of Vietnam's foreign policy approach in the current changing context where it is trying to diversify its international relationships with forging better relationships with countries like India but at the same time is extremely cautious of not openly adopting an unfriendly attitude towards China.

Bharti Chhibber's chapter *Mekong-Ganga Cooperation and India-Vietnam Relations* through the Prism of Act East Policy examines the shifting historical trajectory of India's Look East Policy and existing contours of India's foreign policy which defines India's role in Southeast Asia. In this context she argues that this reinvigoration of Look East Policy into Act East Policy is a clear message that cooperation between India and the ASEAN countries, including Vietnam, has gone beyond functional aspect to include political and security dimensions. The second section of the paper after brief analyses of the historically profound association between India and Vietnam further explores Mekong-Ganga initiative which is a symbol of inter-regional cooperation.

The last section reflects on the way ahead to augment the cooperative venture and argues that to appreciate the dynamics of India-Vietnam relationship, one need to employ the multilateral perspective instead of seeing it only through the narrow prism of bilateral relations.

Do Thu Ha's chapter titled *Indian-Vietnam Cooperation on Non-traditional Security Issues* argues that the co-operative relation between Vietnam and India is challenged by a number of non-traditional security issues including the energy nexus, terrorism, environment, health, trans-national organized crimes and economic performance. This paper categorises and clarifies some key emerging issues between the two countries and looks at their interconnectedness and implications basically from Vietnam's point of view. The paper then discusses the official perceptions of Vietnam's national security challenges and the official perceptions of Vietnam's non-traditional threats. It also discusses the common initiatives taken up by both the countries to tackle these non-traditional threats and comments that Modi's Act East Policy provides a new setting for India-Vietnam Relations in Non-traditional security.

Athira Anand's chapter *Disaster Preparedness and Resilience: Providing Technical Safety* takes up a specific issue of disaster under the larger rubric of non-traditional security dimensions. It argues that as a stretch of land, the eastern seaboard of South East Asia is extremely vulnerable to natural hazards. This paper focuses on discussing scientific and technological safety measures to be initiated for disaster preparedness and resilience in Vietnam with an international outlook when Indo-Vietnam relationship widens to new horizons. It argues that larger part of the disaster is initiated through challenges raised by topography and climatic change in Vietnam which can be mitigated through good governance and advanced science and technology, which is at a blooming stage. One critical issue which the paper brings up is the issue of "diplomatic resilience" which says is possible only when the discussions surrounding disaster preparedness and resilience are taken to the international scenario, and such discussions are incorporated into diplomatic relationships.

Emerging Research Horizons of Indo-Vietnamese Shared Cultural Heritage by Shubham Singh highlights fresh areas of probable research in India's and Vietnam's shared historical heritage and chalks out ways for a more mutually interactive future. The broad research horizons that may open up with dedicated effort in this direction include a study of the shared architecture and religious structures, the organization of towns, the religious influences and practices, a shared culture, the ancient Hindu kingdoms, the degree of assimilation of the people of the two civilizations, parameters of caste and gender, the ancient inscriptions, the art and historical artefacts, and the ancient languages of the two civilizations. How the two nations bear similarity and interdependence in terms of these broad factors is the central discussion point of this paper.

Abira Bhattacharya's chapter *Buddhist Female Iconography in the Art of Ancient Vietnam* sheds light on the subject of Buddhist female iconography, with reference to the art of ancient Vietnam, by taking up an exploratory approach of examining the devotional imageries of Buddhist female divinities and also the depictions of female royalty, while supporting the arguments and interpretations through epigraphic, textual and parallel visual data. Firstly, in order to understand the early incoming influence of Prajnaparamita discourse in Vietnam, the spread of Buddhism from India to Vietnam and the flourishing Buddhist activities, beginning from the early Common Era to the early medieval period, in the vassal states of the Chinese regime in Vietnam and also Indrapura dynasty at Dong Duong and Oc Eo culture is outlined. These ruling entities grew to power in different economic and cultural milieus, due to their distinct ethnicity, identities and local traditions, and moreover, they were political enemies, involved in power confrontations as recorded in the North Vietnamese and Chinese chronicles. An analysis of Buddhist Sanskrit inscriptions and textual sources, suggestive of the diffusion of the Mahayanic cult of Buddhist goddesses and the role of royal patronage in the promotion of the Buddhist practices is also emphasized in the study. Secondly, a descriptive analysis of the iconographic forms of Tara and Prajnaparamita represented in the plastic art of Cham art, while tracing their cross-cultural linkages with Indian art is also shown.

1

India–Vietnam: Mutual Visions, Mutual Efforts

Ram Madhav

Like India, Vietnam too is an ancient civilisation with known history dating back to several millennia while the archaeological remains trace its civilisational origins to the Palaeolithic age around 500,000 BC. India is an ancient civilisation whose history and archaeology date as back as that of Vietnam's, if not more.

We are two nations and peoples connected by land, across Myanmar, Laos and Cambodia; connected by sea, through the great Indian Ocean; and connected through millennia by history and culture. The great Champa dynasty of Vietnam had interactions with the kingdoms in India at least 18–19 centuries ago and we can find the remnants of those cultural engagements in the form of ancient temple complexes in parts of Vietnam. It is true that the initial engagements were probably through naval expeditions by the Indian kings like Bhadravarman. But the lasting engagements had been those of culture and religion. In his path-breaking work *The Indianised States of Southeast Asia*, the early 20th century French historian George Cœdès records the evidence about this religio-cultural engagement between the two countries in the first and second millennia. Referring to a ninth century inscription he concludes that the kings of Champa had claimed themselves to be the descendants of Maharishi Bhrigu of Mahabharata period. He also refers to the inscriptions of Bhadravarman that reveal the dominance of the 'cult of Siva–Uma' in the Cham kingdom. It is heartening to revisit those relationships today that can form an abiding bond between the two countries.

Vietnam is a great nation with a great history. Like India, Vietnam too has seen invaders come and go, dynasties rise and fall and colonialists conquer and recede. Like India, Vietnam's history too is that of a nation never surrendered. Centuries of struggles mark the history of Vietnam that culminates in its final independence in 1954 from the colonial French rule.

It is pertinent to remember here that we in India too have waged continuous wars against invaders and colonialists for more than a millennium before finally securing independence from the British colonial rulers in 1947. We had our Gandhi; they had their Ho Chi Minh and others. Our paths were different; but our objective was the same – freedom from colonialism.

As nations that were subjects of colonisation and the ones to fight it back just less than one century ago, we know the evils of colonialism. It is important for us to make sure that the 21st century versions of colonialism do not return to haunt us and succeed. Geo-politics in the Indian Ocean region makes the possibility of the return of neo-colonialism a reality with countries trying to dominate others through money, markets and military. India and Vietnam should jointly and independently work towards defeating all such tendencies and forces.

The Vietnamese are heroic people. They have passed through countless struggles. They have defeated colonialists; they have defeated colonialist designs subsequently by undoing the artificial partition; they have endured blockades and embargoes. Yet, at the end of all this, they have come out in shining colours. Vietnam today is one of the fastest growing new economies in the region and the world.

A country once shunned by the West is being wooed today by all the important powers in the world. Vietnam has today emerged as an important player in the Indo-Pacific region. It's close to 100 million population is fast coming out of economic backwardness and the country is emerging as a middle income country.

The Indian Ocean region is today home to such progressive and prospering populations and countries. From Japan to South Korea to China to Singapore to Vietnam to India to Indonesia and beyond up to Australia.

The Indo-Pacific region has today emerged as the new global power house. The global power axis has moved away from the Pacific-Atlantic region to the Indo-Pacific region in this century. Several of the world's largest and fastest growing economies are situated in this neighbourhood. We are all linked by sea lines that carry 70 percent of the world's container traffic and transhipments of close to half of the world's energy resources. It is also the region that is home to the biggest militaries, with massive defence budgets and ever increasing military movements and purchases. It is projected that by 2025 half of world's submarines and warships would be roaming around in this region. Trade and tyranny co-exist in the backyards of many countries in the region.

It is important for countries like India and Vietnam to come together to ensure that sovereignty, security and sentiments of all the countries are protected and maritime laws respected. Together and also by mobilising the support of other nations in the region, we should strive to evolve a new Indian Ocean maritime order that ensures peace, stability, freedom of navigation and over-flights, and non-interference of outside powers in the affairs of the region.

India and Vietnam have been working together in many areas including trade, oil exploration, science and technology, space and defence. India cherishes its bonds with Vietnam that started immediately after Vietnam's independence in 1954 and further strengthened through uninterrupted bilateral engagements over the decades.

The relationship touched a new high when Prime Minister Modi visited Hanoi in September 2016 and both the countries signed the strategic partnership agreement. India is committed to supporting Vietnam in its endeavour for self-reliance in defence and space technology area. India and Vietnam enjoy a strong cultural bond also. Humanity and harmony are the hallmarks of traditional Vietnamese culture. The Vietnamese people regard family and community values very highly. It is these values that we in India also cherish deeply.

Working together, India and Vietnam could contribute to ensuring peace and stability in the Indo-Pacific, thereby helping countries located here to concentrate their efforts towards attaining national goals of poverty elimination and economic prosperity.

2

Working Together: Building on Vietnam–India Relations

Ton Sinh Thanh

I believe that the theme "Emerging Horizons in Vietnam–India Relations" provides us with an excellent opportunity to review the achievements of our bilateral relationship over the past 45 years and to find out the ways to bring our relations to higher level in the time to come.

First of all, it is worth to recall that 7 January 1972 was the date when these two countries upgraded the consular relations which started from 1956 to full-fledged Ambassadorial level. This is undoubtedly an important turning point in the thousand years of interactions between the two peoples.

Since then, despite many ups and downs that have taken place in the world and the region, the relations between Vietnam and India have not been shaken. Moreover, our relations have been continuously growing, upgrading and expanding. Especially, the last 10 years have proved to be the best period of our relationship, which reached the highest level – the Comprehensive Strategic Partnership.

It is not exaggerated to say this is a rare and unique relationship that I expect researchers from both countries should explain. In my opinion, there are some features that make our relations special.

Firstly, the two countries enjoy many cultural similarities as a result of thousand years of religious and commercial interactions. There have already been quite many studies on these similarities. So I don't need to elaborate on this.

Secondly, an important factor that binds our two countries together was the mutual sympathy between the people who both suffered from colonialism and imperialism. The two countries continued to support each other even after they regained independence and started the process of national construction and defence. The Vietnamese people have received not only spiritual and diplomatic support but also material assistance from the Indian people and government during our struggle for national liberation and reunification and in the period of post-war embargo imposed by the US in the 1980s. We can even now feel very clearly the good sentiment of most Indians extended to Vietnam and Vietnamese people.

Thirdly, the relationship between Vietnam and India has been almost free from any problem and always "as clear as sky without cloud" as described by late Prime Minister Pham Van Dong. Moreover, the two countries have very high level of mutual trust, and convergence of strategic interests. That is why the two countries enjoy a very good political relationship and strong security-defence cooperation. We can say that Vietnam and India are not only two reliable partners but also two brothers, willing to share almost all bilateral and multilateral issues, including the South China Sea.

Fourthly, the past 10 years have also witnessed the expansion of our economic relations many times more than previous decades. Two-way trade has increased more than 5 times. India now is among top 10 trading partners of Vietnam. In the first five months of 2017, bilateral trade was growing much faster than the world trade, reaching more than US $3 billion, which gives prospect of reaching US $7 billion for the whole year.

The expansions of our economic relations are attributed to positive impact of economic development of the two countries since the renewal in Vietnam and reform in India. The average GDP growth of the two countries since then has been about 7 percent, which is almost at the top of the world. Vietnam and India have become two most attractive destinations for foreign investments. India has made impressive achievements in service sector, especially IT industry, while Vietnam has made a great leap in exports, the volume of which is now 150 percent more than our GDP. Obviously, the economic development in each country has provided a lot of opportunities for cooperation between our two countries.

Fifthly, our foreign policies have many aspects in common. Vietnam and India share the same objectives of creating a stable and peaceful environment for the national development. Both countries follow multilateralisation and diversification of external relations, advocating forming an open and balanced regional structure. We both give priority to relations with our neighbours. While Vietnam and other ASEAN countries have promoted their dialogue partnership with major world partners, particularly welcome India's more active engagement in Southeast Asia, since Prime Minister Modi came into power has developed many concrete programs to implement the Act East Policy. It is the special relationship with India that gives Vietnam an advantage to assume the role of coordinating the ASEAN-India dialogue relations from 2015-2018.

I believe that the above-said factors will continue to be solid foundation for the development of our relationship in the future. We need to continue consolidating our good political ties, strengthening defence-security cooperation in a more effective manner, and coordinating more closely in international forums. We should focus on making our strategic partnership truly comprehensive. This means we need to put more efforts on economic and science-technological and culture-educational cooperation which are equally important pillars in our comprehensive strategic partnership.

These are the areas where a lot of potentials remained untapped. I hope that researchers of both countries would help to explain why our bilateral trade is still much lower than our trade with other partners. Is it because we don't have enough promotion activities to introduce our products to each other's market, or should we need a breakthrough measure such as a bilateral FTA between the two countries? In short, what should we do in order to achieve trade target of US $15 billion by 2020? Why has India's investment in Vietnam since 1988 been only US $775 million, ranking as low as 27th among international investors in Vietnam? Is it necessary to have more investment promotion activities or more attractive conditions for Indian investors?

Regarding tourism, I believe that once direct flights from Ho Chi Minh City are launched, it would significantly solve the problem of air connectivity between the two countries. But the question is what should be done to increase the flows of Indian tourists to Vietnam to catch up with other Southeast Asian nations?

There are so many issues that the scholars of the two countries need to study, find solutions and make recommendations to both governments to better uilitise the potentials and promote cooperation to meet the aspirations of the two peoples. This 45th Anniversary of Diplomatic Relations and 10 years of strategic partnership between our two countries should be used as a staging point to push up our bilateral relations to a higher level.

3

India in Vietnam's Foreign Policy in the New Context

Huynh Thanh Loan

After nearly 30 years of "*doi moi*" (renewal), Vietnam's position and strength has been constantly consolidated and enhanced. Vietnam has firmly maintained the environment of peace and stability, creating favourable conditions for national construction and defence. Thanks to "*doi moi*", the country has got out of socio-economic crisis and has created necessary prerequisites for the shift to a new period of development – the period of accelerated industrialisation and modernisation. Besides, after 20 years of implementation of the 1992 Constitution, Vietnam has witnessed many changes in the international context of great, profound and complicated developments.

Based on the objective assessment of the domestic, regional and world situations and on practical experience in external activities, the 11th National Congress of the Communist Party of Vietnam (CPV) mapped out the foreign policy in the new situation. Vietnam has maintained the goal of building itself into a strong country with elements of social justice, democracy, and civilisation. Vietnam consistently implements a foreign policy of independence, self-reliance, peace, cooperation and development; multilateral and diversified relations; is pro-active in international integration; is a reliable partner and a responsible member of the international community. Also, documents of the 12th National Congress of the CPV reconfirmed that one of the key tasks of Vietnam in the coming period was the thorough and effective handling of relations including the relation between independence, self-reliance and international integration..

In its foreign policy, Vietnam has expanded its multifaceted cooperation bilaterally and multilaterally with other countries and territories, giving priority to developing relations with neighbouring countries and regions, and with powerful countries, international organisations and regions in line with the fundamental principles of international law.

With India, which has the age-old friendly relations and multifaceted cooperation with Vietnam, it has put great importance in developing its relation. Vietnam highly appreciates India's capabilities and potentials as an important rising power and a responsible player in the region and the world. The CPV and the State of Vietnam has always been consistently supporting India since it started implementing the 'Look East Policy' which is now transformed into the 'Act East Policy', and laid down a policy of supporting India's growing role in the region and the world; and promoting Vietnam-India relations bilaterally and in multilateral forums.

This paper aims at analysing changes and transitions of Vietnam's foreign policy, especially with the view of highlighting the position of India in it, and concludes that Vietnam has increasingly put greater attention on India's rising role in the region and the world and has applied a number of measures to strengthen the bilateral relations between the two countries.

Overview of Vietnam's Foreign Policy

After the course of national liberation and unification in 1975, Vietnam entered period of construction and protection of socialism, a goal which is chosen by the CPV and people of Vietnam. In mid-1980s Vietnam faced serious difficulties. The prolonged centrally-planned, bureaucratic and subsidized economic mechanism stifled development motivation; the country was isolated, subject to embargo and dependent on external aid. People's life became very difficult, poverty rocketed, the economy could collapse at any time, and worries spread. The political regime was confronted with big challenges.

Facing these difficulties, prior to and during the renewal process, the CPV set out goals, viewpoints and orientations on foreign relations with a new vision of the world and clearer perception on national interest and demands for national development in each stage.

Each Party Congress put forth goals of foreign relations in different forms but successfully and consistently identified the interests of the nation. Ensuring security, maintaining a peaceful environment and creating favourable conditions for development and thereby raising the country's status were the core elements of this new foreign relations mechanism.

Adapting to the fast changing environment, the CPV made significant changes at the core of its foreign relation principles and adopted the motto of "diversification and multilateralisation of foreign relations in the spirit of "more friend and less enemy". This was in favour of ensuring independence, sovereignty and mutual benefit. Accordingly, the 7th Party Congress (June 1991) put forward the policy of equal cooperation with and mutual benefit of all countries, irrespective of different socio-political regimes, on the basis of the principles of peaceful coexistence. The motto was, "Vietnam wants to be friend with all countries in the world community, strive for peace, independence and development".

Achieving national "strength" and "position" after 15 years of renovation, the 9th Congress further developed the earlier motto of the 7th Congress, "Vietnam wants to be friend with countries in the world community to strive for peace, independence and development" into "Vietnam is ready to be a friend, a reliable partner of countries in the international community, striving for peace, independence and development". Later it was further developed from the 10th Congress of "a reliable friend and partner" to the 11th Congress of "a reliable member" of the international and regional community. On orientation of foreign relations, each congress of the CPV marked a new step of supplement and development, especially on international integration.

The 8th Congress of the Party in 1996 for the first time mentioned the policy of international economic integration, "Build an open economy with regional and international integration". However, the implementation of commitments on regional economic integration in that period was still very slow due to the fear of competition, hesitation and worry of negative impact from outside, especially when the financial-monetary crisis in Asia broke out.

In the documents of the 9th Party Congress (April/2001), for the first time, the phrase "Pro-actively integrate into international and regional economy in the spirit of maximising inner-strength and enhance effectiveness of international cooperation" was introduced, marking a paradigm shift in thinking about development and integration of Vietnam. The viewpoint on international economic integration was later defined concretely in Resolution 07-NQ/TW of the Politburo of the CPV Central Committee, 9th Tenure in 2001.

The 10th Congress in 2006 added the word "actively" and set out the line: "Proactively and actively integrate in international economy while broadening international cooperation in other fields". Though the supplement was not really a breakthrough, it clearly affirmed confidence in the necessity and benefits of international integration. The 10th Congress set out the guiding stance that the international economic integration "must be carried out with appropriate roadmap, positive and firm steps, without hesitation, haste, and simplicity".[1]

Ever since becoming an official member of the World Trade Organization (WTO) in 2007, Vietnam's economy has fully integrated into the global economy. Vietnam's commitments with WTO are a common framework to promote domestic reforms, perfecting the socialist-oriented market economy. On that basis, the 11th Congress in 2011 marked a fundamental change in perception on international integration by identifying: "...be proactive and active in international integration". This was also specified by Resolution No. 22-NQ/TW of the Politburo, 11th Party Congress in April 2013 to assert that international integration was no longer confined to economic field, but was extended to all other areas, including political, defence, security cultural and social fields. Ensuring independence, self-reliance, firm maintenance of national sovereignty and combination of national strength with that of the time.

Parallel with the development of perception on international integration, Vietnam has become fully aware of the need to satisfactorily settle relations between international integration and ensuring independence, self-reliance, firm maintenance of national sovereignty and combination of national strength with that of the time.

The 6th Congress of the Party in 1986 initiated a comprehensive renewal of the country which advocated "joining international division of labour", "expanding economic and scientific-technical relations" with other countries.[2] The spirit of the 6th Congress led to a new approach that shows independence and self-reliance does not mean isolation, and "closed door" to the world, thereby opening up a new way of thinking about international economic integration in the first years of renewal.

The 7th Congress in 1991 affirmed, "in the new conditions, it is necessary to attach importance to applying the lesson of combining national strength with the strength of the time, inner-strength with international strength, tradition with modern elements for the cause of socialist construction and defense"[3] and "Broaden, diversify and multilateralise foreign economic relations in the principle of firmly maintaining independence, sovereignty, equality and mutual benefit, attract external resources to strongly promote advantages and inner-resources...". The Resolution of the 3rd Plenum of the Party Central Committee, 7th Tenure in 1992 also identified one of the mottos for resolving international issues was firmly maintaining independence, self-reliance and promoting multilateralisation and diversification of foreign relations.

The 8th Congress in 1996 pointed out: "Broadening of international relations should be based on firm maintenance of independence, self-reliance, equality and mutual benefit, preservation and promotion of identity and fine traditions of the nation".[4] The 9th Congress elaborated on the relations between independence, self-reliance and international economic integration, "Proactively integrate into international and regional economy in the spirit of maximising inner-strength, enhancing the effectiveness of international cooperation, ensuring independence, self-reliance and socialist orientation, protecting national interest and security, preserving national cultural identity and protecting environment".[5]

The CPV has also early drawn lessons on the necessity to promote inner-strength to ensure successful international integration. The 10th Congress conceded mistakes and weaknesses in the way of thinking on building an independent and self-reliant economy and international economic integration while pointing to the lesson learnt: "Only by intensifying inner-strength could we ensure economic independence and self-reliance and successful international economic integration".[6]

By the 11th Congress, the CPV affirmed that the relationship between independence, self-reliance and international integration was one of the big issues which needed special attention. Resolution 22-NQ/TW dated 10th April 2013 of the Politburo on international integration also emphasised the leading viewpoint: "Be proactive and active in international integration on the basis of firmly maintaining the foreign policy of independence and self-reliance for the interest of the country and the nation, peace, cooperation and development, open foreign relation policy, multilateralisation and diversification of international relations...".

Documents of the 12th Congress continue confirming that the thorough and effective handling of relations including the relations between independence, self-reliance and international integration is one of the key tasks of Vietnam in the coming period.

For successful international integration, Vietnam has made important renovation in perception on comprehensive diplomacy. The 3rd Plenum of the Party Central Committee, 7th Tenure, defined major contents of comprehensive diplomacy as foreign relation activities in political, economic, cultural and social domains. By the 11th Congress, the comprehensive diplomacy was understood as unified diplomacy under the leadership of the Party to mobilise all foreign relation forces/sectors/channels; apply all foreign relation forms/tools; operate in different aspects/areas, aim at different targets to bring to play aggregated strength and effectively realise foreign relation goals of the Party and State. This diplomacy is built on the three major foreign relation forces including Party's foreign relations, the State's diplomacy and people-to-people diplomacy, synchronous implementation of three pillars of political diplomacy, economic diplomacy, and cultural diplomacy together with the work on overseas Vietnamese and citizen protection.[7]

In addition, Vietnam's foreign policy is based on a consistent principle of peace, independence and self-reliance, not joining alliances with any country or group of countries against other countries. In the 2009 Vietnam's National Defence White Paper, Vietnam declared its defence policy as "three nos": "Vietnam consistently advocates neither joining any military alliances nor giving any other countries permission to have military bases or use its soil to carry out military activities against other countries."[8]

During the process of establishment, expansion and consolidation of its international relations, Vietnam has consistently adhered to the following principles: Firstly, respect for independence, sovereignty and territorial integrity, non-interference in each other's internal affairs and peaceful coexistence. Secondly, follow the principle of equality and mutual benefits in the relations with other countries. This is the principle which is written in the UN Charter, is the result of the humanity's common struggle and in conformity with Vietnam's national interest and culture. Thirdly, abjure from the use of or threat of using force in international relations. Fourthly, settlement of disagreements and disputes is done by means of peaceful negotiations; resolution of the border and territorial disputes in conformity with international laws and regional practices.

The full awareness and successful handling of the relations between independence, self-reliance and international integration have made important contributions in Vietnam's tremendous achievements of historical significance during the 30 years of renovation. Vietnam has entered a new orbit of international integration, performed basic adjustments, raised the position, size and competitiveness of the economy; national independence has been strengthened, and national self-reliance has been consolidated. In 1986, Vietnam had diplomatic relations with more than 30 countries. At present, Vietnam has established diplomatic relations with 187 countries and economic relations with more than 223 countries and territories.[9] Vietnam's relations with all big countries have been developing well; in particular, in-depth, substantive and effective relations with some countries have been established through comprehensive cooperation and strategic partnership.[10] From standing aloof, Vietnam has become a member of more than 70 regional and international organisations. Departing from loose bilateral economic agreements, Vietnam has reached agreements with economic institutions at all levels, including new generation Free Trade Agreements (FTA), such as the Agreement on Trans-Pacific Partnership (TPP), and the Vietnam-European Union Free Trade Agreement (VEFTA). These show Vietnam's proactive and positive efforts to accelerate the process of in-depth and extensive international economic integration.[11]

Vietnam's Foreign Policy in the New Context

The early years of the second decade of the 21st century have witnessed more complicated and unpredictable developments in the regional and world situation.

Regarding economic aspect, the fourth industrial revolution has taken place quickly, especially with technological breakthroughs in areas such as artificial intelligence, robotics, the internet, 3D printing technology, nanotechnology, biotechnology and energy storage among others. This has resulted in tremendous changes in the quality of life, employment, production and socio-political relations. The trend of technological innovation has taken place at high speed, posing several issues on development models and "shortcuts" to countries. With the application of new technologies such as robots, labour-intensive production will shift back to developed countries; due to greater cost reduction, these countries will have the advantage of exporting their goods to Vietnam. New generation FTAs such as TPP or VEFTA run the risk of becoming the "Trojan horse" and the "integration trap" for Vietnam's development in the coming period.

Regarding political-security aspect, the international environment and world security are also unpredictable, posing risks for development. Big countries have competed fiercely with each other to expand their influence. The balance of strength among big countries have rapidly changed, thus small countries have faced difficult policy choices. The complexity of relations between big countries requires Vietnam to be cautious, flexible and prudent to balance relations, intermingle interests, maintain independence and self-reliance, avoid confrontation, dependence or pressure or being dragged by other countries to create a favourable external environment for development. Situated in a strategically important location, it would be very difficult to have a strategy to choose partners and be "neutral". Establishing "strategic trust" and respecting the independence and sovereignty of each other has always been a challenge of small countries in relations with big countries.

China as a big country and the second largest economy in the world China has stepped up competition to occupy development space.[12] China's sea and ocean strategy sets the economic objectives of rapidly shifting its priorities from "mainland" to breakthrough at "sea", turning coastal areas into "bridges" and "gateways" to the outside world, while increasing seizure and control of disputed areas at sea, causing tension in its relations with neighbouring countries. By implementing a series of initiatives on economic linkages, China has shown its attempt to regulate development process in the Mekong Sub-region and Southeast Asia, using it as a springboard to reach out to the world. The formation of the new mechanisms proposed by China from border gate economic zones, North-South economic corridor of the Mekong Sub-region, trans-Asian railway to entities of global influence such as "One Belt, One Road,"[13] Asia Infrastructure Investment Bank (AIIB), and internationalisation of the renminbi are opportunities, and challenges, for adjacent countries creating great pressure in choosing participating policy options.

With changes in policy, moving from foreign investment reception to active investment to foreign countries, China is "shifting" energy- and raw material-consuming, labour-intensive and environmental polluting industries to less-developed countries. In addition, China is still in need of raw materials, energy, and market for redundant goods. With the motto: preserve national resources, increase harnessing and use of external resources, first from afar and latter from nearby, China's imbalanced development and huge shortage will put pressure on adjacent countries in the region.[14]

The situation in Southeast and East Asia has also been changing rapidly with the formation of the ASEAN Community (AC), which has shown strong efforts to become the focus of integration in Asia. However, ASEAN centrality in managing regional security are of great concern to Vietnam due to lack of policy cohesiveness among its constituents[15] and due to the close relationship of some members of the ASEAN Community with China.[16] The East Sea dispute, the Trump Presidency, China's rise, the divisions in ASEAN, etc., contain many unpredictable challenges for Vietnam. However, there is one definite thing: Vietnam would continue on the path of multilateralisation and diversification of foreign relations while continuing to modernise its armed forces to prevent all risks.[17]

In this current context, Vietnam has proactively and actively implemented external relation activities with focus and priority, paying attention to efficiency, effectively serving foreign policy objectives "to ensure supreme national interest" as set out by the 12th National Party Congress following the five major directions:

First, Vietnam has promptly disseminated and concretized major lines on foreign affairs mapped out by the 12th National Party Congress, especially supplements and new development on international integration. Shortly after the Congress, the Government instructed relevant agencies to carry out overall review of international economic integration, frankly pointing out causes to constraints of the international integration in the past.

Second, Vietnam has strongly carried out external relation activities, particularly at high level, considering it as an important direction to strengthen in-depth and stable relations, bringing about practical benefits for the country. Vietnam gave priority to the exchange of high-level visits with neighbouring and ASEAN countries; with big countries like the United States, Russia, Japan, India, and traditional friendly countries. These important diplomatic activities were implemented, aiming at increasing overlapping interests between Vietnam and partners, improving the efficiency of the cooperation mechanisms and enhancing political trust between the two sides.

Third, Vietnam has stepped up the work on the border and strengthened the country's defence line. On maritime matters, Vietnam has conducted negotiations on the delimitation of the exclusive economic zone with Indonesia, the government-level talks on borders with China, and together with ASEAN promoted the effective implementation of the Declaration on the Conduct of Parties in the East Sea (DOC), and the early development of the Code of Conduct of Parties in the East Sea (COC).

Fourth, in multilateral diplomatic activities, Vietnam has shifted from "attendance" to substantially "active and positive participation in" the process of building and shaping general rules of organisations, and regional and international forums. Vietnam's proposals and initiatives in ASEAN, APEC, ASEM, among others, have been responded to positively by friends and partners.[18]

Fifth, Vietnam has expedited the "Overall Strategy for International Integration through 2020, vision to 2030" in most of the fields, affirmed "the overall objective of international integration through 2030 is to contribute to strengthening national aggregated strength".[19] Vietnam needs to be cautious but not slow in applying the concept of independence, and self-reliance in the context of deeper international integration while being flexible, smart, and open for appropriate adjustments to ensure security, development and to raise the country's position.

Accordingly, the recent directions of foreign affairs is to deepen external relations, increase level of interwoven interests with neighbouring and bordering countries, with major countries, and the ASEAN countries; carry out programmes to implement Resolution No. 06-NQ/TW to smoothen the process of international economic integration; maintain socio-political stability; be actively prepared to handle problems arising in relations with other countries.[20]

Importance of India in Vietnam's Foreign Policy

For Vietnam, the relationship with India has been placed in its overall foreign policy of openness, mutilateralisation, and diversification of external relations, proactive integration into the world under the motto: Vietnam is willing to become a friend and reliable partner of all countries in the world community; intensifying and deepening relations with its strategic partners and major powers while promoting the traditional ties with other countries. Therefore, Vietnam prioritizes the expansion of bilateral, regional and global cooperation with India in line with the interests of Vietnam.

Though many changes have taken place, as mentioned above, as far as the new regional and international context is concerned, one thing not new is that India continues to hold an important position in the global political map. India has an advantage which few countries have, and that is the trust of most other countries in the world. Over the past decades, India has been regarded as a friend by both the West and the East, by both developed and developing countries. Even countries which have territorial disputes with India now attach importance to India's position in the region and the world. After nearly 30 years of economic reform, India has made significant progress, becoming a market economy and extensively integrating into the world. India has become a major agricultural producer, being capable of self-reliance in food security and even being the world's leading rice exporter. India is also the country that has attained a high level in the fields of financial services, banking, information technology, telecommunications, software outsourcing, nuclear weapons etc.[21]

In the region, China's growing economic and military might and its territorial expansion ambitions, especially in the South China Sea, have made Vietnam more concerned and cautious with its complicated relationship with China. Thus, in its foreign policy strategy, Vietnam attaches importance to developing relations with all countries in order to create an overlap of interests and counterbalance between the major countries. In this connection, India plays an important role in assuring the security and balance of power in the region, particularly in Southeast Asia.

The importance of India in Vietnam's foreign policy can be seen via different aspects, as follows:

Political Aspects: Vietnam considers India a trustworthy, faithful, and traditional friend. This friendship was started by President Ho Chi Minh and Prime Minister Jawaharlal Nehru. Right after India's independence in 1947, President Ho Chi Minh's message congratulating the victory of the Indian people, on behalf of the Democratic Republic of Vietnam, emphasised the solidarity and friendship between Vietnam and India. During the visit to Vietnam by Prime Minister Nehru in October 1954,[22] President Ho Chi Minh stated that "(T)he people and Government of Democratic Republic of Vietnam are delighted to welcome Prime Minister Pandit Nehru, the beloved leader of great India, the warrior dedicated to the peace of Asia and the world, the good friend of the Vietnamese people".[23]

In February 1958, President Ho Chi Minh and the delegation of the Government of Vietnam paid an official visit to India. During the visit, President Ho Chi Minh made the following statement: "We visit your great country with affection deeply attached to our two peoples"... "As one of the leading flags of the Non-Aligned Movement and the colonial liberation movement, India has always supported Vietnam in the struggle for national liberation. On behalf of the Government of Vietnam, President Ho Chi Minh expressed his thanks to the Government and people of India for supporting the Vietnamese people's resistance war against French colonialism..."[24]

During the Cold War period, Vietnam and India remained close friends. India supported Vietnam in the Cambodia issue, and Vietnam always stood by the side of India in the Indo-China border disputes. India assisted Vietnam in its post-war national reconstruction and economic development. Strong cultural link, intimate friendship, sincere affection and sharing common values of independence, freedom, equality and humanity created a lasting solid foundation for the close faithful relationship of the two peoples as late Prime Minister Pham Van Dong once said "Vietnam-India relationship is as pure as a cloudless sky".

With a peaceful, independent and non-aligned external strategy, striving for a regional environment of peace, stability and development that both Vietnam and India have continued to pursue and the traditional friendship that both of them share, India has become one of the most reliable and prioritized partners in Vietnam's foreign policy. Vietnam's position on relations with India was determined by General Secretary Nguyen Phu Trong: "Vietnam attaches great importance to traditional friendship and strategic partnership with India; supports India's Act East policy and India's all-round connectivity with Southeast Asia as well as India's increasingly important role in the region and the world". At the same time, Vietnam also supports India as a permanent member of the UN Security Council once the mechanism is expanded.

In addition, a very important aspect is that Vietnam, a member country of the Association of Southeast Asian Nations (ASAEN), has a lot of potential and important position and role in the region, is assessed by India as one of the most important pillars of the India's Look East Policy with a focus on expanding relations with neighbouring countries.[25] Indian leaders have repeatedly affirmed the importance of Vietnam. In January 2008, Consul General Jitendra Nath Misra said that Vietnam plays a very important role in India's Look East Policy.[26] In 2011, Speaker of the Lok Sabha, Meira Kumar, said that Vietnam is the main supporter of India's implementation of the Look East Policy.[27] In April 2011, the Indian External Affairs Minister also emphasised that Vietnam plays an important role in the implementation of the India's Look East Policy. India hoped that the two countries' strategic partnership would be upgraded to new heights.[28] Preeti Saran, Secretary (East) of the Indian Ministry of External Affairs said: "Government of India has placed the new context and vision of the bilateral relationship in the framework of India's 'Look East' and 'Act East' approaches of which Vietnam is an important pillar, and that of ASEAN, which is also important to us in terms of the history, geography, and the economic and strategic space that we share" and "(W)e welcome and appreciate the significant contribution of Vietnam to ASEAN-India engagement in its capacity as the ASEAN Coordinator for India for the period of 2015-2018".[29]

Given the recognition from India, Vietnam has repeatedly affirmed its support for various policies of India. For instance, addressing the meeting with the Indian External Affairs Minister in August 2011, Foreign Minister Phạm Binh Minh emphasised that Vietnam supported India's implementation of the Look East Policy, and expected India to play a more active role in international and regional affairs.[30]

During his visit to India (2014), Prime Minister Nguyen Tan Dung affirmed that the Party, State and people of Vietnam always bear in mind the great support and assistance extended to Vietnam by India in the years of struggle for national independence and reunification as well as today's national construction and defence. The Government of Vietnam expects India to further support Vietnam in the fields of economics, trade, investment, tourism, science-technology, education-training and defence-security. Vietnam supports India's Look East or Act East Policy. Vietnam has pledged its support to India to strengthen its relations with ASEAN, to engage in East Asian cooperation, and to support India becoming a permanent member of the UN Security Council.

Currently, looking from the regional and world perspective, India has a great potential to develop into a regional and global power in the future. India's economic rise is considered by experts to be one of the most important events of the 21st century. In 2015, India surpassed China as the world's fastest-growing economy and by 2030 it has the prospect of becoming the world's third-largest economy. It can be clearly seen that, along with the strong economic, military, political and security rise, India is playing an increasingly important role in the region and in the world.

Therefore, Vietnam sees India as a major strategic partner to balance its relations with other major powers and to protect its national interest. For Vietnam, the national interest is to firmly defend the independence, sovereignty and territorial integrity, protect the regime and preserve the environment of peace, stability and to take advantage of all international favourable conditions to facilitate the cause of industrialisation and modernisation of the country while continuously enhancing the prestige and position of Vietnam in the international arena.[31]

Economic Aspects: Vietnam has been trying to proactively promote the process of international economic integration, increasing participation and implement free trade agreements.

On the Indian side, with a rapid pace of reform and development, the country is emerging as a leading economic power in the Asia-Pacific region as well as globally. Vietnam regards India as one of the most important economic partners. Not only is India the third largest economy in Asia, the fifth in the Asia–Pacific region, the 11th in the world; but also, with an area of about 3.3 million kilometre square and a population of about 1.25 billion people, is now a member of the G20 and a potential big economy for Vietnam. This densely populated market is a potential market for Vietnam's consumer goods of Vietnam.

On the other hand, while the tensions between Vietnam and China over the East Sea issue is increasing, the threat of economic sanction serves as a measure which has been used by China to put pressurize Vietnam. This compels Vietnam to find and expand new markets to reduce the dependence on China. In this context, India has shown its willingness to replace China in the supply of textile materials to Vietnam so that the latter does not depend on China. Prime Minister Nguyen Tan Dung's visit to India in October 2014[32] opened a new era of economic cooperation, especially with India's offer to the supply of raw materials for textile and footwear in case of China's border closure. This is also the guideline of Vietnam's foreign policy, which is strengthening cooperation with India, Japan, South Korea, etc., to develop supporting industries so as to reduce dependence on supplies from China.

In addition, in the context that the TPP Agreement is in danger of collapsing as the US officially withdrew from it, Vietnam needs to plan for alternatives. TPP is currently not in effect while many studies have predicted Vietnam as a country which would receive many advantages. Therefore, in the case that the TPP is not implemented, Vietnam should take the initiative to create new opportunities in trade relations[33] and India would be a priority choice.

Security and Military Aspects: India is now emerging as a significant military power, especially in the geo-political context of Asia which now requires greater coordination between the two countries for peace and security in the region. Vietnam attaches great importance to strengthen security-military cooperation with India to improve its capacity and capabilities, thereby implementing its strategies of military development. Especially, strengthening defence cooperation with India is also a part of the policy of increasing investment in defence equipment, combining weapons of different origins to enhance defensive capability. Firstly, cooperation in weapon deals with India would help Vietnam to diversify its imports of weapons. Furthermore, deep defence cooperation with India would also enable Vietnam to access new but affordable defence technologies. India's weapons development programmes are very diverse as it signed many joint development projects with Russia, the United States, France, Israel, etc.[34] The issue is how Vietnam coordinates weapons of different origins to create national synergy to defend the homeland. The rich experience of India would help Vietnam answer that question.

During the visit of the then Indian President Pranab Mukherjee to Vietnam in 2014, India signed several defence agreements with Vietnam; and agreed to grant Vietnam a US $100 million credit line to buy four off-shore patrol vessels. Although the US $100 million credit line is not that large, it points out to India's defence cooperation. In September 2016, Prime Minister Narendra Modi announced a new defence credit line of US $500 million for Vietnam for further facilitating defence cooperation between the two sides.

The East Sea Issue: Vietnam appreciates India' strong stance on the East Sea issue. In an interview with the Vietnam News Agency, Secretary (East) of the Ministry of External Affairs Preeti Saran confirmed that "Our position on the East Sea has been consistent. As can be seen in the Joint Statement issued during the Prime Minister Modi's visit to Vietnam in September 2016, we reiterated our desire and determination to work together with Vietnam to maintain peace, stability, growth and prosperity in Asia and beyond".[35] Facing China's threat over Vietnam's territorial sovereignty, besides implementing multilateral diplomacy, Vietnam aimed at fostering its ties with India, urging India to play a more active role in dealing with the issue and Vietnam is in "the hope that India, as a regional and global power, will actively support the parties concerned in resolving the disputes peacefully".[36]

Technological aspects: India's IT industry is developing very fast and strongly, and Vietnam sees India as an important partner in scientific and technological cooperation and has been promoting cooperation in this area. Meanwhile, Vietnam has also set out the strategy that by 2020 Science and Technology would reach the development level of leading ASEAN countries. In order to make this target come true, Vietnam needs the support of a country like India which has a developed information technology network.

Therefore, we can see that in the new context in accordance with the development needs as well as the shared goodwill of both countries coupled with the traditional relationship which they share, India has become a reliable partner and occupies a priority position in Vietnam's foreign policy.

Conclusion

Vietnam has repeatedly affirmed its foreign policy of "diversification", "multilateralisation", "being a friend, reliable partner and responsible member of the international community". This is essential for Vietnam to respond to the geopolitical situation in the region, in order to protect the national territorial integrity in a sustainable manner. Vietnam identifies the strategic partnership with India as a priority in its foreign policy.[37] Indian appreciation of Vietnam is very important to Vietnam and it attaches great importance to continuously strengthening and deepening the traditional friendship and comprehensive cooperation with India.

The emerging new context of the region in particular and the world in general poses many opportunities and challenges for both Vietnam and India to further deepen their cooperation, strengthen national synergy and enhance their competitiveness for development. The challenges of the new international context can be seen as an opportunity for Vietnam and India to move closer and cooperate more closely with each other.

NOTES

1. "Documents of the 10th National Party Congress," *Communist Party of Vietnam* (Hanoi: The National Political Publishing House, 2006), 112, 180-181.
2. "Documents of 6th National Party Congress," *Communist Party of Vietnam* (Hanoi: The Truth Publishing House, 1987), 81.
3. "*Documents of the 7th National Party Congress," Communist Party of Vietnam* (Hanoi: The Truth Publishing House, 1991), 88.
4. "*Document of the 8th National Party Congress,*" *Communist Party of Vietnam* (Hanoi: The National Political Publishing House, 1996), 74.
5. "*Document of the 9th National Party Congress," Communist Party of Vietnam* (Hanoi: The National Political Publishing House, 2001), 120.
6. "*Document of the 10th National Party Congress," Communist Party of Vietnam* (Hanoi: The National Political Publishing House, 2016), 179.
7. Pham Binh Minh, "Viet Nam's external relations in renovation period: some theoretical and practical issues," *Communist Review*, no. 862 (August 2014).
8. *Vietnam's National Defense White Book* (Hà Nôi: Vietnam Ministry of National Defense, 2009), 19.
9. The Ministry of Foreign Affairs, The proposed scheme "Effective implementing international integration, maintaining socio-political stability while Vietnam participates in new generation FTAs, including the TPP and the ASEAN Economic Community" on 16 July 2016, Hanoi.
10. Vietnam has established strategic partnerships with 15 countries, and comprehensive partnership with 10 countries.
11. By now, Vietnam has participated in and is negotiating 16 FTAs.
12. Pham Sao Mai, "China and external relation strategy to 2020", in *The World Arena by 2020*, ed. Pham Binh Minh (Hanoi: The National Political Publishing House, 2010), 454.
13. Including: "Silk Road Economic Belt" and "The 21st century Marine Silk Road".
14. Nguyen Hong Son, Nguyen Manh Hung, "ASEAN Economic Community in the new international context," *Review of World Economic and Politic,* Issues 7, no. 219 (2014).
15. Abhay Kumar Singh, "Maritime Security Environment in Western Indo-Pacific: Challenges and Prospects," in International Conference Proceedings *45 years of Vietnam-India relations: Achievements and prospects*, Hanoi, (2017), 15.
16. Former Prime Minister Nguyen Tan Dung, *Vietnam's foreign strategy of balance*, Retrieved on Nguyentandung.org, 16 February, 2017, http://nguyentandung.org/chien-luoc-doi-ngoai-can-bang-cua-viet-nam.html.
17. Ibid.
18. Pham Binh Minh (Member of the Politburo, Deputy Prime Minister, Minister of Foreign Affairs), "Vietnam diplomatic sector has proactively implemented the foreign policy of the 12th Party Congress", *Communist Review*, 6 April, 2017, http://english.tapchicongsan.org.vn/Home/Foreign-Relations-and-International-Intergration/2017/1033/Vietnam-diplomatic-sector-has-proactively-implemented-the-foreign-policy-of-the-12th.aspx.
19. The Overall Strategy on International Integration through 2020, Vision to 2030, issued together with Decision No. 40/QD-TTg, on 7 January 2016 of the Prime Minister, p. 8.
20. Nguyen Xuan Thang (Member of the Party Central Committee*)*, "Effectively handle the relation between independence, and self-reliance and international integration of Vietnam in the new context," *Communist Review*, 9 March 2017, retrieved from http://english.tapchicongsan.org.vn/Home/Foreign-Relations-and-International-Intergration/2017/1029/Effectively-handle-the-relation-between-independence-and-selfreliance-and-international-integration-of.aspx.

21. Vu Hoang Cong, "Bring into play the political advantages and choose the priorities in Vietnam–India Cooperation," in the International Conference Proceedings *Vietnam – India: 45 years of Diplomatic relations and 10 years of strategic partnership,* (Hanoi: The National Political Publishing House, 2017), 53.
22. Pandit Jawaharlal Nehru was one of the first visitors to Vietnam after its victory against the French at Dien Bien Phu in 1954.
23. *Ho Chi Minh: Full Collection*, the 9th book, CPV Central Committee's Secretariat (Hanoi: The National Political Publishing House, 2011), 92.
24. *Ho Chi Minh: Full Collection*, the 11th book, CPV Central Committee's Secretariat (Hanoi: The National Political Publishing House, 2011), 255-256.
25. Tran Nguyen Tuyen, "Developing Vietnam – India strategic comprehensive partnership in the new context," *The Communist Review Online*, 31 March 2017, retrieved on http://www.tapchicongsan.org.vn/Home/Doi-ngoai-va-hoi-nhap/2017/44197/Phat-trien-quan-he-doi-tac-chien-luoc-toan-dien-Viet-Nam.aspx.
26. *India focuses on cooperation with Vietnam*, Vietnam Breaking News.Com, 27 January, 2008, retrieved on https://www.vietnambreakingnews.com/2008/01/india-focuses-on-cooperation-with-vietnam/.
27. Hai Minh, "Vietnam – Important Partner in India's Foreign Policy", *VGP News* – Online News Paper of the Government, 17 May, 2011, retrieved on http://news.chinhphu.vn/Utilities/PrintView.aspx?ID=10565.
28. *Vietnam, India seek to boost strategic partnership*, The Voice of Vietnam, 8th March 2016, retrieved on http://english.vov.vn/diplomacy/vietnam-india-boost-strategic-partnership-327138.vov.
29. Secretary Preeti Saran's interview with Vietnam News Agency, *Vietnam greatly values relations with India,* 2 April, 2017, http://english.vov.vn/politics/india-greatly-values-relations-with-vietnam-342775.vov.
30. Meeting between Foreign Minister and Indian Deputy Foreign Minister, August 2011.
31. Le Thi Thu Hong, "The current world context and Vietnam–India Strategic Partnership," in the International Conference Proceedings *Vietnam – India: 45 years of Diplomatic relations and 10 years of strategic partnership* (Hanoi: The National Political Publishing House, April, 2017), 38.
32. Vietnam Government News, http://baodientu.chinhphu.vn/Thu-tuong-tham-chinh-thuc-An-Do/387.vgp.
33. Dinh Trung Son, "Driving force and prospects for enhancing Vietnam–India relations," in the International Conference Proceedings *Vietnam – India: 45 years of Diplomatic relations and 10 years of strategic partnership* (Hanoi: The National Political Publishing House, April, 2017), 147.
34. Nguyen The Phuong, "Vietnam–India security – defense cooperation: Overcome Bilateral synergy," *East Sea Studies Org,* 19 September, 2016, retrieved on http://nghiencuubiendong.vn/y-kien-va-binh-luan/6136-hop-tac-an-ninh-quoc-phong-viet-nam-an-do-vuot-qua-xung-luc-song-phuong.
35. Secretary Preeti Saran's interview with Vietnam News Agency, *Vietnam greatly values relations with India,* 2 April, 2017, http://english.vov.vn/politics/india-greatly-values-relations-with-vietnam-342775.vov.
36. Tran Nam Tien, *India with Southeast Asia in the new international context* (Ho Chi Minh City: The Culture and Art Publishing House, 2016), 133.
37. Vietnam Embassy in Hungary, *Vietnam–India Relations keep on growing*, retrieved on http://www.vietnamembassy-hungary.org.

REFERENCES

"Document of the 10th National Party Congress," Communist Party of Vietnam (Hanoi: The National Political Publishing House, 2016).

"Document of the 8th National Party Congress," Communist Party of Vietnam (Hanoi: The National Political Publishing House, 1996).

"Document of the 9th National Party Congress," Communist Party of Vietnam (Hanoi: The National Political Publishing House, 2001).

"Documents of 6th National Party Congress," *Communist Party of Vietnam* (Hanoi: The Truth Publishing House, 1987).

"*Documents of the 7th National Party Congress,*" *Communist Party of Vietnam* (Hanoi: The Truth Publishing House, 1991).

Ho Chi Minh: Full Collection, the 11th book, CPV Central Committee's Secretariat (Hanoi: The National Political Publishing House, 2011).

Ho Chi Minh: Full Collection, the 9th book, CPV Central Committee's Secretariat (Hanoi: The National Political Publishing House, 2011).

India focuses on cooperation with Vietnam, Vietnam Breaking News.Com, 27 January, 2008, retrieved on https://www.vietnambreakingnews.com/2008/01/india-focuses-on-cooperation-with-vietnam/.

Mai, Pham Sao, "China and external relation strategy to 2020," In *The World Arena by 2020*, edited by Pham Binh Minh. Hanoi: The National Political Publishing House, 2010.

Minh, Pham Binh (Member of the Politburo, Deputy Prime Minister, Minister of Foreign Affairs), "Viet Nam's external relations in renovation period: some theoretical and practical issues," *Communist Review*, no. 862 (August 2014).

Minh, Pham Binh (Member of the Politburo, Deputy Prime Minister, Minister of Foreign Affairs), "Vietnam diplomatic sector has proactively implemented the foreign policy of the 12th Party Congress," *Communist Review*, 6 April, 2017, http://english.tapchicongsan.org.vn/Home/Foreign-Relations-and-International-Intergration/2017/1033/Vietnam-diplomatic-sector-has-proactively-implemented-the-foreign-policy-of-the-12th.aspx.

Nguyen, Tan Dung (Former Prime Minister), *Vietnam's foreign strategy of balance*, Retrieved on Nguyentandung.org, 16 February, 2017, http://nguyentandung.org/chien-luoc-doi-ngoai-can-bang-cua-viet-nam.html.

Nguyen, The Phuong, "Vietnam–India security – defense cooperation: Overcome Bilateral synergy," *East Sea Studies Org*, 19 September, 2016, retrieved on http://nghiencuubiendong.vn/y-kien-va-binh-luan/6136-hop-tac-an-ninh-quoc-phong-viet-nam-an-do-vuot-qua-xung-luc-song-phuong.

Nguyen, Xuan Thang (Member of the Party Central Committee), "Effectively handle the relation between independence, and self-reliance and international integration of Vietnam in the new context," *Communist Review*, 9 March 2017, retrieved on http://english.tapchicongsan.org.vn/Home/Foreign-Relations-and-International-Intergration/2017/1029/Effectively-handle-the-relation-between-independence-and-selfreliance-and-international-integration-of.aspx.

Secretary Preeti Saran's interview with Vietnam News Agency, *Vietnam greatly values relations with India*, 2 April, 2017, http://english.vov.vn/politics/india-greatly-values-relations-with-vietnam-342775.vov.

Singh, Abhay Kumar, "Maritime Security Environment in Western Indo-Pacific: Challenges and Prospects", in International Conference Proceedings *45 years of Vietnam-India relations: Achievements and prospects*, Hanoi, May, 2017.

Son, Dinh Trung, "Driving force and prospects for enhancing Vietnam–India relations", in the International Conference Proceedings *Vietnam–India: 45 years of Diplomatic relations and 10 years of strategic partnership* (Hanoi: The National Political Publishing House, 2017).

Son, Nguyen Hong and Nguyen Manh Hung, "ASEAN Economic Community in the new international context," *Review of World Economic and Politic Issues* 7, no. 219 (2014).

Tien, Tran Nam, *India with Southeast Asia in the new international context*. Ho Chi Minh City: The Culture and Art Publishing House, 2016.

Tuyen, Tran Nguyen, "Developing Vietnam–India strategic comprehensive partnership in the new context," *The Communist Review Online*, 31 March 2017, retrieved on http://www.tapchicongsan.org.vn/Home/Doi-ngoai-va-hoi-nhap/2017/44197/Phat-trien-quan-he-doi-tac-chien-luoc-toan-dien-Viet-Nam.aspx.

Vietnam, India seek to boost strategic partnership, The Voice of Vietnam, 8th March 2016, retrieved on http://english.vov.vn/diplomacy/vietnam-india-boost-strategic-partnership-327138.vov.

Vietnam's National Defense White Book, Vietnam Ministry of National Defense. Hà Ni, 2009.

4

Growing Significance of Vietnam in India's Act East Policy

Subhadeep Bhattacharya

Last September (2016), on the eve of his visit to Vietnam, Prime Minister Narendra Modi said that his government gave high priority to the bilateral relations with Vietnam (India-Vietnam partnership to benefit Asia, 2016). This statement of the Indian Prime Minister is very significant. The Act East Policy of the Narendra Modi Government is giving India's traditional Look East Policy a proactive character in the twenty-first century. The Ministry of External Affairs has defined the Act East Policy as a proactive policy "which envisages accelerated across-the-board engagement between the two growth poles of vibrant Asia" (cited in Bhattacharya, 2016, p.145). The current government in New Delhi has given priority to its Southeast Asian neighbours since it came to power in 2014. Both the Prime Minister and the Foreign Minister visited most of these countries, including Vietnam. Apart from the ministers, the Indian President Pranab Mukherjee visited Vietnam in September 2014 while India received the Vietnamese Prime Minister in late October, the same year. Vietnam is fast emerging as an important partner of India's Act East Policy. The Policy, which has both strategic and economic aspects, is a new boost to the decades old Look East Policy meant to make India more active in the East Asian scene. It bears the connotation of enthusiasm and activeness on the part of the Indian leadership to reap the maximum benefit from the economic vibrancy of this part of Asia which houses the leading Asian economies – China, Japan, Korea and Singapore – and the emerging economic power-houses like Malaysia, Indonesia and Vietnam.

Vietnam is a fast-growing economy of Southeast Asia which prioritises foreign investments to boost its economy while its natural resources are vital for an energy-hungry economy like India. Apart from the economic aspect, the Act East Policy bears a strategic character as well. The Asian geopolitical scene is simmering with the latent tension between the two Asian rivals – India and China – which is sending ripples all around the Indo-Pacific world. India's Act East strategy is China-oriented. And in order to provide a counter balance in the aforementioned region, India needs an ally which it finds in Vietnam. But how far this alliance would go to serve each other's geopolitical objectives? Is India-Vietnam relations of today only a part of larger "contain China" mission of the Act East Policy or the Southeast Asian country has any relevance outside this strategic objective of India? What is the character of the growing significance of Vietnam in India's Act East Policy?

Harsh V. Pant has claimed that according to some quarters in New Delhi India sees Hanoi as a counterweight to Beijing, the same way China sees Islamabad (Pant, 2011, para 4). He has even opined that India considers its policy towards East Asia as a counter-move against China's venture in the Indian Ocean region and South Asia and in this venture of India towards the East, Vietnam can be the linchpin (ibid, paras 3,4). Such a perception is justified. Vietnam-China bilateral relations are no better than India-Pakistan relations, if not worse. Although Sino-Soviet feud during the Cold War period proved that comradeship among the communist regimes was a myth, the Sino-Vietnam relations are more complicated. The Vietnam-China clash is far deep-rooted in the history of Vietnam, mixed with the modern day memory of invasion from the north. India is aware of the wariness that prevails among the Vietnamese policymakers about China. And such wariness is mutual. In this context, it is natural to assume strategic closeness between the two countries in handling the China affairs.

India's Southeast Asia policy has been China-oriented since 1947, especially after China fell to the communists in October, 1949 and it became more prominent after the war of 1962. Jawaharlal Nehru's concern was the growing influence of radical communism of China on the then ongoing communist upheaval in the region. When he managed to thwart it in some countries there, he failed to do so in Vietnam. However, he tried his best to limit such influence with his Panchsheel Doctrine ensuring non-interference of one country in the internal affairs of the other although the doctrine, too, failed him eventually in Indochina. Throughout the Cold War period, India struggled to contain the Chinese influence in the Southeast Asian region although the latter's meddling in the regional affairs there has reduced since 1964 with India getting more and more engaged in its immediate South Asian neighbourhood while managing a two-front strategies with Pakistan and China. It, however, did not delink itself with Southeast Asia and continued with its mission to contain China in the region.

There was a clear reflection of tension in Sino-India relations on India's policy towards the Vietnam War, especially with the border tension between these two Asian giants erupting by late 1950s. At the International Control Commission (ICC), constituted to restore peace in Indochina, India started voting against North Vietnam (China's instrument to thwart the US influence in Indochina) during this time although India officially denied that this had anything to do with its dispute with China. However, this was privately admitted as "only natural" (Thakur, 1979, p.963). Later, with the end of the war and unification of Vietnam in 1975, India improved its relations with Hanoi. Post-unification, India could see another rival of China emerging in Southeast Asia when relations between China and Vietnam deteriorated with the Chinese invasion of Vietnam in February 1979. And this happened when the Indian Foreign Minister Atal Bihari Vajpayee was visiting Beijing. The Rajya Sabha's unanimous resolution of condemnation of Chinese aggression (ibid, p.972), which compared it with the "betrayal" of 1962, reflected the aspiration for future collaboration with Vietnam against China. This incident sowed the seed of future India-Vietnam strategic closeness to contain China. The special place of Vietnam in India's foreign policy was well depicted in India's strong support to Vietnam-installed Heng Samrin regime of Cambodia. This regime was disapproved by most of the regional countries, including China. India went to the extent of ignoring the advice of ASEAN countries not to recognise the regime in Phnom Penh, which was supported by Vietnam and USSR, both being strongly anti-China during that time. Thus Vietnam became an important partner, although not overtly, of India's traditional mission to contain the Chinese influence in the Southeast Asian region long before the rise of China as a major power.

It is undeniable that India's Act East Policy has a definite mission to limit the influence of China in East Asia. The East Asian maritime zone is China's only maritime opening and it houses the major sea lanes of communication for the country. With China's international trade soaring (RMB 24.33 trillion in 2016[1]) these sea lanes are becoming important for China and thus the urge to invest in naval power to protect its maritime interests (Chinese government's focus on strengthening the naval wing of its military with the commissioning of its first aircraft carrier and working fast on the second carrier, indigenously constructed, are worthy of mention here). This also serves China's goal to be a major power in Asia and in the world. China knows that in order to be a genuine power, it has to strengthen its naval might in order to become a formidable power in East Asia, which is a maritime region. Moreover, the rise in domestic demand for natural resources is driving China to underwater explorations in nearby maritime zones thus drawing protests from the neighbours, involvement of external powers and complicating the regional geopolitics. China's naval investment should be viewed from these angles as well.

India's Act East Policy thus has an exceptional challenge in the form of China. And India knows that China also has to encounter tough challenges from some countries in the East who, like India, are equally uncomfortable with its rise. India is thus investing in developing rapport with these countries. There are two countries in East Asia with whom India is developing strategic relations, within this context-Japan in the north and Vietnam in the south.

As mentioned earlier, India's strategic relations with Vietnam during the Cold War years were China-oriented. The legacy of 1962 and 1979 Chinese invasions of India and Vietnam respectively became a point of convergence for both the countries. However, India shied away from developing any defence partnership with Vietnam during the Cold War period although Vietnam did take interest in this direction at least once. General Vo Nguyen Giap, on his way to Moscow in 1978, halted in New Delhi and requested the Indian leadership for assistance for his country to develop local arms manufacturing capability to reduce Vietnam's reliance on USSR. But India politely turned down the request (Jha, 2011, p.118). During that time it was neither possible nor necessary for India to develop any special security relations with Vietnam to contain China, since India's Southeast Asia policy during the Cold War years was more diplomatic and political than strategic, and secondly, given the close relations between Moscow and Hanoi (both sharing mutual wariness about China and the Soviet Union had their naval presence in Vietnam) there was no need for India's involvement since the purpose was anyway served. However, the end of Cold War and the disappearance of Soviet Union from the scene, saw a changed geopolitical ambience of Southeast Asia, with the USA inclining towards disengagement, the Philippines asking USA to withdraw from Subic Bay and the rise of China as the lone regional power. On the other hand, the unveiling of the Look East Policy by India in 1994 confirmed India's post-Cold War Southeast Asia policy. India now took interest in the regional framework of Southeast Asia and as Prime Minister Narasimha Rao said, "India would like to be part of the evolving security framework in the region to assuage doubts arising from its potential military might as well as to contribute to the security edifice that was being crafted by the Asia-Pacific powers" (cited in ibid, p.119). Thus India was now coming out of her traditional politico-diplomatic posture vis-à-vis Southeast Asia. India now had to ensure security of its interests in the region on its own since there was no Soviet Union now to do so.

Like India, Vietnam was also a close ally of Moscow and thus experienced the same difficulty, like India, in coping with the new regional geopolitical scenario. With the collapse of Soviet Union, Vietnam, like India, lost a major source of arms. Meanwhile, both India and Vietnam had embarked on economic reform initiatives (although Vietnam started much earlier, in 1986 and India in 1991) and thus a tranquil ambience was required. Besides, given the economic priorities of the governments of both the countries, de-escalation of tensions with the neighbours was essential. Thus both India and Vietnam attempted to normalise relation with China. This, however, did not stop both sides from harping bilateral strategic relations. Vietnam's significance for India's Look East Policy became prominent as India's economic interest in South China Sea grew.

Like China, India is an emerging economy and is equally hungry for resources. After India faced difficulties in importing oil from the Gulf region during the First Gulf War (1991), India looked for alternative sources which drew her attention to the South China Sea. Although India was involved in oil exploration in Vietnam since 1980s, the opening of oil and gas sector by Vietnam in post-Cold War period in 1990 and 1992 led to its increased involvement in oil exploration in the South China Sea. India's ONGC Videsh Ltd. (OVL), jointly with British Petroleum (BP) and Petro Vietnam, carried out exploration in South China Sea in 1992 and 1993 (Bhattacharya, 2017, p.230). Increasingly South China Sea became important for India. In view of Vietnam's sovereignty dispute with China over the possession on the uninhabited islands in the Sea, it is important for India to convey to Beijing the message that India's rejection of Chinese claims by conducting oil explorations around the disputed islands. This would also send a message of cooperation to Vietnam. Vietnam considers India's presence vital, given the rivalry it has with China in the Indo-Pacific region apart from its traditional hostility to China's aggressive postures. Vietnam, thus, does not hesitate to invite India for exploration since by doing this it exhibits its right to exercise sovereignty over the territorial water it claims. In February 2016 Vietnam invited India to explore natural resources within 200 nautical miles of its exclusive economic zone (EEZ). The country's ambassador to India, Ton Sinh Thanh emphasised his country's determination to defend its rights and continue with its activities in its "sovereign waters" and vowed to collaborate with countries like India to search for and use resources under the sea within its Exclusive Economic Zone (Vietnam invites India to explore resources in South China Sea, 2016).

Vietnam wants India to explore more in these disputed waters. On the eve of Vietnamese Prime Minister Nguyen Tan Dung's visit to India in October, 2014, Ambassador Ton Sinh Thanh expressed hope that there would be more oil and gas exploration with India and promised to create complimentary ambience for that. (Vietnam wants more Indian oil exploration projects in South China Sea, 2014). Vietnam's leadership wants India to play a more active diplomatic role in addressing territorial disputes in the South China Sea. Talking to Press Trust of India, the Vietnamese Prime Minister had expressed his hope that India would actively support countries who want peaceful resolution of the dispute (Bhattacharya, 2017, p.231). Thus, Vietnam's India policy is a major tool to counter China.

As India's trade with East Asia is increasing, the sea lanes of the region are becoming important; its security is a priority of the Indian government as it provides the link to Southeast and the larger East Asia. China's growing assertive posture in the South China Sea as seen by its undertaking massive constructions in the disputed islands of Paracel and Spratly archipelagos. Such constructions causing unease to the extra-regional countries like India who are concerned about the freedom of navigation through the South China Sea. India's main concern is unhindered access to the East Asian market as well as the supply of oil from Sakhalin (Asian Russia) which passes through the South China Sea. Thus, the security of the sea lanes of communication in the South China Sea is vital for India. This importance can be judged from the reference of the issue in the Modi-Obama 2014 joint statement issued during the debut visit of the former to USA. This statement referred to the meeting between the two leaders which discussed the problem of the maritime disputes and vowed to safeguard maritime security and freedom of navigation. The joint statement also urged the disputing parties to resolve the matter peacefully adhering to the international law including the UN Convention on the Law of Seas (Joint Statement during the visit of Prime Minister to USA, para 41).

India, thus, sees Vietnam as a major partner in containing Chinese expansionism in the East Asian scene and in ensuring unhindered navigation in the South China Sea. This is clear from a reading of the joint statement issued on the occasion of the visit of Vietnamese Prime Minister to India in October, 2014. The statement mentioned the decision of the two Prime Ministers to coordinate in maintaining peace, stability and prosperity of Asia and agreed that over-flights and navigation in the South China Sea should be unimpeded and urged the contending parties to opt for peaceful and non-military solution of the dispute following the UNCLOS 1982 (Joint Statement on the state visit of Prime Minister of Socialist Republic of Vietnam, para 15). The emphasis on non-impeding of over-flights over the East Asian maritime zone was a tacit reference to the imposition of Air Defence Identification Zone (ADIZ) over the disputed islands in East China Sea by China in 2013 which sent ripples all around the region. In July 2016 China threatened to impose similar arrangement on South China Sea after the international tribunal rejected China's claims over the islands in South China Sea (China threatens to impose air defence zone on disputed area of South China Sea, 2016). During Prime Minister Modi's visit to Vietnam in 2016 the communiqué issued also reiterated the importance of freedom of navigation and over-flights and also unimpeded commerce (Joint statement between India and Vietnam during the visit of Prime Minister to Vietnam, September 3, 2016).

India's interest in forging strong security relations with Vietnam started developing at the dawn of the new millennium. Visiting Vietnam in March 2000, India's the then Defence Minister George Fernandes proposed policing of sea lanes of communication in the South China Sea. He said, "A strong India, economically and militarily endowed, will be a very solid agent to see that sea lanes are not disturbed and the conflict situations are contained". (cited in Pankaj Jha, p.124). Therefore, India has been considering patrolling the sea lanes of South China Sea for long. Previously, India thought of itself undertaking the responsibility of the patrol operations. Presently, it is assisting Vietnam develop her patrolling capabilities. During the visit of Vietnamese Prime Minister Ngyun Tan Dung's visit to India in 2014, India agreed to supply naval vessels to Vietnam as part of modernising Vietnamese military Prime Minister Modi announced a US $100 million Line of Credit to Vietnam to help the country procure new naval vessels from India (India to supply naval vessels to Vietnam amid China dispute, 2014). On the occasion of Prime Minister Modi's visit to Hanoi in 2016 India signed contracts for the supply of high-speed patrol boats (Joint statement between India and Vietnam during the visit of Prime Minister to Vietnam, September 3, 2016). India wants to strengthen Vietnam militarily to deal with the Chinese challenges in the disputed waters.

During Prime Minister Modi's visit to Vietnam in 2016 India approved Defence Line of Credit worth US $500 million to Vietnam in order to strengthen mutual defence ties. India finds Vietnam a major ally in her Act East Policy where she wants Hanoi to be a collaborator in countering the challenges emanating in the context of China's activities. This was clear from the statement of Prime Minister Modi who, during his visit to Hanoi in 2016, emphasised on the need for cooperation to counter growing regional challenges. This was a veiled reference to the Chinese challenge in the East Asian scene, especially in South China Sea waters. India is well aware of Vietnamese wariness about its giant neighbour and its desire to prepare itself to encounter any adverse situation. And thus India finds Vietnam an appropriate partner in her Act East strategy. The regular visits of the Indian leaders (from the President to the Prime Minister and Foreign Minister) to the Southeast Asian country since the Modi government took charge in May 2014 are noteworthy.

Vietnam is certainly the most useful partner of India in Southeast Asia. Like India, Vietnam is also concerned about the security of sea lanes of communication in her adjacent maritime zone amidst the assertive Chinese policy. Therefore, Vietnam currently is focusing on strengthening its naval capability given its national interests in the South China Sea. The seas around Vietnam holds an estimated reserve of 1.2 billion barrels of oil equivalent, fish stock of 2,744,900 tons (allowable catch 1,372,400 m tons) and a large amount of other resources. With the depleting resources of fishes in the coastal region, the Vietnamese fishermen are forced to venture beyond the EEZ (Exclusive Economic Zone) which trigger clashes in the disputed waters. Since late 1990s Vietnam is concentrating on augmenting its maritime economy and there was proposal for development of off-shore fisheries (Bhattacharya, pp.177, 178). Thus protection of sea lanes is becoming important for Vietnam in the face of regular clashes with the Chinese. Not only with the Chinese but skirmishes sometimes occur with fellow ASEAN countries as well. Recently Vietnamese fishing vessels were intercepted by Indonesian patrol vessels in Indonesia's EEZ, near the Natuna Islands in South China Sea (*The Statesman*, 24th May, 2017, p. 9). Thus Vietnam needs to strengthen its naval patrolling capacity and in this India has a role. India is trying to meet other defence requirements of Vietnam in order as part of its efforts to boost its defence export. The present government has emphasised on developing specific strategies to encourage defence exports within the ambit of the Foreign Trade Policy (Strategy for Defence Export, Ministry of Defence). In 2016, Larsen & Toubro (L&T), a company manufactures defense equipments got an order worth US $99.7 million from Vietnam Border Guard to supply high-speed patrol vessels (L&T bags US $100 million Vietnam ship order, 2016). However, USA and Japan have already supplied patrol boats to Vietnam. It must be mentioned that India and Vietnam have signed a Joint Vision Statement for period of 2015-2020 on Defence Cooperation and a MoU on cooperation between the Coast Guards of the two countries (Annual Report, 2015-16, p. x).

In addition to supplying patrol vessels, Vietnam is also an important potential customer of Indian defence items like missiles. India has acquired capacities in producing missiles and has decided to produce 100 missiles per month, increasing from current number of 50, per month. With an objective to promote itself from being the largest defence importer to a major defence exporter, India now eyes Vietnam. The Chairman of state-run Defence Research and Development Organisation (DRDO), S. Christopher, confirmed that India is talking to several countries for sale of the surface-to-surface Aakash missiles, which includes Vietnam as well (India says in talks with Vietnam for first missile sale, 2017). There is immense interest among the government and academic circles regarding India's plans to supply BrahMos missiles to Vietnam.

China, however, is anyway uncomfortable with increased arms imports of its neighbours. The *Global Times* (GT), an English daily in China considered the mouthpiece of the ruling Communist Party, expressed its displeasure with the trend of arms imports of India, Vietnam and South Korea. It admitted that Vietnam and the Philippines (before Rodrigo Duterte's presidency) were concerned with the increasing power of the Chinese navy (Asia arms import on rise as...2016). China's discomfort with sale of Indian arms to Vietnam was also expressed by the said mouthpiece. Its January 11, 2017 edition mentioned the growing military ties with Vietnam and implied that China was the main cause behind this closeness. Acknowledging that Vietnam was the key pillar of India's Act East Policy, it warned that "...such ties should be built for the sake of peace and stability in the region, rather than stirring up troubles or anxiety for others" (India's arms sales to Hanoi disturbing if aimed at China, 2017, para 2). However, while criticizing the Indian media for creating panic, it acknowledging Indian aspiration to be a great power, and that in the present circumstances it was not possible for any country to achieve such goal on its own. According to GT, India, therefore, needed "a more pragmatic cooperation with other countries" (ibid, para 9). India is doing just the same and the reactions of the Chinese ruling circles show their anxiety about this development with the China-wary countries in the neighbourhood. GT warned that China "will hardly sit idle with arms crossed" if Indian government enhances military cooperation with Vietnam as a strategic arrangement or as a "revenge against Beijing" (ibid, para 4).

Apart from the strategic cooperation to contain China, defence assistance to promote India's export-oriented defence production and also strengthening the Southeast Asian country as a buffer against China, Vietnam is important for India's vision of boosting connectivity with Southeast Asia, another prime objective of the Act East Policy. The Trans-Asian Railway network, a project of the United Nations Economic and Social Commission for Asia and the Pacific (UN-ESCAP), comprises of 117,500 km of railway lines passing through 28 member countries. This is meant to develop cultural exchanges and trade between Asian and European countries (Trans Asian Railway, UN-ESCAP). India became a signatory of this agreement in 2007. The proposed Delhi–Hanoi rail link is part of this project. The idea was, however, first floated by former Prime Minister Atal Bihari Vajpayee while attending the ASEAN meeting in 2003 (Delhi to Hanoi 2003, para 3). India by that time was working on trilateral connectivity between India, Thailand and Myanmar.

Two routes were considered, one, Delhi to Hanoi via Assam and Myanmar and two, Delhi to Hanoi via West Bengal, Bangladesh and Myanmar (ibid). The connectivity via Northeast India seems to be the choice of the current government in New Delhi.

Prime Minister Modi has emphasised developing infrastructure in the region in order to make it the gateway to Southeast Asia (PM Modi bats...2017). His government is investing in developing the Broad Gauge lines in the northeastern states while his Railway Minister Suresh Prabhu has asserted that connectivity in the North East is the priority of the Central Government (Prabhu assures BG connectivity, 2017). However, not much progress has been done on the Delhi-Hanoi rail link yet. The restive northeastern region of India is still not ready for any connectivity project, let alone international connectivity project. The National Highway Infrastructure Development Corp. Ltd. (NHIDCL), which was established in July 2014 to expedite the road construction in Northeast India, admitted that it could only construct a little over 300 km roads in the region till 2016 against the target of 4,000 km. For any international connectivity project to materialise, the Indian government has to ensure that the region is equipped to act as a medium for the linkage. The northeastern Indian region still needs a long way to go before any such connectivity project like Delhi–Hanoi rail link can actually materialise. However, if the Agartala–Akhaura rail connectivity between India and Bangladesh is any indication, the future of Delhi-Hanoi rail link is bright. However, in order to do so development of internal infrastructure of Northeast India and similar initiative in Myanmar is required.

Trade and investment is another field where Vietnam is gaining importance for India. The Act East Policy has both strategic and economic aspects. India wants to promote its economic engagement with its Southeast Asian neighbours further in the new century. In this context India's economic engagement with Vietnam is important. India is currently one of the top ten trading partners of Vietnam. According to GOI data, total trade between the two countries during April–November of fiscal year 2016-2017 was US$6244.92 million. The two sides agreed to set the target of bilateral trade at USD $15 billion by 2020 (Embassy of India, Hanoi). However, India lags far behind China. The trade between the two communist countries is currently US $72 billion and Vietnam wants to take it up to US $100 billion per year. This was the proposal put forward by the Vietnamese President Tran Dai

Quang when he visited Beijing in May 2017 (Vietnam president plans to push trade with China to US$100 billion a year, 2017). China is Vietnam's largest trading partner.

The picture is also not very bright in the field of investment. China is one of Vietnam's ten largest investors, with total investment of US$11.2 billion. The Vietnamese President, during his visit, assured China of favourable conditions for Chinese enterprises in Vietnam (ibid). Indian investments in Vietnam have been around US$1 billion but is expected to rise in the coming years. During 2016, according to figures from the Foreign Investment Agency of Vietnam, Indian companies identified 17 new projects with a total capital of US$98.12 million in the areas of food processing, fertilisers, auto components, textile accessories etc. With these projects, India now has 131 major projects with total investments of about US$707.95, ranking 25th among 110 countries and territories investing in Vietnam. Major sectors of investment are energy, mineral exploration, agro-processing, sugar manufacturing, agro-chemicals, IT and auto components (Embassy of India, Hanoi). Vietnam wants investments from India. Addressing a conference jointly organised by the Vietnamese Embassy in India and the Federation of Indian Chambers of Commerce and Industry (FICCI) on April 12, 2016, the Vietnamese Ambassador to India Ton Sinh Thanh said that his government welcomes Indian investment oil and gas industry (which has a strategic connotation as well), textile, support industries, pharmaceuticals, food processing, IT, mechanics, infrastructure development and renewable energy (Vietnam welcomes Indian investors: ambassador, 2016).

The strategic significance of Vietnam in India's Act East Policy is growing continuously as day-by-day India-China competition in the region is becoming visible. India's growing strategic closeness with Japan, Prime Minister Modi's visit to Fiji in 2014 announcing economic aid to the tiny Pacific country which was followed by the visit of Chinese President to the country, all point to the growing competition between India and China in East Asia. India holds strategic importance to Vietnam and is seen as a major help to contain the enemy. It is reminiscent of Singapore's urge for military help from India after coming out of the Malaysian Federation in 1965 (Ray, 2009, p.102). Vietnam is important for India in keeping the South China Sea free of Chinese dominance. To do this, India needs to strengthen Vietnam militarily and in that way, there emerges potential of the latter becoming a customer of India's defence products boosting India's dream to be a defence exporter. Thus, relations with Vietnam serves India's two purposes. However, to make India's relations with Vietnam more fruitful, it is important for India to concentrate on trade and investment opportunities. India still is far away from China in the economic relations with not only Vietnam but with the entire ASEAN. China's main dividend vis-à-vis her neighbours is her economic largesse. That is why Vietnam, despite historical animosity, welcomes Chinese investment. Therefore, India also has to enhance its economic engagement with Vietnam further.

NOTES

1. Review of China's Foreign Trade in 2016, General Administration of Customs, Republic of China, 01.13.2017, http://english.customs.gov.cn/statics/6cd634d6-e8f2-4aa3-80d6-2eb2b97199d3.html (accessed on 22 May 2017).

REFERENCES

14th ASEAN-India Summit and 11th East Asia Summit in Vientiane, Lao PDR, 2016, Ministry of External Affairs, Government of India, September 08, 2016, http://mea.gov.in/press releases.htm?dtl/27354/14th_ASEANIndia_Summit_and_11th_ East_ Asia_ Summit_ in_Vientiane_Lao_PDR_September_08_2016 (accessed on 23 May 2016).

"Asia arms import on rise as India buys new jets," 2016, http://www.globaltimes.cn/content/1009300.shtml (accessed on 28 May 2017).

"At least 21 dead in Vietnam anti-China protests over oil rig," https://www.theguardian.com/world/2014/may/15/vietnam-anti-china-protests-oil-rig-dead-injured (accessed on 29 May 2017).

Bhattacharya, Subhadeep, *Looking East Since 1947: India's Southeast Policy*, New Delhi: KW Publishers, 2016.

Bhattacharya, Subhadeep, *Understanding South China Sea Geopolitics*, New Delhi: Pentagon Press, 2017.

"China threatens to impose air defence zone on disputed area of South China Sea," 2016, http://www.telegraph.co.uk/news/2016/07/13/china-declares-right-to-set-up-air-defence-zone-in-south-china-s/ (accessed on 25 May 2017).

Datta-Ray, Sunanda K., *Looking East to Look West: Lee Kuan Yew's Mission India*, Gurgaon: Penguin Books, 2009.

"Delhi to Hanoi? Possible, says Railways," 2003, http://timesofindia.indiatimes.com/india/Delhi-to-Hanoi-Possible-says-Railways/articleshow/192952.cms (accessed on 28 May 2017).

Embassy of India, Hanoi, http://indembassy.com.vn/cms.php?id=8 (accessed on 29 May 2017).

Government of India, Ministry of Commerce and Industry, Department of Commerce, Annual Report, 2016-17, http://commerce.gov.in/writereaddata/uploadedfile/MOC_636281140249481285_annual_report_16_17_eng.pdf (accessed on 25 May 2017).

Government of India, Ministry of Commerce and Industry, Department of Commerce, Foreign Trade (North East Asia), http://commerce.gov.in/InnerContent.aspx?Id=75 (accessed on 25 May 2017).

Government of India, Ministry of External Affairs, Joint Statement during the visit of Prime Minister to USA, http://www.mea.gov.in/bilateral-documents.htm?dtl/24051/Joint+Statement+during+the+visit+of+Prime+Minister+to+USA (accessed on 25 May 2017).

Government of India, Ministry of External Affairs, Joint Statement on the state visit of Prime Minister of Socialist Republic of Vietnam, October 27-28, 2014, http://www.mea.gov.in/bilateral-documents.htm?dtl/24142/Joint+Statement+on+the+ State+ Visit+of+Prime+Minister+of+the+Socialist+Republic+of+Vietnam+to+India+October+2728+2014 (accessed on 25 May 2017).

Government of India, Ministry of External Affairs, Joint statement between India and Vietnam during the visit of Prime Minister to Vietnam, September 3, 2016, http://www.mea.gov.in/bilateral-documents.htm?dtl/27362/Joint+Statement+between+ India+ and+Vietnam+during+the+visit+of+Prime+Minister+to+Vietnam (accessed on 25 May 2017).

"India extends $500 million to Vietnam to bolster defence ties," 2016, http://indianexpress.com/article/india/india-news-india/india-extends-500-million-to-vietnam-to-bolster-defence-ties/ (accessed on 25 May 2017).

"India looks to double missile production to 100 per month," 2016, http://indianexpress.com/article/india/india-news-india/india-looks-to-double-missile-production-to-100-per-month/ (accessed on 27 May 2017).

"India says in talks with Vietnam for first missile sale," 2017, http://in.reuters.com/article/airshow-india-vietnam-idINKBN15U0Y2 (accessed on 27 May 2017).

"India to supply naval vessel to Vietnam amid China dispute," October 28, 2014, http://www.reuters.com/article/us-india-vietnam-idUSKBN0IH0LE20141028 (accessed on 25 May 2017).

"India's arm sales to Hanoi disturbing if aimed at China," 2017, http://www.globaltimes.cn/content/1028164.shtml (accessed on 28 May 2017).

India-Vietnam ties eye bright future: ambassador, 2017, http://en.nhandan.com.vn/politics/item/4918702-vietnam-india-ties-eye-bright-future-ambassador.html (accessed on 29 May 2017).

Jha, Pankaj, "Defence and Security Dimension of India-Vietnam Relations," in *India-Vietnam Strategic Partnership: Exploring Vistas for Expanded Cooperation*, edited by Vijay Sakhuja, New Delhi: Pentagon Press, 2011.

"L&T bags $100 million Vietnam ship order," 2016, http://www.thehindu.com/todays-paper/tp-business/LT-bags-100-million-Vietnam-ship-order/article14995120.ece (accessed on 27 May 2017).

"Modi government's northeast push will only see 7.5% road target achieved," 2016, http://www.oneindia.com/india/modi-government-northeast-push-will-only-see-7-5-road-target-achieved-2161829.html (accessed on 29 May 2017).

Ministry of Defence, Department of Defence Production, Strategy for Defence Export, http://ddpmod.gov.in/defenceexports/strategy-defence-export (accessed on 27 May 2017).

Ministry of External Affairs, Annual Report 2015-16, https://www.mea.gov.in/Uploads/PublicationDocs/26525_26525_External_Affairs_English_AR_2015-16_Final_compressed.pdf (accessed on 28 May 2017).

Pant, Harsh V., "The India-Vietnam Axis," *The Wall Street Journal*, September 22, 2011, https://www.wsj.com/articles/SB10001424053111903791504576584653465899250 (accessed on 19 May 2017).

"PM Modi bats for making Northeast India the 'gateway' to Southeast Asia," http://thenortheasttoday.com/pm-modi-bats-for-making-northeast-india-the-gateway-to-southeast-asia/ (accessed on 28 May 2017).

"Prabhu assures BG connectivity in all states in NE," 2017, http://ptinews.com/news/

8680169_Prabhu-assures-BG-connectivity-in-all-states-in-NE.html (accessed on 28 May 2017).

"Trans Asian Railway, United Nations ESCAP," http://www.unescap.org/our-work/transport/trans-asian-railway (accessed on 28 May 2017).

Thakur, Ramesh, "India's Vietnam Policy, 1946-1979," *Asian Survey University of California Press*, 19, no. 10 (Oct.1979), www.jstor.org/stable/2643848 (accessed on 22 December 2012).

Vietnam invites India to explore resources in South China Sea (2016) retrieved from http://economictimes.indiatimes.com/news/politics-and-nation/vietnam-invites-india-to-explore-resources-in-south-china-sea/articleshow/51130326.cms (accessed on 23 May 2017).

"Vietnam president plans to push trade with China to $100 bn a year," 2017, http://e.vnexpress.net/news/business/vietnam-president-plans-to-push-trade-with-china-to-100-bln-a-year-3583789.html (accessed on 29 May 2017).

"Vietnam wants more Indian oil exploration projects in South China Sea," 2014, http://www.thehindubusinessline.com/economy/vietnam-keen-on-indian-oil-exploration-projects-in-south-china-sea/article6535135.ece (accessed on 23 May 2017).

"Vietnam welcomes Indian investors: ambassador," 2016, http://en.nhandan.com.vn/business/investment/item/4194402-vietnam-welcomes-indian-investors-ambassador.html (accessed on 29 May 2017).

"Vietnam-India partnership to benefit Asia," (2016), retrieved from http://www.financialexpress.com/india-news/india-vietnam-partnership-to-benefit-asia-world-pm-narendra-modi/365391/ (accessed on 19 May 2017).

Zhu, Zhiqun, *US-China Relations in the 21st Century: Power transition and peace*, London and New York: Routledge, 2006.

5

Prominent Features of the Vietnam-India Comprehensive Strategic Partnership

Nguyen Phu Tan Huong

After the diplomatic normalisation of the Vietnam-United States relationship in July 1995, Vietnam, for the first time in its 50 year-long history, had "normal" relations (neither confrontation nor alliance) with all great powers in the world. Since then, Vietnam's foreign policy has adjusted to balancing the relations with great powers. The People's Democratic Republic of Vietnam was established on September 2, 1945. However, neither countries nor international organisations recognised the newly formed state until 1947. In the beginning of 1950s, Vietnam took a stand in the Cold War, declared itself to be a socialist country and became an ally of the Soviet Union and China. Vietnam struggled against France from 1946-1954 and against the US from 1954-1973. The Treaty of Friendship and Cooperation between Vietnam and the Soviet Union in November 1978 helped bring the two allies closer which lasted till 1991. After the Cold War and being next to a giant neighbour who has been developing dramatically for the past 30 years, Vietnam has chosen a foreign policy based on non-alignment and more specifically, the "three No" policy of non-alliance, non-confrontation and no military bases in its territory. Enhancing the relationship with India is not only in conformity with Vietnam's strategy of multi-lateralisation and diversification as well as the above mentioned "three No" policy, but also contributes to balance its foreign policy towards major powers. The relations between Vietnam and India were elevated from "strategic partnership" to "comprehensive strategic partnership" in September 2016 during the Indian Prime Minister Narendra Modi's official visit to Vietnam. Therefore, India became the third partner after China and Russia to enjoy this highest level in Vietnam's bilateral relations.

Understanding "Balance of Power" Theory, Vietnam's Foreign Policy of Balancing in Relations with Great Powers and "Comprehensive Strategic Partnership"

Balance of power is one of the most prominent theories of realism. Morgenthau understood power as relative, that is: the power of one state is evaluated in "terms of its capabilities relative to the capabilities of other states". Balance of power can be understood as a situation or as a policy. As a situation, the balance of power could be in equilibrium or disequilibrium. A balance of power in equilibrium refers to conditions whereby the power of one state or set of states is literally "balanced" by the equivalent power of another state or set of states. A balance of power in disequilibrium describes a condition in which the distribution of power among the contending states is not balanced. This condition clearly favours the leading hegemon and may result in the abuse of power by the strongest state, "which neutralizes other states" and may feel "free to be the deciding force and the deciding voice". The balance of power as a policy often refers to actual efforts to encourage the preservation of equilibrium. This policy to reach equilibrium would be most commonly found in a system that acknowledges that unbalanced power is unsafe.[1] The balance of power and policies aiming at the preservation of the international balance of power are not only inevitable but are essential stabilising factors in a society of sovereign nations; and that the instability of the international balance of power is not due to the faultiness of the principle but to the particular conditions under which the principle must operate in a society of sovereign nations.

In the 21st century, Robert Ross sees balance of power in the new context of East Asia. Because of the combination of bipolarity and geography, great power competition between China and the United States should experience minimal pressure for arms races, crises and war. U.S.-China bipolarity will be far less costly and dangerous than the U.S.-Soviet Cold War rivalry. Furthermore, neither China nor the United States would be able to challenge each other's dominance in their respective spheres of influence. The rise of China does not portend instability and the emergence of a new balance of power.[2] He concludes with a discussion of the prospect for restoring a global balance of power not through the rise of China but through Sino-Russian cooperation, just as Sino-Soviet cooperation balanced American power after World War II.

Since 1995, Vietnam has pursued a foreign policy of balancing its relations with all great powers. On the one hand, Vietnam has kept diversifying and deepening bilateral relationships with major powers as well as strengthening cooperation with them in international forums. On the other hand, Vietnam has stressed on preserving its independence, territorial integrity, national interests, socialist direction and preventing interference or pressure by great powers. The purpose of the balancing foreign policy based on maximizing our internal strengths is to maintaining a peaceful environment and avoiding political or military escalation in the region, so that Vietnam could concentrate on developing its economy and heightening its image and position in the international arena. Living next to an ambitious giant neighbour, Vietnam – based on the "three No" policy – will neither seek for an alliance against the rising power nor bandwagon with it.

This foreign policy adopted by Vietnam towards major powers has been in line with its general policy adopted by the National Congress of the Communist Party of Vietnam: Vietnam is a friend and reliable partner of all countries in the international community, actively taking part in international and regional cooperation, striving for peace, independence and development. In the research named: "Vietnam's Foreign Policy: In Search of a New Delicate Balance", the two authors offer proof for this argument. The speculation is that Hanoi wants to lessen the effects of negative external challenges, and more importantly, proactively exert some influence over ongoing regional political developments. Seeking a delicate balance between great powers, and among other regional states, is a necessity to keep Vietnam's national interests and relationships with other countries undamaged.[3]

In international relations, there are many ways to interpret "strategic partnership". According to Ayush Rai, it defines a bilateral relationship more important than the others, but stops short of an actual alliance. The term "strategic" further implies a future convergence of interests in areas that are vital: security, defence and investment.[4] Russian Professor Valery Loskin explained that the full meaning of the term "strategic partnership" includes:

no war among the partners, no alliance against another, no interference into each other's internal affairs and mutual trust.[5]

The term "comprehensive strategic partnership" generally indicates a relationship at a higher level than "strategic partnership". The Singaporean Ministry of Foreign Affairs understands "comprehensive strategic partnership" as deepening economic integration, expanding defence cooperation, jointly promoting innovation and entrepreneurship and strengthening people-to-people ties by facilitating tourism, cultural exchanges and educational opportunities.[6] In short, a comprehensive strategic partnership is built on the basis of strong mutual trust, convergence of views on various regional and international issues, development of all fields of cooperation, especially economic and defence ones.

Nowadays, Vietnam has good relations with all great powers but at different levels. China, Russia and India have enjoyed the highest level of comprehensive strategic partnership. The Vietnam-Japan relationship has seen the extensive strategic partnership for peace and prosperity in Asia, meanwhile, the Vietnam-US ties have been only at the level of comprehensive partnership since 2013. In the relations with the EU, Vietnam also upgraded the strategic partnership with its key members, including Germany, France, UK, Italy and Spain.

Basis of the Vietnam-India Relations

From the perspectives of constructivism, Vietnam and India have long shared values in cultural aspects, the Buddhist religion, civilisation and also a long history of struggle against colonialism. The foundation of this bilateral relation was laid by two prominent leaders – Vietnamese President Ho Chi Minh and Indian Prime Minister Pandit Jawaharlal Nehru after their first meeting in 1954. In 1958, President Ho Chi Minh was welcomed by Prime Minister Nehru as a great international revolutionary and a legendary national hero. Through mutual trust, understanding and shared national interest in regional as well as international forums, Vietnam and India have strengthened this traditional friendship. During his state visit to Vietnam in September 2016, Prime Minister Modi, in his banquet speech, remarked that Delhi-Hanoi bilateral ties are based on "strong mutual trust, and understanding, and convergence of views on various regional and international issues".[7]

The traditional friendship has been developing for the past 45 years. In

February 1956, Vietnam and India established their first diplomatic ties at the consulate level.[8] Then, in 1972, while Vietnam was severely struggling against the US invasion, China (one of the two biggest donors to Vietnam during the Vietnam War) started approaching the US, after the ping-pong diplomacy in 1971 and the US-China jointly statement in Shanghai in 1972, the two countries leveraged the relationship to full diplomatic ties at the Embassy level. India's actions were considered a good sign of their support for Vietnam in the war against colonialism. On April 24, 1972, in the Asian Union meeting in New Delhi, Prime Minister Indira Gandhi said: "The Vietnamese struggle against foreign invasion is a precious lesson for us – a small nation against one of the two biggest superpowers in the world. The need for peace, freedom and prosperity of nationalists created the strength of unity".[9] Prime Minister Pham Van Dong, on his visit to India in 1980, stated that the Vietnam-India ties were as clear as the sky without any cloud. Although Vietnam was still under the economic embargo and political isolation by the US, China and their allies, India continued supporting Vietnam and was the first country to sign a contract to cooperate in gas and oil exploration in the South China Sea within Vietnam's 200-nautical mile exclusive economic zone, just after Vietnam adopted the first law on foreign investment in 1988.

Vietnam's renovation policy since 1986 and India's "Look East", then "Act East" policies also have helped bring the two countries closer. In Vietnam's foreign policies adopted from the 8th to 12th National Congress of the Communist Party of Vietnam (from 1996 to 2016), India was among the priority group and was as defined as a major world power and a traditional friend. Vietnam's wish to leverage the friendship with India conforms to its multi-lateralisation and diversification strategy, the policy of balancing relations with all major powers and that of non-alliance which has been in place since 1995. Developing relations with India not only contribute to achieving Vietnam's objectives of development and security but also improving its role and position in the regional and international arena. In the meeting in 2012, on the occasion of the 40th anniversary of the establishment of diplomatic ties with Vietnam, Foreign Minister Pham Binh Minh said: "The consistent policy of the Vietnamese Government towards India is appreciating and giving priority to improve the traditional friendship and strategic partnership".[10]

The "Look East" policy, born after the end of the Cold War, aimed at enhancing economic ties with India's Eastern neighbours and further participating in regional forums in East Asia in general and Southeast Asia in particular. Southeast Asia has been considered India's strategic region, in addition to its neighbouring countries, because of the region's geopolitical position, the dynamic of economic development, the existence of major powers and the building of a regional ASEAN Community. The "Look East" policy comprised of two stages: from 1991-2002 when India took part in the first ASEAN-India Summit held in Phnom Penh, and from 2002 to 2014 marked by the establishment of the ASEAN-India Regional Trade and Investment Area (RTIA) in 2003 and ASEAN-India Free Trade Area (AIFTA) in 2010.[11] In Modi's Act East Policy Vietnam is an important pillar and by enhancing the India-Vietnam ties Modi has tried to meet his people's expectations of improving their vibrant economy and leading India to become a responsible stakeholder in the Asia-Pacific region.

Development of the Vietnam-India Comprehensive Strategic Partnership

Although the Vietnam-India relationship has reached its highest level ever, it must be seen that it has not developed consistently in all fields. Among the five aspects of cooperation between the two countries, politics and defence are growing faster than economics, culture-education and science & technology. Therefore, one can conclude that the prominent features of the Vietnam-India comprehensive strategic partnership are traditional friendship, mutual trust and understanding, political and defence ties. Meanwhile, those of the Vietnam-China partnership are shared border, socio-cultural similarities, economic ties and national integrity disputes in the South China Sea. For the Vietnam-Russia partnership, we will first think of cooperation in gas and oil exploitation, defence (particularly Vietnam's military has been equipped by the Soviet Union before and Russian weapons since 1991) and traditional friendship (Vietnam and the Soviet Union enjoyed good relationship from 1950 to 1978 and were allies from 1978 to 1991).

The political-diplomatic ties in the Vietnam-India relationship have been growing both in breadth and depth, contributing to the national interest of both sides and the larger peace and stability in the Asia-Pacific region. From both sides many high profile visits have taken place (especially since the end of the Cold War) to step up relations between the two Governments and their institutions, and also to establish bilateral cooperation mechanisms and effectively implement agreements signed by the countries' leaders. In the State visit to India by Vietnamese General Secretary Nong Duc Manh in April 2003, the two sides signed a Joint Declaration on the Framework of Comprehensive Cooperation between the Republic of India and the Socialist Republic of Vietnam in the 21st century. During the visit of Vietnamese Prime Minister Nguyen Tan Dung in 2007, India and Vietnam signed the Joint Declaration on the strategic partnership in order to diversify and deepen the relationship in a rapidly changing environment in the political, economic, security, defence, cultural, science and technological dimensions and steer their cooperation in regional and multilateral forums in years to come.[12] To realise the Declaration, both sides agreed on the establishment of a strategic dialogue, a Joint Working Group on Counter Terrorism, closer defence cooperation. India further committed itself to assisting Vietnam through grants and concessional Lines of Credit, and committed to work together for the expansion of bilateral trade, enhancement of science and technology, cultural cooperation and also closer collaboration in multilateral forums. Indeed, 2017 is considered the year of Vietnam-India friendship to celebrate the 45th year of establishment of diplomatic ties and 10 years of strategic partnership.

Multilaterally, Vietnam and India have closely cooperated and supported each other in regional and global institutions such as the United Nations (UN), Non-Aligned Movement (NAM), Asia-Europe Meeting (ASEM), India-ASEAN Summit, East Asia Summit (EAS), Asian Regional Forum (ARF), ASEAN Defence Ministers' Meeting Plus (ADMM+) and the Mekong-Ganga Cooperation (MGC). Vietnam supports India to become a Permanent Member of the open UN Security Council, and in return, India voted for Vietnam in the election to be a Non-Permanent Member of the UN Security Council in the term of 2008-2009.

As an active member in ASEAN, Vietnam has contributed to the ASEAN-India dialogue partnership. Vietnam is the ASEAN Coordinator for India for the period of 2015-2018, during which both countries have closely cooperated and quickly implemented various initiatives and schemes to further consolidate ASEAN-India Strategic Partnership. There is need to expedite work on priority projects identified for implementation during 2016-18 from the ASEAN-India Plan of Action for the period 2016-20 adopted in August 2015, which identifies concrete initiatives and areas of cooperation among the three pillars of political-security, economic and socio-cultural arenas.

Besides political ties, defence cooperation is one of the most prominent features of the relationship. Although the diplomatic ties were established in 1972, the first MoU in this field signed by the two Governments was in 1994 as Prime Minister Narasimha Rao paid a State visit to Hanoi. However, the bilateral defence relationship did not develop much until the agreement on Vietnam-Indian defence cooperation was concluded in March 2000. The 15 points of the agreement can be broadly divided into four types. The first touched on bilateral exercises which the navies of India and Vietnam have conducted, albeit intermittently. Second, the two Defence Ministries agreed to exchange military personnel regularly for training, notably Indian soldiers would get in Vietnam for guerrilla warfare and Vietnamese ones would involve in submarine operation and exchanging officers at training centres of higher learning. Third, Vietnam expressed its interest in certain systems that India produced and spare parts for common systems they had acquired from Russia. Fourth, India committed itself to sell multi-role advanced light helicopters (ALH) to Vietnam. Since the Vietnamese military is also equipped with Russian weaponry, Vietnam sought to "study the catalogue of the Ordnance Factory Board and explore possibilities of using the products and services being provided by India's defence manufacturing industries".[13] Vietnam and India also commenced the expansion of military training, including pilot training for the Sukhoi Su-30 MK aircraft and underwater combat training for Vietnamese navy personnel to operate Vietnam's new advanced Kilo-class submarine fleet. On October 28, 2014, India and Vietnam signed a memorandum of understanding (MOU) to found the joint Vietnam–India English Language and Information Technology Training Center at the Ministry of National Defence's Telecommunications University in Nha Trang.[14]

During his official visit to Vietnam in September 2016, Prime Minister Modi extended a new Line of Credit for Vietnam of US$500 million.[15] The two Prime Ministers signed agreements on patrol vessel building, cyber security, UN peacekeeping operations and naval information sharing. When Prime Minister Nguyen Tan Dung arrived at New Delhi in late 2016, Prime Minister Modi underscored: "Our defence cooperation with Vietnam is among our most important ones. India remains committed to the modernisation of Vietnam's defence and security forces. This will include expansion of our training programme, which is already very substantial, joint exercises and cooperation in defence equipment. We will quickly operationalise the 100 million dollars Line of Credit that will enable Vietnam to acquire new naval vessels from India. We have also agreed to enhance our security cooperation, including counter-terrorism".[16] Vietnam and India cooperated multilaterally at regional forums such as ASEAN Defence Ministers' Meeting Plus (ADMM+).

Both Vietnam and India have vital interest in the South China Sea, which has made the two countries come closer, especially in the context of China's announcing its territory within the 9 dotted lines. India's maritime strategic interests in the region are well established, including the fact that 55 percent of India's trade with Asia-Pacific passes through the South China Sea.[17] Meanwhile, Vietnam is one of the six claimants of the Spratly Islands and the Paracel Islands. In an interview with the Press Trust of India on October 27, 2014, prior to the meeting with Prime Minister Modi, Prime Minister Nguyen Tan Dung stated: "Vietnam hopes that India, as a major power in the region and the world, will actively support parties concerned to peacefully resolve all disputes".[18]

In a Joint Communiqué between Vietnam and India released on the occasion of President Pranab Mukherjee's visit to Vietnam in September 2014, the two leaders stressed on the direction of action in order to maintain peace and stability in Asia regarding the disputed waters of the South China Sea. The two leaders agreed that freedom of navigation in the sea should not be impeded and called the parties concerned to exercise restraint, avoid threat or use of force and resolve disputes through peaceful means in accordance with universally recognised principles of international law, including the UNCLOS 1982.[19] They also welcomed the concerned parties to work towards the implementation of the 2002 Declaration on the Conduct of Parties in the South China Sea.

Vietnam-India economic cooperation is not growing as fast as the two above-mentioned fields of politics and defence. The fact is that India is not in Vietnam's top 5 trading partners, which is topped by China. In recent years, the trade turnover between the two countries has had relatively high growth rate, at an average of 20 percent per year. The trade volume in 2015 was US$7.8 billion and expected to a target of US$15 billion by 2020.[20] That amount of money is only less than 15 percent of the trade volume between Vietnam and China. "Bilateral trade volume will reach US$100 billion in 2017" is the common goal written in the Joint Statement after a two-day visit to Vietnam by Chinese President Xi Jinping.[21]

In spite of the fact that leaders of both sides emphasised on enhancing bilateral economic engagement as a strategic objective, Vietnam-India trade is far below the actual potential. The key trading sectors are hydrocarbons, power generation, renewable energy, infrastructure, tourism, textiles, footwear, IT, medical and pharmaceuticals, electronics, agriculture, chemicals, machine tools and other supporting industries. With regard to investment, India has 114 projects valued at US$1.1 billion. In 2013, Tata power was awarded a US$1.8 billion thermal power project in Soc Trang province, which is the largest Indian investment project in Vietnam till date. Vietnam has three investment projects in India with total value of US $23.6 million.[22] Regarding sea connectivity, both sides have nominated their members to the Joint Working Group (JWG) being established under India-Vietnam Maritime Shipping Agreement. The two countries also have entered into an agreement on cooperative oil exploration in Vietnam's EEZ in the South China Sea.

The bilateral cultural-educational cooperation has developed, notably since the beginning of the 21st century. During his visit to Vietnam in September 2016, Prime Minister Modi underlined the connections between Buddhism and the monuments of the Hindu Cham civilisation. He said that while some came to make war, India had come with the message of peace – the message of Buddha, which had endured.[23] In the seminar themed: "India-Vietnam Cultural Relations: Retrospect and Prospect" held in New Delhi on 20-21 February 2016, Vietnamese Ambassador Ton Sinh Thanh stressed that cultural ties should pioneer to pave the way for cooperation in other fields, adding that Vietnam and India have many advantages to boost cultural relations as they share a lot of similarities of their rich cultures.[24] Many Vietnamese people have been granted scholarships at both undergraduate and post-grade levels in various fields of IT, advanced Buddhist studies, English language, nuclear energy, pharmacy, educational management, etc. Nevertheless, this field of cooperation has faced some challenges, including the lack of correct and complete information about each other. Therefore, not so many Vietnamese people are attracted to India's culture and opportunities and vice versa. Even the natural beauty of Vietnam and the warmth of its people are not widely acknowledged in India. Coupled with this there are no direct flights connecting the big cities of the two countries. These factors together hinder tourism prospects between Vietnam and India.

In this part, I would like to suggest some solutions to strengthen Vietnam-India relations which are as follows: (i) India should continue cooperating with Vietnam in exploring gas and oil in the South China Sea, and support freedom of navigation and over flight through the disputed waters based on principles of international laws; (ii) the two countries should culturally cooperate in carrying out conservation work to preserve Hindu tower temples of the My Son Sanctuary – the remains of the Champa Kingdom in the South of Vietnam; (iii) the countries need to create more joint subcommittees on commerce, culture, tourism, and education to promote import and export volume, attract more investment and greater business and leisure travel flow between the two countries; (iv) Vietnam and India should advertise more about their rich cultures, Buddhism country and natural beauty via mass media, movies and Embassy channel, that would help develop tourism between the two countries; (v) More cultural seminar and scientific workshops should be held in both countries to connect scholars and encourage research on Vietnam-India bilateral relations; (vi) Exchange programs between students from Universities of the two countries and more scholarships on various fields should be conducted.

Contribution of the Vietnam-India ties to Vietnam's Foreign Policy of Balancing in Relations with Great Powers

The centre of gravity in the world has been shifting from the West to East and the Asia-Pacific has emerged as the most active developing region. In the context of a rising China, notably escalating territorial tension in the South China Sea and the US's continuation of its pivot to Asia strategy, Vietnam does not want to take sides. Elevating the bilateral relations with India can both increase Vietnam's internal strength economically, militarily and culturally, and help Vietnam diversify its relations, reduce its dependence on China, thus materialise its foreign policy of balancing in relations with great powers. As neighbouring countries of China, both Vietnam and India have shared common concerns over a revisionist power and faced with territorial disputes with the giant. India has supported Vietnam maintaining its positions over regional and international issues. Concerning disputed issues, notably the territorial dispute in the South China Sea, India agrees with Vietnam's stance of freedom of navigation, resolving the dispute by peaceful means and avoiding the use of force. In return, Vietnam is serving as a bridge connecting India to the ASEAN community.

Conclusion

After over 20 years of implementing the foreign policy of balancing in relations with great powers, Vietnam has gained significant success, contributing to achieving objectives of development, security and improving national image and position. Vietnam not only has good relations with all of the major powers but has also deepened bilateral relationships with them and leveraged to a new height. India has become an important major power to help realise the above-mentioned foreign policy thanks to the geographical proximity, firm basis for further development and common concerns over a revisionist power.

Vietnam-India relationship was revitalised after the end of the Cold War and reached the highest level of bilateral relations in September 2016. Different from Vietnam-China and Vietnam-Russia comprehensive strategic partnerships, Vietnam-India relations have seen prominent features of mutual trust and understanding, traditional friendship, faster growth of political and defence cooperation than economic and cultural-educational ties. In order to develop the relationship comprehensively, both sides need to carefully consider suggested solutions and based on potential future areas of cooperation including maritime economy and security, cyber security, space, civil nuclear energy, defence production and technology and renewable energy. Upgrading Vietnam-India relations is not only consistent to Vietnam's external strategy of multi-lateralisation and diversification, and India's "Act East Policy" but also contributes to realising Vietnam's balancing foreign policy towards great powers, ensuring regional peace, stability and prosperity.

NOTES

1. Peter Toledo, "Classic Realism and the Balance of Power Theory," *Gledon Journal of International Studies,* Vol. 4, 2005, http://gjis.journals.yorku.ca/index.php/gjis/article/view/35205/31924.
2. Robert S. Ross, "Bipolarity and Balancing in East Asia," in *Balance of Power: Theory and Practice in the 21st Century*, ed. T.V. Paul, James J. Wirtz, and Michel Fortmann, http://www.hiunpar.org/wp-. ...content/uploads/2015/10/Balance-of-Power-Theory-and-Practive-in-the-21st-Century.pdf.
3. Truong Minh Vu and Nguyen Thanh Trung, "Vietnam's Foreign Policy: In Search of a New Delicate Balance," *Asia Maritime Transparency Initiative,* Nov. 10, 2016, https://amti.csis.org/vietnams-foreign-policy-search-new-delicate-balance/.
4. Ayush Rai, *What is meant by a strategic partnership between two countries?*, https://www.quora.com/What-is-meant-by-a-strategic-partnership-between-two-countries-How-is-it-different-from-a-normal-relationship.

5. Đinh Công Tuấn, *Quan hệ đối tác chiến lược trong quan hệ quốc tế hiện nay: Lý thuyết, thực tiễn thế giới và Việt Nam*, https://www.toancanhthegioi.co.vu/2014/03/quan-he- doi-tac-chien-luoc-trong-quan-he.html?m=1.
6. Singapore Government, Ministry of Foreign Affairs, Singapore, MFA Press Statement: *Singapore-Australia Comprehensive Strategic Partnership Package*, 6 May 2016, https://www.mfa.gov.sg/content/mfa/media_centre/press_room/pr/2016/201605/press_20160506.html.
7. Government of India, Ministry of External Affairs, *Banquet Speech by Prime Minister during his visit to Vietnam*, 03 September 2016, http://www.mea.gov.in/SpeechesStatements.htm?dtl/27364/Banquet_Speech_by_Prime_ Minister_ during_ his_ visit_ to_Vietnam_ September_03_2016.
8. Nguyen Canh Hue, *The Vietnam–India relations from 1956 to the first years of the 21st century*, The Ho Chi Minh Teaching Pedagogy University, June 2010, p.26.
9. Ibid, p.35.
10. Tran Xuan Hiep, "The Vietnam–India relations in the first decade of the 21st century," *India and Asia Studies*, no.2 (2014): 12-26.
11. Tran Tuan Minh, "India's Look East Policy Review," *Indian and Asian Studies*, no.4 (2016): 17-24.
12. Piyush Srivastava, "India-Vietnam: Expanding Strategic Engagement in 21st Century," paper presented at the conference on *Vietnam-India: 45 years of Diplomatic Relations and 10 years of Strategic Partnership*, 2017.
13. Do Thanh Ha, "Vietnam–India defense – security cooperation under the new global context," *India and Asia Studies*, no. 4 (2016): 1-7.
14. Carl Thayer, "India and Vietnam Advance Their Strategic Partnership," *The Diplomat*, December 11, 2014, http://thediplomat.com/2014/12/india-and-vietnam-advance-their-strategic-partnership/
15. Le Thi Hang Nga, "The state visit by Indian Prime Minister Narendra Modi to Vietnam and its effects on the Vietnam-India relations," *India and Asia Studies*, no. 10 (2016): 1-7.
16. Thayer, "India and Vietnam Advance Their Strategic Partnership," http://thediplomat.com/2014/12/india-and-vietnam-advance-their-strategic-partnership/.
17. Rajeev Ranjan Chaturvedy, "South China Sea: India's Maritime Gateway to the Pacific," *Strategic Analysis*, Vol. 39, no.4 (2015): 360-377.
18. Thayer, "India and Vietnam Advance Their Strategic Partnership," http://thediplomat.com/2014/12/india-and-vietnam-advance-their-strategic-partnership/.
19. Piyush Srivastava, "India-Vietnam: Expanding Strategic Engagement in 21st Century," paper presented at the conference on *Vietnam-India: 45 years of Diplomatic Relations and 10 years of Strategic Partnership*, 2017.
20. Le Thi Hang Nga, "The state visit by Indian Prime Minister Narendra Modi to Vietnam and its effects on the Vietnam–India relations," *India and Asia Studies*, pp.1-7.
21. *2017 Trade turnover: Vietnam–China strive to reach 100 billion USD*, https://vnembassy-roma.mofa.gov.vn/en-us/About%20Vietnam/General%20Information/Economic/Pages/2017—Trade-turnover-Vietnam---China-strives-to-reach-100-billion-USD.aspx?p=2.
22. Phan Thi Hong Xuan, "Vietnam-India relationship in the 21st century," *India and Asia Studies*, no.11 (2013): 13-27.
23. Rajeev Ranjan Chaturvedy, "India-Vietnam Ties: The Stamp of "Modi Doctrine", *ISAS Insights*, no. 346 (2016).
24. "Fostering cultural ties between Vietnam and India," *Vietnam Breaking News.com*, February 22, 2016, https://m.vietnambreakingnews.com/2016/02/fostering-cultural-ties-between-vietnam-and-india/.

REFERENCES

Chaturvedy, Rajeev Ranjan. "India-Vietnam Ties: The Stamp of 'Modi Doctrine'." *ISAS Insights*, no. 346, (2016).

Chaturvedy, Rajeev Ranjan. "South China Sea: India's Maritime Gateway to the Pacific." *Strategic Analysis* 39, no.4 (2015): 360-377.

Ha, Do Thanh. "Vietnam–India defense – security cooperation under the new global context." *India and Asia Studies*, no. 4 (2016).

Hiep, Tran Xuan "The Vietnam–India relations in the first decade of the 21st century." *India and Asia Studies*, no. 2 (2014).

Hue, Nguyen Canh "The Vietnam–India relations from 1956 to the first years of the 21st century." The Ho Chi Minh Teaching Pedagogy University, (2010).

Minh, Tran Tuan "India's Look East Policy Review." *Indian and Asian Studies*, no.4 (2016).

Nga, Le Thi Hang. "The state visit by Indian Prime Minister Narendra Modi to Vietnam and its effects on the Vietnam–India relations." *India and Asia Studies*, no. 10 (2016).

Nga, Le Thi Hang. Nguyen Ngoc Quynh, "Vietnam–India Cultural Cooperation since establishment of the strategic partnership (2007-2015)." *India and Asia Studies*, no.7 (2016).

Phan Thi Hong Xuan, "Vietnam-India relationship in the 21st century." *India and Asia Studies*, no.11 (2013).

Ross, Robert S. "Bipolarity and Balancing in East Asia," In *Balance of Power: Theory and Practice in the 21st Century*, edited by. T.V. Paul, James J. Wirtz, and Michel Fortmann, 267-304, Stanford, CA: Stanford University Press, 2004, http://www.hiunpar.org/wp-content/uploads/2015/10/Balance-of-Power-Theory-and-Practive-in-the-21st-Century.pdf.

Srivastava, Piyush. "India-Vietnam: Expanding Strategic Engagement in 21st Century." paper presented at the conference on *Vietnam-India: 45 years of Diplomatic Relations and 10 years of Strategic Partnership*, (2017).

Thayer, Carl. "India and Vietnam Advance Their Strategic Partnership." *The Diplomat*, 2014, http://thediplomat.com/2014/12/india-and-vietnam-advance-their-strategic-partnership/.

Toledo, Peter. "Classic Realism and the Balance of Power Theory." *Gledon Journal of International Studies*, Vol. 4, 2005, http://gjis.journals.yorku.ca/index.php/gjis/article/view/35205/31924

Vu, Truong Minh and Nguyen Thanh Trung, "Vietnam's Foreign Policy: In Search of a New Delicate Balance." *Asia Maritime Transparency Initiative*, November 10, 2016, https://amti.csis.org/vietnams-foreign-policy-search-new-delicate-balance/.

6

India, Vietnam and the South China Sea

Munmun Majumdar

Introduction

As a semi-enclosed sea as defined in Article 122 of the UN Convention on the International Law of the Sea (UNCLOS), the South China Sea hosts numerous islets and reefs as well as abundant living and non-living marine resources. It also provides key sea routes for maritime shipping and naval mobility and is traversed by a quarter of global shipping. Hence, it is an important economic and strategic sub-region of the Indo-Pacific that carries the bulk of international trade as well as provides crucial lifelines of energy and resource supplies. Stretching from Singapore and the Strait of Malacca in the southwest to the Strait of Taiwan in the northeast, the SCS is one of the most important trade routes in the world. It is bounded by the coast of Asia from Ca Mau, the southern tip of Vietnam, to Taiwan Strait, the southwest coast of Taiwan and the west coast of the Philippines to Balabac Island, the north coast of Sabah and the coast of Brunei and Sarawak, the northern façade of Indonesia's Kepulauan Natuna and the north coast of peninsular Malaysia. Because of its important strategic location and abundant resources, it has become a target of contention between/among bordering countries and the disputes in the SCS are regarded as one of the most difficult regional conflicts in the Asia Pacific.[1]

There are overlapping claims made by China, Vietnam, Malaysia, Brunei, the Philippines, and Taiwan[2] to the sovereignty over the islands and reefs, other outlying islands and islets are disputed and maritime jurisdictional disputes relating to maritime claims exists. Notwithstanding China's ratification of UNCLOS, the Chinese claim, articulated to the UN in 2009 but extending back to the 15th century, is by far the most extensive and provocative.[3] Beijing has dusted off a 1947 so-called nine-dash line claim map that encircles islands, waters, and other features of the South China Sea encompassing approximately 2,000,000 square kilometres of maritime space.[4] China while asserting that it has indisputable sovereignty over the SCS and the islands,[5] is using a range of diplomatic, economic and military levers to strengthen its position in the SCS against the other claimants.[6] It is in this aforesaid context that India and Vietnam's position are of relevance and will be discussed in the following section.

India and the South China Sea

Although India is not a claimant state, it has interests at stake in the South China Sea. India's interest in the SCS has been articulated by several Indian policy-makers who emphasised freedom of navigation in the SCS, as India considers unimpeded right of free passage in accordance with international law, as essential for peace and prosperity in the Asia Pacific region. India has been calling for the peaceful resolution of dispute between Beijing and its maritime neighbours, with whom it has conflicting claims in accordance with international law, including the UNCLOS.[7] India hoped that the parties to the dispute would abide by the 2002 Declaration on the Conduct of Parties (DoC) in the SCS and work towards the adoption of the Code of Conduct (CoC). India's position on maritime matters essentially highlights the following points: opposition to the use or threat of use of force and exercise self-restraint in the conduct of activities that could complicate or escalate disputes affecting peace and stability, adherence to the 2002 Declaration on Conduct in the South China Sea and peaceful resolution of disputes, in accordance with international law, including the UNCLOS 1982 and supports freedom of navigation and overflight, and unimpeded commerce, based on the principles of international law, as reflected notably in the UNCLOS.

India's dependence on the security of the Indian Ocean has compelled it to reach out beyond its own littoral. The entire Indian Ocean region stretching from the east African coast to the waters of the SCS is critical for India's foreign trade, energy and national security interests. More than 55 percent of India's trade with the Asia Pacific passes through the SCS. The significant dependence of India's trade on maritime traffic gives the sea a substantial influence on its destiny.[8] As such protection of the sea-lanes has become a fundamental feature of India's engagement with the countries of Southeast Asia and beyond.

India also recognises the strategic importance of Southeast Asia particularly because several Indian islands territories are as close as 90 miles from the Strait of Malacca. Another reason that explains Indian interest in the area is that it is worried about the way in which China has moved unilaterally to strengthen its hold in the SCS, which could enable it to exert unlawful coercive measures against smaller nations who are seeking to avoid domination by China. China's sustained military build-up, its anti-access/area-denial (or A2/AD) capabilities and its assertiveness in the East and South China Seas[9] are causing the Indian government to look beyond specific threats to it and to consider risks to broader regional stability as a result of China's rise. India, therefore, views with caution Chinese creeping maritime assertiveness, supported by its modernised and capable navy and marine paramilitary units. India is worried that if China controls this sea space it will dictate maritime traffic, both civilian and military. On July 22, 2011, INS Airavat was accosted by an unidentified Chinese warship (in the South China Sea 45 nautical miles off Vietnam's Nha Trang port), which asked it to identify itself. It was a clear signal (or warning?) that China does not want any foreign vessel in what it regards as its sovereign maritime domain. It is, therefore, rightly worried that China will use its growing maritime might to dominate not only the resource-rich waters of the SCS but also the crucial shipping lanes. As such India's priority has always been to maintain freedom of navigation in the sea for both merchant and naval ships, thus protecting the sea-lanes as it considers open and stable maritime commons essential to international trade and prosperity.

Apart from this, China has also been objecting to oil exploration by India's public sector company, ONGC Videsh (OVL) in Vietnam's territorial waters. China's insistence that essentially all the waters in the South China Sea fall within its jurisdiction, without providing any legal rationale, has led to several disputes over oil and gas concessions. These incidents have provided further impetus to New Delhi to deepen its engagements with the SCS littoral states in order to commercially participate in the exploration of vital energy resources. More so, since India also views the SCS region as a key to its energy security and any major conflict in the region is bound to impact Indian economic and strategic interests, which it cannot allow. Hence, India would like to maintain its presence in the SCS to track potential developments that could affect its national interest.

The Indian navy has underlined the importance of a forward maritime presence and sees naval partnership as critical to deter potential adversaries. Furthermore, involvement in the SCS could have implications on other territorial disputes. Particularly because it has unsettled borders with China in the Himalayas and therefore China's assertiveness in the SCS is troubling for India. Hence, interest in the SCS is not only about legality or historical pride but also pragmatism. What must also be clearly understood is that India's relationships with South East Asian countries are not geared only towards checking the Chinese presence in the region, but also reflective of India's global interests.

Under the Narendra Modi Government, India's policy hint at a greater political will in playing a part in shaping the changing security architecture. At the 2014, India-ASEAN and East Asia Summits, Indian officials emphasised freedom of navigation, peaceful resolution of disputes, and importance of international law. For the first time, India made a direct comment on dispute resolution in the South China Sea in a joint statement at the end of Prime Minister Narendra Modi's visit to the US in September 2014. The statement read: "The leaders expressed concern about rising tensions over maritime territorial disputes, and affirmed the importance of safeguarding maritime security and ensuring freedom of navigation and over-flight throughout the region, especially in the South China Sea". The statement also urges all parties to resolve the dispute in a peaceful manner in accordance with international law, drawing criticisms from Beijing. In September and January 2015, Prime Minister Narendra Modi and US President Barack Obama jointly affirmed common interests in the disputed SCS and in June 2015, India and the US also signed a defence framework.[10]

Furthermore, when the Vietnamese Prime Minister paid an official visit to India, the South China Sea was mentioned once again in their joint statement and Beijing's angst became even more evident. The statement had called for freedom of navigation through the South China Sea and urged all disputing parties to work toward the implementation of the Code of Conduct.[11] The joint communiqué between India and Vietnam also opposed threats to freedom of navigation and use of coercion in the SCS. With growing India-Vietnam defence ties, Hanoi in particular is keen on India's presence in the region, whether it is for economic or strategic reasons.[12]

Prime Minister Modi again emphasised the need to stabilise the South China Sea in the 12th India-ASEAN Summit and the 9th East Asia Summit in Myanmar. At both forums, Prime Minister Narendra Modi stressed on the need to follow international norms to maintain peace and stability in the South China Sea, a comment directed at China.[13] The document which Vietnam issued after Prime Minister Narendra Modi's visit to Vietnam was unique because apart from the usual references to freedom of navigation and overflight, and respect for international law, it also noted "the Award issued on 12 July 2016 of the Arbitral Tribunal constituted under the Annex VII to the 1982 United Nations Convention on the Laws of Sea (UNCLOS)".

India's repeated mention of the South China Sea in joint statements is definitely a shift from its previous statements on maritime security. Although New Delhi has previously remarked on the need to ensure maritime security and freedom of navigation in the region, it has never named any country or an area in dispute. What is also of significance is India's choice of platforms in making these comments. Similarly, the joint statement with Vietnam is a re-assurance to one of India's closest friend in the Southeast Asia engaged in a sharp dispute with China. Since almost half of India's trade with Asia passes through the critical waterway and that is the reason India has been pushing for a resolution of the matter based on international norms. In fact, right after the Permanent Court of Arbitration ruled against China in a case taken up by the Philippines, India issued a statement urging concerned parties to show utmost respect for the verdict. China dismissed the verdict questioning the legality of the tribunal itself. Besides, India's Act East policy demands an increase in Indian presence in the waters of the SCS, both economically and politically. More so India has to demonstrate and deliver for its ASEAN friends.

Vietnam and the South China Sea

Unlike India, Vietnam is a claimant in the SCS disputes. Its claims for sovereignty of islands and maritime regions overlap either wholly or partially with those of Brunei, China, Taiwan, Malaysia, and the Philippines. After its unification in 1975, Vietnam asserted its longstanding claims to sovereignty over the entire Paracel and Spratlys cluster of islets-referred to Vietnamese as Hoang Sa and Truong Sa respectively.

The disputes in the SCS stand out as the single most challenge that has seen China and Vietnam against each other in armed confrontation on more than one occasion.[14] While the quarrel over Paracels is between the two, the Spratlys involve Philippines, Malaysia, Brunei, Taiwan and China as well. The claims made by Vietnam as well as China are mainly grounded in historical evidence that both sides present. Vietnam has published three White papers in 1979, 1981, and 1988 and presented a wide range of historical data to prove its peaceful and continuous administration over these islands since the 17th century. Additionally, it contested the legitimacy of China's use of force to expel Vietnam from the Paracel Archipelago in 1974 and Spratlys reefs in 1988. In its two submissions to the Committee on the Limits of the Continental Shelf (one jointly with Malaysia, one on its own) in early 2009, Vietnam implicitly held the position that features in the two archipelagos do not meet criteria set out under Article 121, and thus they possess no EEZ or continental shelf of their own. However, in its Note Verbale to the UN Secretary-General protesting the joint submission by Malaysia and Vietnam, China stated that it "has indisputable sovereignty over the islands in the South China Sea and the adjacent waters, and enjoys sovereign rights and jurisdiction over the relevant waters as well as the seabed and subsoil thereof."

The current round of tensions in the South China Sea can be traced to the 2009 joint submission to the United Nations by Vietnam and Malaysia of a section of their extended continental shelves in the area [15] with China responding by submitting an objection to the UN Commission on the Limits of the Continental Shelf (CLCS) decrying Vietnamese and Malaysian infringement of its claims, which it defined via an ambiguous map that encompassed nearly the entire sea.[16] This difference in the views is derived from divergent interests of the two countries which show that while China wants to maximise the disputed areas to include the EEZ and Continental shelf of other claimants, Vietnam seeks to minimise them to protect its economic interests in its lawful EEZ and continental shelf.

Since February 1974, when China invaded the Crescent group of the Paracels then held by South Vietnamese forces[17] China has controlled 130 features southwest of Hong Kong. Vietnam has continuously confirmed its undisputable sovereignty of the Paracels and requested China to open negotiations to peacefully resolve the dispute to which China has turned a deaf ear. Modern Vietnam still claims what it lost. The 42nd anniversary of the 1974 naval battle between China and then South Vietnamese troops over Paracel Islands was marked by shouts and anti-China slogans on 19 January 2017. However, according to Carl Thayer, emeritus professor of politics at The University of New South Wales in Australia, "No one can force China out of the Paracels" and added that "The most you could hope for is if Vietnam took arbitral action," such as a petition with the world court in The Hague. What is important to point out is that China has always refused to seek international arbitration regarding its claims in the area.[18] Similarly, Vietnam lost more islands to China in a naval fight in 1988. The fact that China has not clarified its claims and the nine-dash line cuts into Vietnam's EEZ and Continental shelf has further aggravated tension between the two.

Although bilateral normalisation in 1991 has seen certain agreements between the two, efforts to resolve maritime issues launched in 1995 were cancelled in 2006 as the two countries disagreed over the meeting agenda. While Vietnam had insisted on the inclusion of the Paracels, China refused to do so. Finally, an agreement was arrived at in 2011, under which bilateral expert-level meetings on maritime issues were revived in a new format that consisted of two simultaneous series of meetings, one on the delimitation and joint development of the sea area beyond the mouth of the Tonkin Gulf and the other on bilateral cooperation in less sensitive fields in the SCS.[19]

Incidents of cutting Vietnamese seismic survey ships cable by Chinese maritime surveillance vessels within Vietnam's EEZ, China's offering of nine blocks within Vietnam's EEZ to international bidders, firing on Vietnamese trawlers by Chinese patrol ships near Paracels, China's issuance of unilateral fishing moratorium, seizure of Vietnamese fishing boats etc., have generated incessant tension between the two countries. The constant irritant between the two regarding the SCS can be gauged by statements issued by spokesperson of the Vietnamese Ministry of Foreign Affairs.

On the right to board boats in Chinese maritime territory claimed in regulations issued by the Hainan authorities, the Chinese declaration has alerted the regional countries. Vietnam and Philippines opposed the application of the regulations beyond 12 nautical miles since it had implications for the freedom of navigation, especially innocent passage as provided under International law. There have been massive demonstrations in Vietnam supporting Vietnamese claims in the SCS. The Declaration on the Conduct of parties in the South China Sea (DoC) that has been signed by both Vietnam and China has not been effective in showing restraint in the disputed area.[20]

Vietnam is concerned about its traditional national security as well as about human and regional security.[21] Despite the disputes in the SCS Vietnam is simultaneously trying to get along better with China on its own. Since mid-1980s economic development has become a priority. To this end Vietnam sought to improve relations with neighbouring countries including China. Hanoi placed its interest in promoting settlement of the dispute since it was no longer in a position to press its claims forcefully given its modest naval capabilities vis-à-vis China and in the absence of a counter-balancing ally. While physical control of the disputed islands became less pressing, the right to maritime resources and safety at sea gained importance and priority. Anti-Chinese sentiment however still runs high among Vietnamese people, but the government in Hanoi is talking with Beijing outside the ASEAN context about the maritime issue while enjoying economic benefits derived from its relations with China. Vietnam on its part has been undertaking projects on the Spratly Islands that include the extension of 600-meter runway to 1200 meters and the construction of two large hangars, in addition to the two that already exists. On completion of these projects the island will be able to accommodate most of the Vietnamese air force's aircraft. The new features are no match for China's military build-up in the SCS but they are notable for their position.

It is unlikely that China would bring in the subject of Paracels in ASEAN meeting with Vietnam and its ASEAN colleagues, as China considers the Paracels a bilateral issue between itself and Vietnam.[22] Cambodia and Laos who are also ASEAN members are pro-China and Philippines has presently set aside its maritime dispute with China. In such a situation ASEAN would possibly pursue a line that would not risk rifts. Further ASEAN may even see that inclusion of Paracels as an unnecessary complicating factor. Lack of mention or inclusion of the Paracels in the eventual Code of Conduct of parties in the South China Sea (CoC) would be a loss to Vietnam while it would give China absolute sway over the islets where it has huge military infrastructure.

Vietnam's top leaders have lauded India's principled position on the South

China Sea issue and sought its participation in oil and gas sectors of the Communist nation, as they hailed the upgradation of bilateral ties to Comprehensive Strategic Partnership.[23] India is poised to sell its sophisticated Akash missile defense system to Vietnam, the latest development in a broad strategic relationship that has grown rapidly in recent years. India has also agreed to train Vietnamese pilots on Russian-built SU-30s and Sukhoi fighter jets and currently trains Vietnamese submarine operators on Russia-produced Kilo-class submarines.[24] India has already offered military support to Vietnam, which is a direct and important claimant in the South China Sea, and has signed two major naval projects with Vietnam and has also offered a hand on modernising and upgrading their military equipment along with training the Vietnamese submariners. These are important developments at a time when both the countries are talking of China's growing assertiveness in the Asia-Pacific region. It has raised eyebrows since both India and Vietnam do not subscribe to China's claims in the SCS.

Given that 55 percent of India's trade passes through the SCS, the Indian Navy has of late come to prioritise energy security and sea-lane protection. Beijing has been protesting Vietnamese-Indian energy exploration project in the disputed waters of the South China Sea. Ignoring Beijing's warnings, India has publicly supported Vietnam and continues to cooperate with Hanoi on hydrocarbon exploration in the South China Sea. Both India and Vietnam share strategic concerns over China and wish to see a resolution to South China Sea sovereignty disputes. India has oil exploration operations in Vietnam-claimed areas of the sea. The two countries also have joint-exploration plans. Both India and Vietnam see China as the common perceived threat and whether all this would add a new twist to the spiralling power contest in the South China Sea, however, remains to be seen.

Conclusion

It may be said that the challenge for India is to be able to deal with the rise of a hegemonic China while keeping its own growth trajectory intact. New Delhi has reasons to support freedom of navigation in the region and prevent Chinese hegemony from taking hold since Chinese military dominance in the South China Sea offers the People's Liberation Army-Navy a formidable launching pad for more frequent operations into the Bay of Bengal and the eastern Indian Ocean, threatening Indian interests. Therefore, while establishing India's maritime interest in the SCS, New Delhi is also determined to work towards cooperative and rule-based security architecture in the region that would in turn enhance regional and global security. As for Vietnam, it is gearing up to face the Chinese challenge on the one hand by stepping up ties with India, US and Japan in trying to balance ties to increase leverage with China. At the same time, it is also exploring ways in which it could manage the dispute without having to derail its focus on economic development and its efforts to expand cooperation with China, which has seen phenomenal economic growth providing it the wherewithal for the modernisations of its defence forces.

NOTES

1. Shen Dingli, "Reconciliation in the South China Sea", in *CSCAP Regional Security Outlook 2014,* ed. Ron Hutsken (Kuala Lumpur: The Council for security Cooperation in the Asia Pacific (CSCAP), 2013), 37, available at http://www.cscap.org/uploads/docs/CRSO/CRSO2014.pdf. .
2. China and Taiwan see this as an internal conflict and not a conflict over maritime borders. It is interesting to note that China and Taiwan have cooperated in several disputes in the SCS where their claims are identical and both claim the SCS as being Chinese waters, not PRC or Taiwanese waters. See for example Mark Valencia, "China and the South China Sea Disputes: Conflicting Claims and Potential Solutions in the South China Sea." *Adelphi Paper 298,* Oxford: Oxford University Press, 1995; Bob Catley and Makmur Keliat, Spratlys, "The Dispute in the South China Sea." *Aldershot,* UK: Ashgate Publishing, 1997, and Lee Lai To, "China and the South China Sea Dialogues." *Westport,* CT: Praeger Publishers, 1999.
3. US Department of State, Office of Ocean and Polar Affairs, *China: Maritime Claims in the South China Sea,* Limits in the Seas, No. 143, Washington, DC: Bureau of Oceans and International Environmental and Scientific Affairs, December 2014, p. 4, available at http://www.state.gov/documents/organization/234936.pdf (accessed 4 February 2015).
4. US Department of State, Office of Ocean and Polar Affairs,*China: Maritime Claims in the South China Sea,* Limits in the Seas, No. 143, Washington, DC: Bureau of Oceans and International Environmental and Scientific Affairs, December 2014, p. 4, available at http://www.state.gov/documents/organization/234936.pdf (accessed 4 February 2015).
5. As asserted by China's Ministry of Defence spokesperson Geng Yangsheng: see Asia News, 'China's claims in South China Sea cause sparks with United States and Vietnam, Asia News [website], 30 July 2010, available at http://www.asianews.it/news-en/China%E2%80%99s-claims-in-South-China-Sea-cause-sparks-with-United-States-and-Vietnam-19075.html (accessed 25 August 2015).
6. Robert D. Kaplan, *Asia's Cauldron: the South China Sea and the end of a stable Pacific,* (New York: Random House, 2014), p. 18.
7. PM's statement at the 8th East Asia Summit in Brunei Darussalam, 10 October 2013. pib.nic.in/newsite/PrintRelease.aspx?relid=99951.
8. K.M. Panikkar, *India and the Indian Ocean: An Essay on the Influence of Sea Power on Indian History* (London: George Allen & Unwin Ltd, 1951), p.14.
9. See C. Fred Bergsten, Bates Gill and Nicholas R. Lardy, *China: The Balance Sheet – What*

the World Needs to Know about the Emerging Superpower (Washington DC: Public Affairs 2007), pp. 118-154; Donald K. Emmerson, "US, China role play for ASEAN," *East Asia Forum*, November 25, 2011, http://www.eastasiaforum.org/2011/11/25/us-china-role-play-for-asean/ (accessed November 11, 2014).

10. Jim Garamone, "U.S., India Sign 10-Year Defense Framework Agreement" www.defense.gov/News/Article/Article/604775, See http://archive.defense.gov/pubs/2015-Defense-Framework.pdf. (accessed on 10 August 2016). See http://archive.defense.gov/pubs/2015-Defense-Framework.pdf.
11. Joint Statement between India and Vietnam during the visit of Prime Minister to Vietnam September 03, 2016, http://www.mea.gov.in/bilateraldocuments.htm?dtl/27362/Joint_Statement_between_India_and_Vietnam_during_the_visit_of_Prime_Minister_to_Vietnam.
12. Joint Statement on the State Visit of Prime Minister of the Socialist Republic of Vietnam to India, 28 October 2014 http://pib.nic.in/newsite/PrintRelease.aspx?relid=110864.
13. See Prime Ministers remarks at the 9th East Asia Summit, Nay Pyi Taw, Myanmar 13 November 2014. http://mea.gov.in/SpeechesStatements.htm?dtl/24238/Prime+Ministers+remarks+at+the+9th+East+Asia+Summit+Nay+Pyi+Taw+Myanmar.
14. For an analysis of Vietnam's and China's claims, see Mark Valencia, Van Dyke & Ludwig, Sharing the Resources of the South China Sea, University of Hawaii Press, 1997.
15. Malaysia and the Socialist Republic of Vietnam, Joint Submission to the Commission on the Limits of the Continental Shelf Pursuant to Article 76, Paragraph 8 of the United Nations Convention on the Law of the Sea 1982 in Respect of the Southern Part of the South China Sea (May 2009), http://www.un.org/Depts/los/clcs_new /submissions_files/submission_mysvnm_33_2009.htm.
16. People's Republic of China, Note Verbale CML/17/2009 (May 7, 2009), http://www.un.org/Depts/los/clcsnew/submissions_files/mysvnm33_09/chn_2009re_mys_vnm_e.pdf.
17. See Chi-kin Lo, China's Policy Towards Territorial Disputes: The Case of the South China Sea Islands, (London: Routledge, 1989), 53-83.
18. Perlez, Jane, "Tribunal rejects Beijing's Claims in South China Sea," *The New York Times*, 12 July 2016. https://www.nytimes.com/2016/07/13/world/asia/south-china-sea-hague-ruling-philippines.html?r=0.
19. The Vietnamese text of the agreement is available in the Official Gazette of the Socialist republic of Vietnam, No. 581+582 (11 November 2011) http://congbao.chinhphu.vnlnoi-dung-van-ban-so-58_2011_TB-LPQT-(2561)?cbid=2552.
20. Association of Southeast Asian Nations, 'Declaration on the Conduct of Parties in the South China Sea, http://www.aseansec.org/asean/external-relations/china/item/declaration-on-the-conduct-of-parties-in-the-south-china-sea (accessed on August 28, 2013).
21. Stein Tonnesson, "Vietnam's Objective in the South China Sea: National or Regional Security?" *Contemporary Southeast Asia* 22, no. 1 (2000): 199-200.
22. http://globalnation.inquier.net155397/4day-asean-summit-kicks-off-in-manila.
23. Indian Express, http://indianexpress.com/article/india/india-news-india/vietnam-top-leaders-hail-india-position-on-disputed-south-china-sea-3011671/ Sept. 3 2016.
24. Helen Clark, "Why China Should Fear India's Arms Sales to Vietnam (Think South China Sea)" *The National Interest*, January 11, 2017. http://nationalinterest.org/blog/the-buzz/why-china-should-fear-indias-arms-sales-vietnam-think-south-19025.

7

India and Vietnam: Defense and Strategic Cooperation

Dhrubajyoti Bhattacharjee

In a world that is facing new challenges in the form of actions taken by state actors while being assisted by non-state actors, relations between nations are being forced to balance and counterweigh such expansions and threats. As Waltz has noted these balances are formed in between some or all states, consciously aiming to establish and maintain balance, to deter some powerful states' aim for regional or universal domination.[1] It has been also argued that the risk of major wars increases when there are power shifts between major contenders in the system.[2] A shift in power occurs between a rising challenger and a dominant status quo power is, thus a period of competition for leadership and may be critical for systemic stability, the role of regional alliances become crucial for the maintenance of stability.

India and the nations in Southeast Asia have deep links that date back to pre-history. The countries of South-East Asia were rich in minerals and spices. So this region was also called *Suvarna Bhumi* (the land of gold). The cultural and economic relations that have grown through history, dates back to the ages of the Champa and later with the Mauryan and Gupta civilisations, which built deep-seated strategic relations between India and the nations in South East Asia. With changing national and regional dynamics moulded in their colonial histories, nations have drifted apart but the historical ties keep them connected. The links embedded in Buddhism, language, social structure, as well as mindset have helped re-build linkages much easier. Though it might seem that nations are coming closer to each other as to necessitate strategic balancing in the region, but that is not a major fulcrum on which relations are growing.

Though India has various political, social, economic and strategic relations with most of the Southeast Asian nations, Vietnam remains among the most important Southeast Asian nations for India's security interests. Tagore poetically stated that the closeness of the people of India and Vietnam was embedded in history.[3] People of Vietnam followed and resolutely supported the freedom struggle in India and Mahatma Gandhi and other freedom fighters were held in high esteem.[4] Nehru considered Ho Chi Minh as "a great revolutionary and an almost legendary hero".[5] Even while facing international reprimand, India stood close to its belief to support Vietnam in its testing times during the 1960s and 1970s, which was well appreciated by Vietnam.[6]

India and Vietnam strategically had remained close to the Soviet Union, than to the US or China due to their ideological differences, their individual strategic relations with either US or China, their relations with neighbours and Cold War politics that brought them closer. Though they had historical linkages; the present Indo-Vietnam relations were forged between first Indian Prime Minister Jawaharlal Nehru and President Ho Chi Minh, making State visits to each other's country during the 1950s. Indian Prime Minister Nehru was the first head of government to visit Hanoi, barely a week after the Viet Minh took over from the French in 1954. India supported the Hanoi government during the Vietnam War, souring relations with the United States. Both countries fought border wars with China: India in 1962 (when Vietnam sided with its then-patron in Beijing) and Vietnam in 1979 (when India sided with Vietnam). Throughout the Cold War period, both India and Vietnam maintained close ties with the Soviet Union – and their shared reliance on Warsaw Pact military hardware remains a powerful bond two decades after the dissolution of the USSR.[7] In the various joint communiqués that have evolved between Indian and Vietnamese leadership, strengthening of peace and stability of the region has always been stressed upon. Then External Affairs Minister, and later Prime Minister, Narasimha Rao stated clearly that India and Vietnam have to pave an avenue for a lasting peace without abandoning principles. On the same lines, Prime Minister Rajiv Gandhi pointed out that progress brought new challenges. Both the nations should have the flexibility of mind and spirit which enabled the nations to recognise new challenges and work up befitting responses.[8] Rajiv Gandhi stated "Vietnam is a true and sincere friend of India with whom we enjoy ... many shared geopolitical perceptions. We have established a strong political understanding that will strengthen and safeguard the forces of peace and stability in Asia".[9]

From the time India adopted a policy of developing relations with its eastern neighbours in earnest, the nations that already had close strategic links with India are Singapore and Vietnam. Strategically, the relationship between India and Vietnam started getting a formal shape after India joined the ASEAN Regional Forum (ARF) in 1996. Since then, India established a MoU on defence cooperation with Malaysia, which established a Malaysia-India Defence Cooperation Meeting (MIDCOM) at the senior officer level. MIDCOM meetings started between India and Malaysia from 1993.[10] Politically, Vietnam was a viable option for Indian decision makers as among the other neighbours, Myanmar was under a strong military junta, while Cambodia and Laos had strict communist regimes. India had close economic and strategic links with Singapore, while Thailand's closer ties with China, has instigated India to build a closer link with the nation. Vietnam, after Doi Moi in 1986, had reformed its economic policies in a manner, which smoothened the way for international economic and strategic collaborations.

In 2007, during the State visit of Vietnam's Prime Minister Nguyen Tan Dung to India, Vietnam and India agreed to upgrade the comprehensive cooperation established in 2003 between the two countries to a strategic partnership. The strategic partnership encompassed bilateral relations in the political, economic, security, defence, cultural, scientific and technological dimensions and steers their cooperation in regional and multilateral forums. Both sides expressed their "endeavour to develop a strategic dimension to their partnership for the mutual benefit of their peoples and to contribute to peace, stability, cooperation and prosperity in the Asia-Pacific region and the world at large".[11]

The strategic partnership between Vietnam and India was based on "traditional friendship, mutual understanding, strong trust, support and convergence of views on various regional and international issues."[12] The 2007 Joint Declaration on Vietnam-India Strategic Partnership states that the two sides "agreed to establish a Strategic Dialogue at the level of Vice-Ministers in the Foreign Office" which has been taking place in regular intervals.[13] The present Comprehensive Strategic Partnership has been established to build a platform for attaining a comprehensive understanding of each other's regional strategic compulsions, and a deeper understanding of each other's strategic needs and interests.

India appreciated Vietnam's support for upgrading India-Vietnam relationship to a "Comprehensive Strategic Partnership" during Prime Minister Modi's visit to Vietnam, September 2-3, 2016. Previously, India and Vietnam committed to a strategic partnership between the two countries during a meeting in New Delhi between former Vietnamese Defence Minister Phùng Quang Thanh and Prime Minister Narendra Modi in May 2015. On October 27-28, 2014, the previous Vietnamese Prime Minister Nguyen Tan Dung came to India. During Dung's visit, India agreed to supply four naval patrol vessels to Vietnam, increase the level of training of its military personnel and raise its involvement in Vietnam's energy sector. The sale of India-Russia co-developed cruise missiles Brahmos to Vietnam also came under discussion during this visit.[14] India's entry into the Missile Technology Control Regime (MTCR) would legitimise and speed up the process of selling the BrahMos to Vietnam. Along with Vietnam, countries like the Philippines, South Korea, Algeria, Greece, Malaysia, Thailand, Egypt, Singapore, Venezuela and Bulgaria have shown interest in buying the BrahMos.[15] The recent strategic engagement with Vietnam has been seen by many analysts as the Indian desire to protect its investments in the oil fields off Vietnam's coast while strengthening Vietnamese naval power.

The strategic and defence cooperation between the two nations has shown a steady positive engagement. The Indian government provided a US$100 million credit line in October 2015 to help Vietnam in defence procurement and the modernisation of its armed forces, including submarine training.[16] This line of credit has been utilised by Vietnam for procuring four Offshore Patrol Boats for their Border Guards.[17] This line of credit has been presently increased to US$500 million, basically for major defence purchases along with the upgradation of its existing defence equipments and infrastructure.[18]

India's Strategic and Commercial Interests

India has always stressed on freedom of navigation and over-flight and unimpeded commerce in the South China Sea region. India signed an agreement with Vietnam in October 2011 to expand and promote oil exploration in the South China Sea and then reconfirmed its decision to carry on despite Chinese protests to the legality of the Indian presence. Beijing stated that New Delhi required its permission for India's state-owned oil and gas firm to explore for energy in the two Vietnamese blocks in the South China Sea, which China claims to be its territorial waters. China, to counter the move, put up the same oil blocks that Vietnam had leased to India for international bidding.[19] But Vietnam quickly cited the 1982 United Nations Convention on the Law of the Sea to claim its sovereign rights over the two blocks in question. India decided to support Hanoi's claims and accepted the Vietnamese invitation to explore oil and gas in blocks 127 and 128. India's state-owned oil company ONGC Videsh Ltd is involved in the exploration programme.

India and Vietnam have provided each other diplomatic and institutional support, even at the cost of relations with other countries. When Vietnam invaded Cambodia in 1978 and displaced the genocidal Khmer Rouge regime, the action was fiercely opposed by the United States, China, and ASEAN. India's diplomatic support for Vietnam caused friction with most other Southeast Asian states for over a decade. For its part, Vietnam was one of the only countries in the world to support India's 1998 nuclear tests. Vietnam was an early supporter of India's candidacy for a permanent seat at the UN Security Council, advocated for India's inclusion in the East Asia Summit in 2005, and for a time helped block Pakistan's inclusion in the ASEAN Regional Forum. India supported Vietnam's accession to the World Trade Organization, and helped Vietnam secure a temporary seat in the UN Security Council in 2007.[20]

Vietnam's need for strategic and military cooperation with Russia and India has had different intricacies. Though having profound economic and trade linkages, Vietnam shares a contentious relationship with China regarding territorial assets and maritime interests. The ongoing conflict in the South China Sea has intensified in the last few years. Hanoi fought a brief war with Beijing in 1979 and has been wary of the northern neighbour's increasing economic and military weight. The two sides again clashed at sea in 1988 when China occupied its first holdings in the Spratly archipelago of the South China Sea – a retreat that is still acutely felt in Hanoi. China also took full control of another South China Sea island chain, the Paracels, after a naval showdown with the then South Vietnam in 1974, which the present Hanoi administration has protested in many international and regional forums. More recently, China's placement of an oil rig in disputed waters for 10 weeks in the middle of 2014 sparked anti-Chinese riots across Vietnam.[21]

Figure 1: Vietnamese Defence Modernisation (in US$ mn)

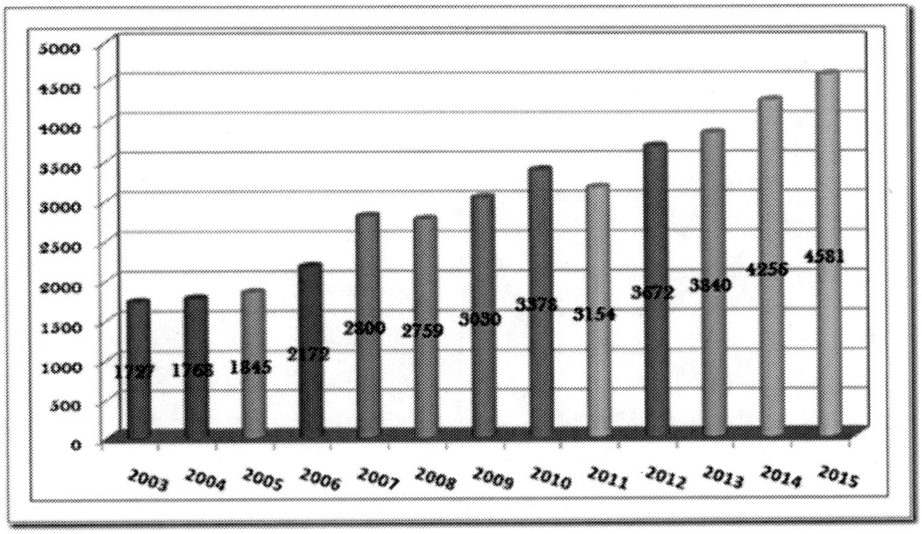

Source: SIPRI.

However, the inveterate economic relations that Vietnam and China shares, and the geographical closeness, makes China an important neighbour, though not strategically unreliable. Vietnamese national interest dictates to tacitly strengthen its position militarily, without disturbing the regional balance. It has been one of the motivators of building a close strategic and defence cooperation with India, which had significant similarity in the defence hardware, as well as had significant leverage in technology and skill.

According to former deputy prime minister of Vietnam Vu Khoan, "We understand that our country, in comparison with China, is a small one...Although they say friendship, they have invaded our territory. Ultimately, China must respect our nation and our sovereignty. Otherwise, Vietnamese will be 'allergic' to China".[22]

Vietnamese Defense Modernisation and India

Vietnam also turned its eye towards military modernisation during the last five years. The chart depicts the importance that has been given for such a modernisation process. Kommersant, an independent Russian newspaper, reported that Hanoi is looking to purchase up to twelve Su-35 fighters to augment its existing Su-30MK2 fleet from Russia.[23] (Indonesia is also interested to buy 10 Su-35.) Vietnam is also partnering with India to build a jointly operated satellite data transmission station. The Asahi Shimbun reports that officials in the Vietnamese Ministry of Defence are using the station as part of a larger plan to "strengthen intelligence-gathering capabilities in the South China Sea."[24]

In the last few years, Vietnam already has acquired 2 Varshavyanka class submarines, 2 Yugo class SSI, 2 Frigates, 6 Corvettes, 8 Tarantul class Corvettes, 54 Patrol and Coastal Combatants, 8 amphibious ships, 30 landing crafts, 13 Mine Warfare and Countermeasures and 29 Logistics and Support mechanisms along with various other naval defence technology and hardware from Russia, North Korea as well has started developing close strategic relationship with Japan and Israel.[25] The visit by the then Defence Minister Manohar Parrikar to Vietnam in June 2016, where he met the President Tran Dai Quang, Prime Minister Nguyen Xuan Phuc and Defence Minister Gen Ngo Xuan Lich to discuss new initiatives in the military sector, strengthened the bonding between the two nations. Along with other discussions, both defence ministers discussed the need for sharing white shipping information to facilitate exchange of data in the maritime domain. The two sides also focused on enhancing hydrographic cooperation. The major areas identified for working together are for upgrade of Soviet legacy systems, upgradation of Thermal Sights and Fire Control Systems for – BMP, T54 and T55 Tanks, upgrade of MI17/Mi8 Helicopters, Shipbuilding Programmes, Missile Systems from India and Software Defined Radios for Vietnam.[26] The highlight of the meeting was the handing over of the bid document by Vietnam Border Guards to Larson & Toubro Limited. The Indian defence minister stated that he desired Indian private sector to lead the initiative and explore and actively participate in Vietnamese modernisation of defence forces. This will not just strengthen the diplomatic and military bond between both the two nations but also open the doors of strategic exports.[27]

India's joint counter-piracy patrols help shore up its sea lanes of communications (SLOCs), while ministers from India and Vietnam have stressed the importance of the freedom of navigation, safe and peaceful maritime trade routes and security of its strategic assets in the region. Both the countries navies are also part of MILAN, a biennial multinational exercise and interaction hosted by the Indian navy since 1995 with the navies of South East Asia (Singapore, Vietnam, Thailand, Malaysia, Indonesia, Brunei and the Philippines) in the Bay of Bengal.

Regarding the volatile regional situation, Vietnam's strategy has stepped beyond contingency planning. Key units have been placed on "high combat readiness" – an alert posture to fend off a sudden attack – including its elite Division 308, which guards the mountainous north. Hanoi has started strengthening its naval deterrent with the purchase of six advanced Kilo-class submarines from Russia, of which five have already been delivered.[28] As noted by analysts, in relation to the fact evolving crisis in the South Chain Sea, Hanoi's generals are reaching out to a broad range of strategic partners. Russia and India are the main sources of advanced weapons, training and intelligence cooperation. Hanoi is also building ties with the United States and its Japanese, Australian and Filipino allies, as well as Europe and Israel.[29]

The ongoing discussion of transferring/selling major weapons systems to Vietnam between the two governments of India and Vietnam underscores the evolution in India's policy towards the Indo-Pacific. For the moment at least, this stance is being welcomed by states like Vietnam, which fear the growing aggression of China. A more engaged India would also lead to a more stable balance of power in the region.[30]

Prime Minister Modi's Visit to Vietnam in 2016

In the process of enhancing strategic cooperation to Vietnam, Prime Minister Modi, during his last visit in September 2016, pointed to the two-thousand-year-old civilisation linkages between India and Vietnam. While strengthening religion diplomacy, the Prime Minister recalled the historical Buddhist and Hindu roots, inviting Vietnamese to India, the land of Buddha. Twelve MoUs were signed, ranging from cultural, social, economic and defence cooperation, during the visit which remain significant in strengthening the relations between the two nations. The agreements that strengthened defence and strategic cooperation were the agreement on sharing white-shipping information, one of the many avenues that would provide a strategic depth to the bilateral relations between the two nations, as it is a major instrument for checking maritime piracy and increasing the scope of maritime surveillance on the entire region. Similarly, space technological cooperation is another untapped area of cooperation which can strengthen the region, strategically as well as in the fields of communication and maritime security. Especially, both countries could envisage developing a GIS mapping programme of its own while strengthening nano and micro-satellite technologies.[31]

The US$500 million line of credit in the defence sector remains strategically significant in nature. Increasing credit lines opens up multiple avenues for procuring significant defence assets for Vietnam, securing its maritime interests. The grant of US$5 million for the construction of an Army Software Park at the Telecommunications University in Nha Trang is also important as such a grant would enable the pooling of technological expertise and provide skill enhancement to Vietnamese professionals.[32]

Modi also emphasised that the two countries need to clearly forge further ties on regional and international issues of common concern, though specifics were not mentioned. On the issue of the South China Sea, India had clearly stated her standpoint supporting freedom of navigation, over-flight and unimpeded commerce (in the Joint Statements with the USA in September 2014 and Japan in December 2015) which was hailed by the Communist Party General Secretary Nguyen Phu Trong. The Vietnamese leadership in this regard sought further Indian participation in oil and gas sectors of Vietnam.[33]

Suggested Areas of Cooperation

There are multiple avenues that could strengthen defence and strategic cooperation between these two nations.

Training to submariners, particularly with regard to Russian submarines, is an area of defence cooperation between India and Vietnam. Indian Air Force can actively cooperate through the training of technicians of the Sukhoi Aircrafts as well as pilots on an annual basis. A five-member training team can be constituted to provide operational training to the young Vietnamese pilots by swiftly resolving various logistical and cost related bottlenecks.

Vietnam also lacks in manufacturing of small arms which is associated with coastal security. There is significant scope for the manufacture of assault rifles that is used by Indian Coast Guard personnel. The Indian defence establishment can also set up manufacturing facilities of carbines and small range missiles for which the potential buyers will be both from India and Vietnam.

India and Vietnam can also work out a coastal defence mechanism that would integrate coordination between marine or sea police, coast guards and navy as well as coastal radar systems to thwart away attacks on commercial or strategic installations along the coast of both the countries. India and Vietnam could also work in mutually developing ports in Vietnam, which the government of Vietnam has shown keen interest in, especially on the country's international gateway ports in the northern province of Hai Phong and the southern province of Ba Ria-Vung Tau.[34]

After India's decision of setting up a satellite tracking and imaging centre in southern Vietnam, which would give Hanoi access to pictures from Indian earth observation satellites that cover the region, another area of cooperation remains the areas of nano and microsatellite technology.[35] Both India and Vietnam hold a wide range of offshore assets, including oil exploration sites and islands. The security of these assets should be reinforced by better aerial surveillance systems and in this regard, the scientific and technological institutions along with universities that have developed such research can undertake pioneering projects. These satellites can be used for geo-spatial mapping as well as for gathering environmental data and sea explorations.

There is also the scope of electronic and military aerial radar systems, in which India has made substantial technological progress. Especially in the case of vehicle mounted electronic aerial radar systems, which can also work as an electronic guidance for counter measures. India and Vietnam can work on flat surface electronic aerial radar which can be installed in the various islands. The transfer or selling of various weapons systems, aircrafts or arms, like LCA Tejas, BrahMos, HAL's light combat helicopters, or missile defence systems remain to be areas that can strengthen defence relations between the two nations.

There are other defence collaborative possibilities. The case of exporting Dhruv and Kamov helicopters, which are produced under Russian license, to Vietnam would also be beneficial. The versatility of the Kamov helicopters would remain significant as they are efficient for monitoring and undertaking difficult terrain operations. India has also developed the Griffon/GRSE 8000 TD, a multipurpose hovercraft, along with Griffon Hovercraft Ltd, England, which has been inducted by the Indian Coast Guard. Such technology would certainly benefit the Vietnamese Marine Police significantly.

Assessment

With the rise of the Asian century, there is a need to strengthen the ancient bonds. With various strategic regional forums in place in Southeast Asia, India, which has a robust expertise in defence and space technologies and hardware production is slowly turning into an approachable destination as well as a viable partner for such forums. India and Vietnam have come a long way together building and fostering a relationship based on mutual trust and understanding.

With the fast changing strategic scenario in the neighbourhood and the rising challenges that are faced by Vietnam, India can play a larger role in strengthening the regional strategic theatre by coming closer to Vietnam in the strategic and defence sectors. With the sharing of each other's expertise and technological know-how, both together can counter the larger powers at play, the rising challenges threatening regional stability and the strategic maritime routes.

NOTES

1. Kenneth Waltz, *Theory of International Politics* (Michigan: McGraw-Hill, 1979), 119.
2. AFK Organski, *World Politics* (California: Knopf, 1958).
3. Nguyen Dang Thuc, "Tagore in Vietnam", in *Rabindranath Tagore: A Centenary Volume 1861 – 1961*, Quoted in Birendra Prasad, Indian Nationalism and Asia 1940-1947, Delhi 1979, p. 90.
4. Vo Von Sung, "Common Bonds of Friendship and Cooperation", in *India and Indochina: Perspectives of Cooperation*, ed. TN Kaul (New Delhi, 1987), 14.
5. Ton That Thien, *India and Southeast Asia: 1947-1960*, (Geneva, 1960), 112.
6. Dr. C. Ravindranatha Reddy, *India and Vietnam: Era of Friendship and Cooperation 1947-1991*, (New Delhi: Emerald Publishers, 2009), 71.
7. Jonah Blank, Jennifer D.P. Moroney, Angel Rabasa, Bonny Lin, *Look East, Cross Black Waters: India's Interest in Southeast Asia*, (CA: RAND Corporation, 2015), 92.
8. India Vietnam Joint Statement during the visit of Prime Minister Pham Van Dong to April 1980 (Vietnam (Hanoi), Vol. XXI, No.2, 1980, p. 19); Establishment of India-Vietnam Joint Commission in December 1982. During the visit of Vietnamese Foreign Minister in India (BBC, SWB, FE/7213/A311-2, 20 December 1982); Speech of the Prime Minister, Shri Rajiv Gandhi, at the banquet held in honour of His Excellency Nguyen Van Linh, General Secretary of the Socialist Republic of Vietnam, New Delhi, 25 January, 1989 (Directorate of Advertising and Visual Publicity, Ministry of Information and Broadcasting, Government of India, March 1989)
9. Government of India, Ministry of Information and Broadcasting, *Rajiv Gandhi Statements on Foreign Policy*, April-June 1988, (New Delhi, 1988), 9.
10. Pankaj Jha, "India's Defence Diplomacy in Southeast Asia," *Strategic Analysis* 5, no 1 (2011): 53, http://www.idsa.in/system/files/jds_5_1_pkjha.pdf.
11. Ministry of External Affairs (Government of India), Joint Declaration on the Framework of Comprehensive Cooperation between the Republic of India and the Socialist Republic of Vietnam as they enter the 21st Century, May 01, 2003, at http://mea.gov.in/bilateral-documents.htm?dtl/7658/Joint+Declaration+on+the+Framework+of+Comprehensive+Cooperation+ between+the+ Republic+of+India+and+the+Socialist+Republic+of+ Vietnam+as+they+enter+the+21st+Century.
12. Ministry of External Affairs (Government of India), Joint Statement on the State Visit of Prime Minister of the Socialist Republic of Vietnam to India (October 27-28, 2014), October 28, 2014, at http://www.mea.gov.in/bilateral-documents.htm?dtl/24142/Joint_ Statement_on_the_State_Visit_of_Prime_Minister_of_the_Socialist_Republic_of_Vietnam_to_India_October_ 2728_2014.
13. Ministry of Foreign Affairs (Socialist Republic of Vietnam), Vietnam-India joint declaration

on strategic partnership, http://www.mofa.gov.vn/en/nr040807104143/nr040807105001/ns070709164916#IhrFZb14XT4F.

14. Joint Statement on the State Visit of Prime Minister of the Socialist Republic of Vietnam to India (October 27-28, 2014), Ministry of External Affairs, October 28, 2014, http://www.mea.gov.in/bilateral-documents.htm?dtl/24142/Joint+Statement+on+the+ State+ Visit+ of+Prime+Minister+of+the+Socialist+Republic+of+Vietnam+to+India+October+2728+2014; Elizabeth Roche, "India assures Vietnam commitment to strategic partnership," *Live Mint*, May 27 2015, http://www.livemint.com/Politics/HKqx4wKLVUDtz3OEIjLcyN/India-assures-Vietnam-commitment-to-strategic-partnership.html.
15. "India's Missile Technology Group Entry May Be Cause Of Worry For China, Say Strategists," *NDTV*, July 02, 2016, http://www.ndtv.com/india-news/indias-missile-technology-group-entry-may-be-cause-of-worry-for-china-say-strategists-1427140.
16. Vivek Mishra, "Modi's Asia Pacific Push," *Center for International Maritime Security*, April 28, 2016, http://cimsec.org/modis-asia-pacific-push/24919.
17. "Parrikar holds talks with Vietnamese President, Prime Minister and Defence minister", *The Indian Express*, June 6, 2016, http://indianexpress.com/article/india/india-news-india/manohar-parrikar-vietnam-president-prime-defence-minister-military-india-2838016/. ; Scott Cheney-Peters, "India's Maritime Acts in the East," *Asia Maritime Transparency Initiative*, June 18, 2015, https://amti.csis.org/indias-maritime-acts-in-the-east/.
18. Dhrubajyoti Bhattacharjee and Sanghamitra Sarma, "Prime Minister Modi's Visit to Vietnam: An Assessment," Viewpoint, *Indian Council of World Affairs*, September 15, 2016, http://icwa.in/pdfs/VP/2014/PMModisVisittoVietnamVP15092016.pdf.
19. Harsh V. Pant, "South China Sea: New Arena of Sino-Indian Rivalry," *Yale Global*, August 2, 2012.
20. Iskander Rehman, "The Indo-Vietnamese Strategic Partnership," *BBC World Backgrounder*, September 17, 2009; Nhan Dan, "India, Vietnam Pledge Closer Strategic Ties", *Vietnam Communist Government News*, July 7, 2007; Ambassador Rajiv Bhatia, "Statement at the Inaugural Session Seminar on India-Vietnam Strategic Partnership: Future Directions," *Hanoi: Indian Council of World Affairs*, July 17, 2012; and "Vietnam-India Strategic Partnership in Spotlight," *VietNam Net*, July 18, 2012.
21. "Vietnam builds military muscle to face China." *The Economic Times*, December 18, 2015, http://economictimes.indiatimes.com/news/defence/vietnam-builds-military-muscle-to-face-china/articleshow/50230360.cms.
22. Erika Miranda, "Vietnamese Leader Shares Advice on Dealing with China", *Yibada News*, May 23, 2016, http://en.yibada.com/articles/125563/20160523/vietnamese-leader-shares-advice-on-dealing-with-china.htm.
23. Diego, "Vietnam, Pakistan dan Aljazair Ikut Beli Su-35, Saudi Pilih S-400", *Jakarta Greater*, April 1, 2016, http://jakartagreater.com/vietnam-2/ ; Chris Mirasola, "Water Wars: Fishermen Again Steer China into Hot Water," *Law Fare*, April 1, 2016, https://www.lawfareblog.com/water-wars-fishermen-again-steer-china-hot-water.
24. Chris Mirasola, "Water Wars: Fishermen Again Steer China into Hot Water," *Law Fare*, April 1, 2016, https://www.lawfareblog.com/water-wars-fishermen-again-steer-china-hot-water.
25. Carlyle Thayer, "Vietnam's Maritime forces", Presentation to Conference on Recent Trends in the South China Sea and U.S. Policy, Center for Strategic and International Studies, Washington, D.C., July 10-11, 2014, http://www.iacspsea.com/wp-content/uploads/2013/09/Vietnams-Maritime-Forces-July-10-2014.pdf. ; Muhammad Zulfikar Rakhmat, "Vietnam: Israel's closest ASEAN partner", *New Mandala*, December 04, 2015, http://

www.newmandala.org/vietnam-israels-closest-asean-partner/. ; Japan-Vietnam Joint Statement on the Establishment of the Extensive Strategic Partnership for Peace and Prosperity in Asia, March 2014, Ministry of Foreign Affairs of Japan, http://www.mofa.go.jp/files/000031617.pdf.

26. "Parrikar holds talks with Vietnamese President, Prime Minister and Defence minister," *The Indian Express*, June 6, 2016, http://indianexpress.com/article/india/india-news-india/manohar-parrikar-vietnam-president-prime-defence-minister-military-india-2838016/.
27. "Parrikar holds talks with Vietnamese President, Prime Minister and Defence minister," *The Indian Express*, June 6, 2016, http://indianexpress.com/article/india/india-news-india/manohar-parrikar-vietnam-president-prime-defence-minister-military-india-2838016/.
28. "Vietnam builds military muscle to face China," *The Economic Times*, December 18, 2015, http://economictimes.indiatimes.com/news/defence/vietnam-builds-military-muscle-to-face-china/articleshow/50230360.cms. ; Alexander Korablinov, "5th Russian-built Kilo-class submarine arrives in Vietnam," *Russia Beyond the Headlines*, February 9, 2016, http://rbth.com/defence/2016/02/09/5th-russian-built-kilo-class-submarine-arrives-in-vietnam_566041.
29. "Vietnam builds military muscle to face China", *The Economic Times*, December 18, 2015, http://economictimes.indiatimes.com/news/defence/vietnam-builds-military-muscle-to-face-china/articleshow/50230360.cms.
30. Harsh V Pant, "India's strategic gambit in Vietnam," *Live Mint,* June 15, 2016, http://www.livemint.com/Opinion/K4RMcKDJDYtplAwoJcPY9O/Indias-strategic-gambit-in-Vietnam.html.
31. Dhrubajyoti Bhattacharjee and Sanghamitra Sarma, "Prime Minister Modi's Visit to Vietnam: An Assessment," Viewpoint, *Indian Council of World Affairs*, September 15, 2016, http://icwa.in/pdfs/VP/2014/PMModisVisittoVietnamVP15092016.pdf.
32. Dhrubajyoti Bhattacharjee and Sanghamitra Sarma, "Prime Minister Modi's Visit to Vietnam: An Assessment," Viewpoint, *Indian Council of World Affairs*, September 15, 2016, http://icwa.in/pdfs/VP/2014/PMModisVisittoVietnamVP15092016.pdf.
33. Dhrubajyoti Bhattacharjee and Sanghamitra Sarma, "Prime Minister Modi's Visit to Vietnam: An Assessment," Viewpoint, *Indian Council of World Affairs*, September 15, 2016, http://icwa.in/pdfs/VP/2014/PMModisVisittoVietnamVP15092016.pdf.
34. "Deep sea ports to be developed," *Vietnam News*, December 18, 2013, http://vietnamnews.vn/society/249067/deep-sea-ports-to-be-developed.html# W4u4PwwlSUTim CDU.97.
35. Sanjeev Miglani and Greg Torode, "India to build satellite tracking station in Vietnam that offers eye on China," *Reuters*, January 25, 2016, http://in.reuters.com/article/india-vietnam-satellite-china-idINKCN0V309W.

8

India-Vietnam Maritime Cooperation: An Indian Perspective

Om Prakash Dahiya

Introduction

The strategic and defence ties between India and Vietnam have acquired a new force and dimension against the backdrop of the on-going flux in the South China Sea. Since the establishment of diplomatic ties between the two countries in 1972, India-Vietnam relationship has developed intensively and is reflected by the increase in high-level visits. Bilateral ties were upgraded to Strategic Partnership in 2007, underpinning the importance each country attaches to the other. Since May 2014, the Modi government has strongly promoted India's "Look East" policy in which Vietnam is regarded as a "pillar". With maritime security on mind, India has extended Vietnam a US $500 million credit line to purchase military equipment which could bolster Vietnam's military infrastructure and its preparedness to deal with maritime threats and respond to emerging regional challenges. As the two countries elevated their ties to a Comprehensive Strategic Partnership, it would provide a new direction, momentum and substance to the bilateral cooperation. The two sides are now looking to intensify strategic defence dialogue and enhance joint naval exercises to expand maritime security cooperation. Significantly, India and Vietnam see their growing relations as part of the larger drive for regional peace and stability.

India's presence in the South China Sea (SCS) is driven by oil exploration activities, and therefore it needs to protect its strategic interests. India also has a principled stand on freedom of navigation and access to resources as per the 1982 UNCLOS. In that context, the safety and security of merchant traffic through the Straits of Malacca and SCS is important to India. It is worth noting that New Delhi and Hanoi have been careful not to offend Beijing despite strong ties and common concerns in the form of long-pending territorial disputes with China. China is an important economic partner for both the countries. India has an intensive high-level engagement with China, and Vietnam could mark a maturation of India's East Asian Strategy under the Modi government. This translates into a twin-track Indian diplomacy in Asia; build on the new economic possibilities with China; but do not allow Beijing to define the limits of India's partnership with Vietnam.

Vietnam-India strategic dialogue and political consultative meetings are effective cooperation mechanisms for maintaining and enhancing bilateral relations in the strategic and political dimensions. Given the complementarily of Indo-Vietnamese strategic and security interests, strengthening defence cooperation between the two countries does not come as a surprise. With the frequent flaring up of tensions between China and India along the Line of Actual Control, and the fromer's increasing influence in India's neighbourhood, New Delhi also wants to strengthen its ties to Hanoi and further deepen security cooperation especially in the maritime domain.

This paper seeks to identify the opportunities and challenges for India and Vietnam to build maritime cooperation. It also aims to examine convergences to promote cooperation in bilateral as well as multilateral forums like ASEAN. This paper looks at the subject in three sections. First, it looks at the history of the decade of strategic cooperation between the two countries. Then it studies the template of India's various successful defence agreements to see what can be replicable in case of India-Vietnam relations and finally concludes by suggesting areas for future cooperation. The effort here is also to discuss and bring out the possible areas of cooperation where the bilateral perspectives overlap.

Evolution of India-Vietnam Defence Relations

It would not be wrong to state at the outset that there has always been a strategic dimension that shaped India-Vietnam bilateral relations. However, in the past, more often than not, this driving strategic factor was external,

Cold War politics for example. What is different in the present era of India-Vietnam relations is that now the two countries share many elements of their strategic vision of the larger Asian region and are firmly in the driver's seat in guiding their bilateral strategic relationship. The relationship today is being driven more by the choices that they make than by the circumstances around them. If earlier hedging was one of the purposes, at present it is about learning from each other's capabilities and converting overlaps in the areas of common interests into cooperation. It is also about exploring more areas where common interests overlap.

India and Vietnam are natural friends in Asia today. There are a lot of commonalities in the way they approach the issue of national defence. For starters, both India and Vietnam are against alliance partnerships and also against allowing the use of their bases and facilities against any third country. In addition, both countries seek open, balanced, comprehensive and inclusive security architecture in the region. Implicit in these variables is the common desire to maintain the freedom of navigation and overflight, and unimpeded commerce as well as respect for international laws and regulations. Indian Ambassador to Vietnam, P. Harish spoke to this effect before Prime Minister's visit in September 2016.

During his visit to Vietnam in September 2016, Prime Minister Narendra Modi called Vietnam "a strong pillar of India's Act East Policy". India-Vietnam bilateral relations have been important elements of both the country's foreign policies and are diverse and multifaceted. As they celebrate the 45th anniversary of the India-Vietnam diplomatic relations, it is pertinent to take a stock of the bilateral relations. At the same time, the year 2017 also represented the tenth anniversary of the establishment of the strategic cooperation agreement. In that context, this paper reviews the bilateral defence and strategic relations and discusses the way forward. It is important to note that after 10 years of strategic partnership, India and Vietnam have decided to upgrade it to comprehensive strategic partnership. This has been possible on the basis of the experience of the last decade. The deepening of defence relations has been on the back of increasing trust and mutual understanding. It is significant that in the last few years, India and Vietnam have had high-level bilateral visits at regular intervals.

Vietnam's centrality in India's Act East Policy is underscored by the fact that Vietnam has endorsed India's aspirations for the United Nations Security Council (UNSC) permanent membership. It favours India's joining of the

Asia Pacific Economic Cooperation (APEC) and was one of the vocal supporters for India to join the East Asia Summit (EAS). In addition, Vietnam was one of the co-sponsors of the UN resolution to declare 21 June as the International Yoga Day. At multilateral level, Vietnam is also part of Milan, the multinational naval exercise initiated by India.

One of the earliest India-Vietnam defence pacts was signed in 2000 when Vietnamese Prime Minister Phan Van Khai visited India. This paved the way for cooperation on regular exchange of intelligence, joint coast guard training to combat piracy, jungle warfare and counterinsurgency training for the Indian army, repair of Vietnamese aircrafts and helicopters, training of Vietnamese pilots and Indian assistance on small and medium arms production.

Training, joint practice and exercise, exchange of protocols and operating manuals is one area of thrust of India-Vietnam defence cooperation, which is an important component of the bilateral strategic relations. SIPRI reports suggest that Vietnam's defence procurement has gone up by 700 percent in 2015. Such a rapid jump would require support from friends and partners for developing capability for operations and maintaining purposes. Therefore, the core of India-Vietnam defence relations is in the right areas. The other aspects include "repairs and maintenance support, exchanges between think tanks, study tours and ship visits". There was also a provision of assistance of line of credit of US $100 million for infrastructure and defence procurement. In the 2016 visit of Modi, this was raised to US $500 million. Another important agreement reached during the 2016 visit was the announcement of a grant of US $5 million for construction of an Army Software Park at the Telecommunications University in Nha Trang to help develop better communication capabilities of the Vietnamese security forces.

Maritime Cooperation

Maritime cooperation is one of the important aspects of the India-Vietnam strategic partnership. The ongoing territorial disputes among some of the ASEAN nations and China in the South China Sea is challenging the region's peace and tranquillity. India holds a primary interest in the Freedom of Navigation (FON) through the South China Sea. It also has an economic interest in exploring hydrocarbon resources in the area with ONGC Videsh Ltd. (OVL) operating in two oil blocks in Vietnam. China's increasingly assertive navy makes it necessary for New Delhi to maintain its stakes and safeguard its interests in the region. This in turn would require continued naval engagement with the littorals. Beijing's claims go well into the Exclusive Economic Zone (EEZ) of the other disputing nations. China's vigorous pursuance of its territorial claims concern the international community as this affects a major SLOC. China even protests India's oil exploration with Vietnam in Block 128 despite the block falling within Vietnam's EEZ. Beijing nevertheless went ahead and put the block up for bidding to international companies ignoring the fact that it is already being operated by India.

India's naval cooperation with the Southeast Asian nations is an important dimension of the "Look East Policy", launched in the early 1990's. The Indian Navy has been carrying out joint exercises and military drills with the navies of the Southeast Asian nations since the early 1990s. India has enhanced its naval cooperation with the ASEAN nations and seeks to further strengthen its defence cooperation with the countries. Although India and its ASEAN counterparts have yet to realise the full potential of their naval cooperation, there has been incremental progress on this front over the years. New Delhi held its first India-Vietnam security dialogue in 2003 and signed a Memorandum of Understanding (MoU) on defence cooperation in 2009.

Naval goodwill visits are an important element of defence diplomacy. Defence engagements are crucial to build and maintain trust and contribute toward conflict prevention and resolution. In this, India and ASEAN share common ground wherein both parties seek to maintain peace and security in the region. ASEAN nations have welcomed Indian presence in the region and wish to see India pursue its engagements. Both sides have realised the importance of India-ASEAN cooperation. Indian Prime Minister Manmohan Singh underlining the need to further strengthen ties remarked in May 2013 that "...ASEAN countries are our strategic partners and there are enormous opportunities of expanding trade ties, expanding investment relations, expanding maritime cooperation, expanding the scope of trade and investment. And now we have reached a stage where large-scale flow of trade and investment is becoming a reality..." When Beijing put up Block 128 for bidding to international companies, Vietnam was enraged and protested vigorously. Vietnam then requested OVL to stay put in the block and promised more data and help to successfully drill the oil block. India had earlier decided that it may vacate the oil block due to unsuccessful drilling but reconsidered its decision. In January 2013, Vietnamese Deputy Prime Minister Vu Van Ninh invited "Indian companies to continue to invest and enter into Vietnam".

Vietnam has sought India's cooperation in the maritime domain. Both countries have engaged in frequent vessel exchange, while Indian officers have imparted training to Vietnamese submarine forces. Interlocked in a territorial dispute with China and its expansive claims on the South China Sea, Vietnam has struggled to hold its ground amid China's aggressive land reclamation and construction projects on reefs.

One of the important factors of overlap of defence interests is the fact that both India and Vietnam own and operate similar systems that have their origins in Russia. India has over 200 Su-30MKI fighters and nine Kilo-class diesel electric submarines. These are also the two of newest platforms in Vietnamese defence forces. Some form of cooperation in the aspects mentioned above on these two is already underway, or in the advanced stage of discussions. Various reports suggest that 550 Vietnamese submariners have been trained under the previous cooperation agreement.

It is well known that India has been providing spares for some Russian-origin equipment to the Vietnamese Navy and also providing basic training in submarine operations. For instance India has supplied spares for the Russian-origin Petya class warships and OSA-II class missile boats of the Vietnamese Navy. Vietnam has acquired three modern versions of the Kilo class submarine, much advanced though than what the Indian Navy had acquired over two decades back. Vietnamese sailors are being trained in submarine warfare doctrine and tactics at the Navy's submarine school INS Satavahanain Visakhapatnam, since October 2013. Indian naval ships have been regularly making port calls in Vietnam and showing their flag to indicate the right of passage and freedom of navigation in the international waters. There are also plans to provide training for Vietnamese Air Force pilots for flying Sukhoi fighters. Capacity building of Vietnam Armed Forces for improving the security environment is one of the major goals to be achieved.

Maritime engagement has therefore taken on additional importance and symbolism. Thus, a Vietnamese frigate crossed thousands of nautical miles from the East Sea in the Pacific, through the Strait of Malacca, to the Indian Ocean to join the International Fleet Review held in February 2016. More recently, four Indian naval ships made the reverse journey, under the Command of the Flag Officer leading the Eastern Fleet, for a four day visit to Vietnam in May 2016, as part of a deployment to the South China Sea and North Western Pacific.

Possible Areas for Future Cooperation

The possible areas for expanding maritime cooperation in the region are in the areas of hydrography; training in visit, board, search and seizure operations; training on board Indian Sail Training Ships; think tank level exchanges and joint participation in adventure activities. Interoperability, shared maritime information network and identification structures are other important target areas of this cooperation. India can also extend cooperation with Vietnam to broaden its capacity in Humanitarian Assistance and Disaster Relief (HADR).

During the June 2016 visit of Defence Minister Manohar Parrikar, defence industry cooperation was identified as one of the areas of cooperation. The other issues discussed include, defence industry networking, establishing a mechanism for exchange of relevant information and exploration of possibilities for partnership and collaboration between the two countries, sharing of white shipping information to facilitate exchange of information in maritime domain and enhancing hydrographic cooperation.

Border management can be another area where India and Vietnam can cooperate. Smuggling, drugs and human trafficking and small arms movement across land and maritime borders are the challenges faced by both the countries. Coastal watch is an on-going issue as well with recurring challenges like illegal fishing in a country's sovereign waters. Watching and controlling what is going on is an increasingly bigger challenge for many countries in the region. This is another area that can be looked at for future cooperation. Officer deputations and training course slots in academies for higher command courses, exchange of operating manuals and best practices and case studies can be looked into. In addition, prospects of technological cooperation on improved border management can be studied further. The joint statement issued during Prime Minister Modi's visit also talks of various issues including "an early conclusion of the MOU for cooperation between the National Security Council Secretariat of India and the Ministry of Public Security of Vietnam, emphasised the need to establish the Deputy Ministerial level dialogue and to enhance cooperation on traditional and non-traditional security matters, cyber security, counter-terrorism, transnational crimes, disaster management and response, and undertaking training and capacity building programmes". This is a highly comprehensive list in itself and follow up on the points listed above must be hastened as these are not only significant but also early harvest areas of cooperation in general.

The contract for 12 offshore high-speed boats is one significant area of security agreement. This contract has been awarded to the Larsen & Toubro (L&T), a major private sector defence manufacturer in India. It is significant to note that L&T also has a contract for supplying 54 interceptor boats for the Indian Coast Guards. This would create another opportunity for joint training and exercises due to the similarity of platforms. Recent reports also suggests that discussions on the issue sale of indigenously developed surface to air Akash missile and the supersonic Brhamos missile were held recently and are at advance stage of discussions.

Conclusion

India-Vietnam relations have been old as well as deep rooted in history. The defence relations between the two countries are expanding well and are of the nature of capacity building and training and deepening mutual understanding. The joint vision statement of May 2015 for the period of 2015-2020 is the guiding principle of the bilateral defence relations and the progress under that has been fairly satisfactory. The up-gradation of strategic partnership to comprehensive strategic partnership underlines the fact that the two countries attach great importance to this relationship and share an optimistic outlook about one another.

The new direction, momentum and substance that the Indian Prime Minister spoke off at the joint press conference would be achieved when the defence relationship expands to newer areas, some of which have been listed above. The high frequency of bilateral dialogues, meetings and consultations in the recent past suggest that the process towards comprehensive strategic partnership is well and truly underway. The following are the some of the recommendations:

(a) India and Vietnam could cooperate with each other to develop Vietnam's indigenous defence sector especially where India has strengths.
(b) Meanwhile, India should consider for export to Vietnam a variety of missile systems (including various versions of BrahMos Cruise missile) besides Unmanned Aerial Vehicles (UAV) and other defence systems and weapons as earmarked by India for export. Dornier surveillance aircrafts, mini UAVs, etc.
(c) Sharing of intelligence would add to intensification of strategic relationship.

(d) As full complement of Russian Kilo class submarines is still to be inducted, continued training of Vietnamese submarine crew would be necessary.

(e) Support the Vietnam forces in establishing and development of its C4ISR (Command, Control, Command, Computers, Intelligence, Surveillance, Reconnaissance) systems.

REFERENCES

Ajaya Kumar Das, ed., India-ASEAN Defence Relations, *RSIS Monograph No. 28*, 2013.

Bhaskar Roy, "Why India–Vietnam Military Relation Disturbs China," *South Asia Analysis Group*, Paper no. 6213, 01/16/2017.

Carl Thayer, "How India-Vietnam Strategic Ties Are Mutually Benecial," *The Diplomat*, December 03, 2013.

David Brewster, "The Strategic Relations between India and Vietnam: The Search for a Diamond on the South China Sea?", ANU Open Research Paper (2008), at https://openresearch-repository.anu.edu.au/bitstream/1885/13058/1/Brewster,%20D.%20India's %20Strategic %20Partnership%20with%20Vietnam%202009.pdf.

Dinakar Peri, "India to train Vietnam's Sukhoi fighter pilots", *The Hindu*, 6 December 2016, at http://www.thehindu.com/news/national/India-to-train-Vietnam%E2%80%99s-Sukhoi-fighter-pilots/article16765719.ece.

For details see, ANI, "India makes its stand clear ahead of PM's China visit, says all must respect UNCLOS," 2 September 2016, at http://www.aninews.in/newsdetail-Mg/Mjc4Mjk2/india-makes-it-stand-clear-ahead-of-pm-039-s-china-visit-says-all-must-respect-unclos.html.

For details see, Indian Embassy in Vietnam, "Bilateral Visits/Events", (n.d.), at http://indembassy.com.vn/media_center.php?id=24#.

Full Text of Prime Minister's Banquet Speech during Visit to Vietnam at http://indiainbusiness.nic.in/newdesign/index.php?param=newsdetail/15018/2.

In case of India, this was seen recently in Prime Minister Modi's speech at the Raisina Dialogue in New Delhi in January 2017, for the full text see, http://www.firstpost.com/india/pm-modi-inaugurates-raisina-dialogue-in-delhi-read-full-speech-here-3208182.html (In case of Vietnam, this was one of the core points of its National Defence White Paper, 2009. For full text, see http://aseanregionalforum.asean.org/files/library/ARF%20Defense %20White%20Papers/Vietnam-2009.pdf.

India & Vietnam sign a Joint Vision Statement on defence cooperation, *Economic Times*, May 26, 2015.

"India, Vietnam ink 5-year defence pact amid Chinese naval expansion," *Live Mint*, 26 May 2015.

Larsen and Toubro, "L&T bags major order from Vietnam Border Guard for High Speed Patrol Vessels," 22 September 2016, at http://www.larsentoubro.com/media/33614/2016-09-22-lt-bags-prestigious-defence-export-order-from-vietnam.pdf.

Manoj Joshi, "Vietnam Will Never Be for India What Pakistan is to China," *The Wire*, 03 September 2016.

MEA, "NSA level meeting on trilateral Maritime Security Cooperation between India, Sri Lanka and Maldives," March 6, 2014, at http://www.mea.gov.in/in-focus-article.htm?23037/NSA+level+meeting+on+trilateral+Maritime+Security+Cooperation+between+India+Sri+Lanka+and+Mal dives.

Ministry of Defence, *Annual Report 2013-14*, p.31, New Delhi, at http://mod.nic.in/writereaddata/AnnualReport2013-14-ENG.pdf.

Ministry of External Affairs, "India-Vietnam Relations", (2014), p. 3, at https://www.mea. gov.in/Portal/ForeignRelation/Vietnam_13_01_2016.pdf.

Ministry of External Affairs, Government of India, "Joint statement between India and Vietnam during the visit of Prime Minister to Vietnam," 3 September 2016, at http://www.mea.gov.in/bilateral-documents.htm?dtl/27362/Joint+Statement+between+ India+ and+ Vietnam+during+the+visit+of+Prime+Minister+to+Vietnam.

Press Information Bureau, GoI, "Visit of Shri Manohar Parrikar to Vietnam from June 05 to 07", 6 June 2016, at http://pib.nic.in/newsite/PrintRelease.aspx?relid=146003.

PTI, "India, Vietnam hold talks on sale of Akash, Brahmos missiles," *Livemint*, 3 February 2017, at http://www.livemint.com/Politics/dZhZhYuvnpvPBJBphn26zI/India-Vietnam-hold-talks-on-sale-of-Akash-Brahmos-missiles.html.

PTI, "Maldives Water Crisis: India transport 1000 tonnes of Fresh Water to Male", *NDTV*, 7 December 2014, at http://www.ndtv.com/india-news/maldives-water-crisis-india-transports-1-000-tonnes-of-fresh-water-to-male-709771.

Rahul Mishra (2014), "India-Vietnam, New Waves of Strategic Engagement", *ICWA Issue Brief*, 20 January 2014, at http://www.icwa.in/icwa_hindi/pdfs/IBindiavietnam.pdf.

Rajiv Ranjan Chaturvediy, "India-Vietnam Ties: The Stamp of 'Modi Doctrine'," *ISAS Insights*, no. 346, (2016).

Ritu Sharma, "Jet set no go: Plan to train Vietnam Sukhoi pilots grounded", *New Indian Express*, 19 November 2016, at: http://www.newindianexpress.com/thesundaystandard/2016/nov/19/jet-set-no-go-plan-to-train-vietnam-sukhoi-pilots-grounded-1540496.html.

Suhasini Haidar, "India to modernise Vietnam's defence forces," *The Hindu*, 29 October 2014.

Sylvia Mishra, "India and Vietnam Can Rescue Asia's Balance of Power," *The National Interest*, 5 Feb. 2017.

The Saigaon Times Daily, "Vietnam, India upgrade ties to Comprehensive Strategic Partnership", 5 September 2016, at http://english.thesaigontimes.vn/49493/Vietnam-India-upgrade-ties-to-comprehensive-strategic-partnership.html.

9

India-Vietnam Bilateral Economic Ties: The Road Ahead

Rashmi Singh

Introduction

Bilateral relations between India and Vietnam are guided both by their common historical experiences and their mutual concerns in the post-cold war context. Both have suffered aggression and fought wars with China in the past and had good relations with the former Soviet Union. India has had formal diplomatic relations with Vietnam since 1972, at the time when Vietnam was isolated by the ASEAN countries due to the Vietnam War. In fact, India was the only non-communist country to recognise the unified Vietnam and, ever since, they are having a friendly relationship, one that has stood the test of time. In addition, the changing geostrategic dynamics have also forced Vietnam to forge greater strategic cooperation with India.

Vietnam-India economic cooperation did not figure prominently in bilateral relations up to the late 1990s. It started gaining momentum when India started its "Look East" Policy at the beginning of the 1990s. The internal development and restructuring needs of Vietnam during the "Đoi moi" (Innovation) period and India's own economic liberalisation era have caused both sides to make great efforts in expanding bilateral trade and investment. When Vietnam and India enhanced their relations to the strategic partnership level in 2007, bilateral cooperation has been promoted across five areas:

political, defence and security; closer economic cooperation and commercial engagement; science and technology; cultural and technical; and multilateral and regional cooperation. India is among the 17 biggest international trade partners of Vietnam, and Hanoi is the 19th largest foreign trade partner of New Delhi.[1] The Indian government's decision to elevate the Look East Policy to an Act East Policy to promote economic growth with Southeast and East Asian economies in order to expand the global role of India holds out promise for India-Vietnam economic ties as well.

Besides closer economic relations, India and Vietnam have similar security interests, including finding out ways to deal with China and other major powers within their respective regions. India's relations with Vietnam provide a basis for a larger Indian role in Southeast Asia in different areas. India's defence cooperation with Vietnam is mutually beneficial for both the countries in the sense that India gains from the sale of military equipment, platforms, technology and services to Vietnam; Vietnam on the other hand has benefited by the increased ability to moderniseits armed forces and strengthen its capacity for the repair and maintenance of air and naval platforms.

India and Vietnam raised their relationship to a "comprehensive strategic partnership" during the September 2016 state visit by Indian Prime Minister Narendra Modi to Hanoi. India has also helped Vietnam to shore up its defence capabilities. Last year (2016), India extended a US $500 million line of credit to Vietnam.[2] India has also agreed to provide Vietnam with Akash surface-to-air missile systems mainly to act as a deterrent to any possible aggression against Vietnam. The two countries have seen their convergence accelerated in recent years given their mutual concerns over a rising China. India has provided training to the Vietnamese navy's submariners on operating the country's six Russian Kilo-class submarines. Vietnam is also receiving Indian assistance in the modernisation of its Petya-class frigates (specifically for anti-submarine warfare). India has also considered offering Vietnam the considerably more advanced BrahMos supersonic cruise missile to expand its defence relations.

Macroeconomic Performance of Indian and Vietnamese Economy

India's Macroeconomic Performance

India is one of the fastest growing economies and is termed as a bright spot in the world, despite the global slowdown and the recent headwinds being faced by Indian economy due to demonetisation. India's real GDP or GDP at constant (2011-12) prices for the year 2016-17 was estimated at Rs. 121.90 lakh crore showing a growth rate of 7.1 percent over the year 2015-16 of Rs. 113.81 lakh crore.[3] According to the International Monetary Fund, the growth in India is projected to bounce back to 7.2 percent in the fiscal 2017-18 fiscal and 7.7 percent in 2018-19.

However, despite the short period of slow growth, the Indian economy is resilient which is reflected by favourable macroeconomic indicators. The inflows of total Foreign Direct Investment (FDI) in India stood at US$60.08 billion during FY2017, including equity inflows, re-invested earnings and other capital as against US$55.5 billion during FY2016 registered a remarkable growth rate of 8 percent (Y-O-Y).[4] The increased FDI inflows along with a falling import bill is due to lower oil prices which has helped India to raise its import cover ratio, even though it is still lower than that of other BRICS economies i.e. China, Russia and Brazil. The CPI and WPI inflation has come significantly down to 2.2 percent and 3.8 percent respectively due to the falling import prices.[5]

India's merchandise exports reached the value of US$274.64 billion as against US$262.290 billion registering a positive growth of 4.71 percent over the same period last year whereas India's merchandise imports for the period April-March 2016-17 were US$380.367 billion as against US$381.01 billion registering a growth of (-) 0.17 percent over the same period last year. Taking merchandise and services together, overall trade deficit for April-March 2016-17 was estimated at US$40.98 billion which is 16.87 percent lower compared to US$49.29 billion during April-March 2015-16.[6] Considering services as the key for development of the economy, the Government of India has been promoting many types of services. Science and technology are considered the two tools to help bring about equitable growth and economic development. The information technology industry and the software industry in India have emerged as areas with the fastest economic growth.

India has also put special emphasis on serving the needs of industrialisation. Nuclear energy is expected to play a key role in serving India's long-term energy security. India's growth in core infrastructure increased to 4.8 percent during April 2016-17 as against 3 percent during the corresponding period of 2015-2016. Despite the process of demonetisation, India registered a growth at 8.8 percent in the consumer non-durable goods,

5.5 percent in consumer durable goods segment and the growth in manufacturing sector at 4.9 percent in 2016-17[7] which is indicative of steady industrial activity and reflects the visible effect of various reform measures undertaken by the Government.

Vietnam's Macroeconomic Performance

Vietnam had suffered from a prolonged war with both United States and China and it saw economic stagnation during 1950-1990. However, since 1986, the country began rebuilding its economy with the policy of doi moi.[8] Substantial progress was achieved from 1986 to 1997, despite the ravages of war, loss of financial support from the old Soviet Bloc and changeover from a centrally planned economy. Real GDP growth averaged around 9 percent from 1993 to 1997.[9] After a slight dip during 1997 Asian financial crisis, growth averaged 7.5 percent during the years 2000-2007. GDP grew by a robust 8.4 percent in 2007, driven by strong domestic growth as well as higher investment following the country's accession to WTO in January 2007. However, the global recession dampened the export oriented economy in 2008. In 2015, real GDP growth grew at 6.7 percent. In absolute terms, GDP increased to US$193.6 billion in 2015 from US$31.18 billion in 2000, and GDP per capita stood at US$2111.13 in 2015 (Table 1).

Vietnam as a part of ASEAN also shares similar economic characteristics and advantages with other members of ASEAN, such as a strategic location near global supply chains, and a low-cost, young and highly qualified labour force. In addition, the consumer class is increasing and the political and the macroeconomic environment is stable. These advantages have helped Vietnam become not only a major manufacturing hub in ASEAN but also the world's factory. Exports of electronic products, computers, phones, etc. have helped change the trade balance through export surplus and have surpassed the textile industry to become the largest export industry.

Services is the largest sector in Vietnam's economy, accounting for 39 percent of Vietnam's GDP in 2014. The shares of industry and agriculture in GDP during the same year were 33.2 percent and 17.7 percent respectively.[10] Vietnam has substantial energy and mineral resources. Its energy resources are a major source of export earnings and support domestic industries. Some of its major resources include phosphates, coal, manganese, rare earth elements, bauxite, chromate, offshore oil and gas deposits, timber, and hydropower. Inflation has been observed to be high in Vietnam in recent years, owing to easy availability of domestic credit. In 2015, inflation eased to 0.6 percent as compared to a high of 23.11 percent in 2008. Foreign-exchange reserves have risen at a strong pace, improving the ability of the central bank to counteract further downward pressure by intervening in the currency market if necessary. Vietnam has remained an attractive investment destination considering its growing working-age population and low labour cost. Nevertheless, the country faces increased competition for FDI in Southeast Asia, particularly from Indonesia. In terms of volume of imports and exports, both are increasing constantly despite fluctuations in year 2010 respectively. (Table 1)

Current State of India-Vietnam Economic Relations

The India-Vietnam relationship, part of which is based on a set of historical commonalities, has been moving towards addressing shared strategic concerns of energy security and open Sea Lanes of Communication and moving to economic areas, capacity building and technical assistance. On the other hand, Vietnam is poised to play a greater role in facilitating India's Act East policy for relations with Southeast Asia. India's new role would add ballast to ASEAN's efforts to maintain regional autonomy in Southeast Asia and a multipolar balance in ASEAN's relations with external powers.

Currently, India is among the leading trade partners of Vietnam. During a visit to India of Secretary General Nguyen Phu Trong in November 2013, the two countries set a bilateral trade target of US$15 billion by 2020.[11] However, apart from achievements, India-Vietnam economic relations have also faced many difficulties and challenges. The major factors hindering trade relations between the two countries are: similarity in the import/export structure of the two economies; geographical distance and difficulty in transportation; and differences in tastes, customs and business environment.

Geo-strategic interests between India and Vietnam are markedly converging. Both share similar concerns about maritime security and Chinese muscle flexing. Not only has India offered substantial support to Vietnam's navy and air force but also political-diplomatic support for Vietnam's South China Sea policy. Both India and Vietnam will benefit from the development of Vietnam's offshore hydrocarbon resources. India is seeking new markets while Vietnam wants to enhance its economic heft. Indian strategists have long called for stepping up relations with Vietnam to exert pressures on China as a response to China's engagement with Pakistan which brings pressure on India. Recently, Indian strategists have called for stepping up relations with

Table 1: Macroeconomic Snapshot of Vietnam

Subject Descriptor	Units	2000	2002	2004	2006	2008	2010	2012	2013	2014	2015
Gross domestic product, constant prices	Percent change	6.79	7.08	7.79	6.98	5.66	6.42	5.25	5.42	5.98	6.7
Gross domestic product, current prices	U.S. Dollars (Billions)	31.18	35.10	49.52	66.39	98.27	112.77	155.57	170.57	186.05	193.6
Gross domestic product per capita, current prices	U.S. Dollars, Units	401.57	440.21	603.67	796.93	1154.49	1297.23	1752.62	1901.70	2052.85	2111.13
Inflation, average consumer prices	Percent change	-1.77	4.08	7.90	7.50	23.12	9.21	9.10	6.60	4.10	0.63
Volume of imports of goods and services	Annual % growth	16.61	15.78	21.93	11.98	15.01	8.22	9.09	17.34	12.80	18.11
Volume of exports of goods and services	Annual % growth	21.10	10.36	25.61	11.19	13.69	8.44	15.70	17.37	11.56	12.64
Current account balance	Percent of GDP	2.73	-1.79	-3.21	-0.25	-10.98	-3.79	5.96	5.55	5.42	0.46

Source: World Economic Outlook Database, IMF; World Development Indicators, World Bank.

Vietnam as a response to Chinese in-roads in the Indian Ocean region especially with Sri Lanka and other countries. Deeper development partnerships between India and Vietnam are proving to be rewarding for both despite the causes for mutual concern such as China's growing investments in the vicinity of both nations and the tensions in the South China Sea.

This paper is an attempt to analyse India-Vietnam economic ties since the establishment of the bilateral strategic partnership of 2007 with a focus on a few major aspects: (1) the economic advantages of India and Vietnam; (2) the current situation of India-Vietnam economic relations; and (3) prospects for the development of India-Vietnam economic relations.

India-Vietnam Trade

India's bilateral trade relations with Vietnam are marked by growing economic and commercial engagement. Bilateral trade between India and Vietnam reached US$8037 million in 2015, up from US$208.9 million in 2000 (Table 2). Although bilateral trade has been growing at a fast rate, Vietnam's share in India's total trade stands at a meagre 1.2 percent in 2015. In exports, Vietnam's share in India's total exports stands at a meagre 2 percent and in imports it is only 0.7 percent. The two sides have set a target of US$15 billion for bilateral trade by 2020. Vietnam ratified the India-ASEAN FTA in goods with effect from June 1, 2010. The proposed agreement on trade in services and investment, which has entered into force in the year 2014, is likely to impart further boost to bilateral trade and economic relations.

This Agreement is a roadmap for tariff reduction commitments made by ASEAN and India. Besides, on signing the ASEAN-India Bilateral Trade in Goods Agreement (AITIG) on 25 October 2009, India also significantly recognised Vietnam's full market economy status. As a new member of ASEAN (Cambodia, Laos, Myanmar, Vietnam), Vietnam enjoys a tariff reduction roadmap of five years, longer than other ASEAN countries and India. In addition, Vietnam still enjoys full privileges from tariff reduction commitments of India and other ASEAN countries. Added to this, at the request of Vietnam, 80 percent of India's tariff lines of goods to Vietnam will be reduced to 0 percent by the end of 2018. On "sensitive" goods, namely, those products in which both India and Vietnam compete such as tea, coffee, pepper, seafood and garments, the roadmap tariff cuts will be implemented from 2019 with India agreeing to reduce the tariff to 45 percent for coffee and black tea and 50 percent for pepper by 2018.[12] (Table 2)

Table 2: India's Trade with Vietnam (USD million)

Description	2000	2005	2006	2007	2008	2009	2010	2011	2012	2013	2014	2015
Gross exports to Vietnam	195.4	633.5	874.1	1241.5	1812.6	1833.5	2475.6	3466.5	3658.2	5987.6	6526.5	5357.2
% Growth	25.8	18.4	38.0	42.0	46.0	1.2	35.0	40.0	5.5	63.7	9.0	-17.9
India's total Export	42358	100353	121201	145898	181861	176765	220408	301483	289565	336611	317545	264381
% Growth	14.7	32.2	20.8	20.4	24.6	-2.8	24.7	37	-4	16	-6	-17
% Share (Vietnam)	0.5	0.6	0.7	0.9	1.0	1.0	1.1	1.1	1.3	1.8	2.1	2.0
Gross Imports from Vietnam	13.5	127.4	159.8	153.1	371.6	442.9	993.5	1554.3	1945.5	2826.7	2781.7	2680.1
% Growth	16.9	74.0	25.5	-4.2	142.7	19.2	124.3	56.4	25.2	45.3	-1.6	-3.7
India's total Import	52940.3	140862	178212	218645	315712	266402	350029	462403	488976	466046	459369.5	390744.7
% Growth	5.9	42.3	26.5	22.7	44.4	-15.6	31.4	32.1	5.7	-4.7	-1.4	-14.9
% Share (Vietnam)	0.0	0.1	0.1	0.1	0.1	0.2	0.3	0.3	0.4	0.6	0.6	0.7
Total trade with Vietnam	208.9	760.8	1033.9	1394.6	2184.2	2276.4	3469.1	5020.8	5603.7	8814.3	9308.2	8037.3
India's Total Trade	95298.3	241214	299413	364543	497573	443167	570438	763886	778541	802657	776914.1	655125.7
% Share	0.22	0.32	0.35	0.38	0.44	0.51	0.61	0.66	0.72	1.1	1.2	1.23

Source: ITC Trade Map.

The prices and range of Indian exported goods to Vietnam such as Fish, cotton and pharmaceutical products are very competitive in the Vietnamese market. Besides, India has strengths in information technology, biotechnology and nuclear energy while Vietnam is weak in these areas but has a great demand for software products, biological products and products with radioactive isotopes. The main commodities that constituted India's exports to Vietnam in 2015 (Table 3) comprised Fish and crustaceans, molluscs and other aquatic invertebrates (12.1 percent), Cotton (10.6 percent), Pharmaceutical products (10.2 percent), Machinery, mechanical appliances, nuclear reactors, boilers; parts thereof (9.8 percent) & Vehicles other than railway or tramway rolling stock, and parts and accessories thereof (5.3 percent). In the year 2015, India's top fifteen exports to Vietnam constituted about 80 percent of its total exports to Vietnam rising almost two-fold from 45 percent in the year 2003.

Indian exports to Vietnam have registered perceptible change during the past 10 years. In the year 2015, India's exports to the world markets constituted about 50% share of the same top 15 products which it exports to Vietnam and the main commodities that constituted India's exports to the world were natural or cultured pearls, precious or semi-precious stones, precious metals, metals clad with a share of 14.6 percent, vehicles other than railway or tramway rolling stock with a share of 5.3 percent, machinery and mechanical appliances with a share of 5 percent etc. However, if we analyse India's export share to Vietnam in those products, it is greater in all the commodities except for one commodity i.e. natural or cultured pearls. This implies that India enjoys tariff concessions or lower non-tariff barriers with Vietnam than with the rest of the world.

India's key imports from Vietnam during the same period comprised electrical machinery equipment parts thereof (36.6 percent), machinery, mechanical appliances, nuclear reactors, boilers; parts thereof (11.5 percent), coffee, tea, mati and spices (6.7 percent), inorganic chemicals (6.1 percent), rubber and articles (5.8 percent) etc. In the year 2015, India's top fifteen imports from Vietnam constituted about 80 percent share in its total imports from Vietnam.

Indian imports from Vietnam have also registered a major change during the past 10 years. In the year 2015, India's global imports constituted about

Table 3: India's Top 10 Exports to Vietnam in 2015 (% share)

Product Code	Product Label	Value in 2015, USD thousand	Share in India's exports to Vietnam	Share in India's exports to World
'03	Fish and crustaceans, molluscs and other aquatic invertebrates	321512	12.1	1.7
'52	Cotton	282001	10.6	2.8
'30	Pharmaceutical products	269669	10.2	4.7
'84	Machinery, mechanical appliances, nuclear reactors, boilers; parts thereof	259429	9.8	5.0
'87	Vehicles other than railway or tramway rolling stock, and parts and accessories thereof	141893	5.3	5.3
'29	Organic chemicals	108711	4.1	4.3
'23	Residues and waste from the food industries; prepared animal fodder	107456	4.0	0.4
'41	Raw hides and skins (other than furskins) and leather	99654	3.8	0.4
'39	Plastics and articles thereof	96086	3.6	1.9
'85	Electrical machinery and equipment and parts thereof; sound recorders and reproducers, television ...	90531	3.4	3.0
'02	Meat and edible meat offal	85692	3.2	1.6
'72	Iron and steel	79172	3.0	2.4
'38	Miscellaneous chemical products	70096	2.6	1.1
'71	Natural or cultured pearls, precious or semi-precious stones, precious metals, metals clad ...	55079	2.1	14.6
'25	Salt; sulphur; earths and stone; plastering materials, lime and cement	43754	1.6	0.7
	Total		**79.5**	**50.0**

Source: ITC Trade Map.

65 percent share of the same products which it imports from Vietnam and the main commodities that constituted India's imports from the world are coffee, tea, malt and spices with a share of 24 percent, man-made filaments; strip and the like of man-made textile materials with a share of 11 percent, essential oils and resinoids; perfumery, cosmetic or toilet preparations with a share of 10 percent etc. However, if we analyse India's share of imports from Vietnam in top 15 products, it is greater in all the commodities than India's share of world imports (in the same commodities) except for four commodities. This implies that Vietnamese products are more competitive in Indian markets than products from the world markets. (Table 4)

Table 4: India's Top 10 imports from Vietnam in 2015

Product Code	Product Label	Value in 2015, USD thousand	Share in India's imports from Vietnam	Share in India's imports from World
'85	Electrical machinery and equipment and parts thereof; sound recorders and reproducers, television ...	979873	36.6	3
'84	Machinery, mechanical appliances, nuclear reactors, boilers; parts thereof	308749	11.5	1
'09	Coffee, tea, maté and spices	179780	6.7	24
'28	Inorganic chemicals; organic or inorganic compounds of precious metals, of rare-earth metals, ...	163860	6.1	3
'40	Rubber and articles thereof	155510	5.8	5
'74	Copper and articles thereof	98155	3.7	3
'54	Man-made filaments; strip and the like of man-made textile materials	82938	3.1	11
'44	Wood and articles of wood; wood charcoal	65623	2.4	3
'33	Essential oils and resinoids; perfumery, cosmetic or toilet preparations	60075	2.2	10
'25	Salt; sulphur; earths and stone; plastering materials, lime and cement	47250	1.8	2
			79.9	65.0

Source: ITC Trade Map.

India-Vietnam User-based Category-wise Exports and Imports

Majority of the exportable goods from India to Vietnam are raw material goods, viz. nearly 60.6 percent. The rest, viz. consumer goods, intermediate goods, and Capital goods, comprise only 39.4 percent of the share. The trend in the basket of goods, based on level of processing, has undergone a significant shift over the years as the share of intermediate goods has come down from 66.3 percent to 18.4 percent over a period of ten years. This signifies that Vietnam is largely importing goods from India to serve its manufacturing and processing sectors, as well as to meet the needs of daily life.

India's Category-wise Exports to Vietnam

Conversely, baskets of imports from Vietnam have gradually shifted from raw materials and consumer goods to capital and intermediate goods. In 2006, nearly 75.3 percent of the imports from Vietnam comprised of raw materials and consumer goods; followed by 24.7 in other categories. However, for 9 years, capital goods captured the majority share in overall imports from

Vietnam to India, viz. 48.3 percent, followed by 23 percent share of intermediate goods, 16.1 percent share of consumer goods, and 12.6 percent of raw materials. Among the main imports from Vietnam, telephones and accessories have become the largest imports to India since 2009. Rubber is the third largest Vietnamese import item to India, since 2008. Since India annually imports more than 500,000 tonnes of all kinds of spices with a total value of annual imports reaching over US$1.7 billion.

Figure 1: India's Category-wise Exports to Vietnam

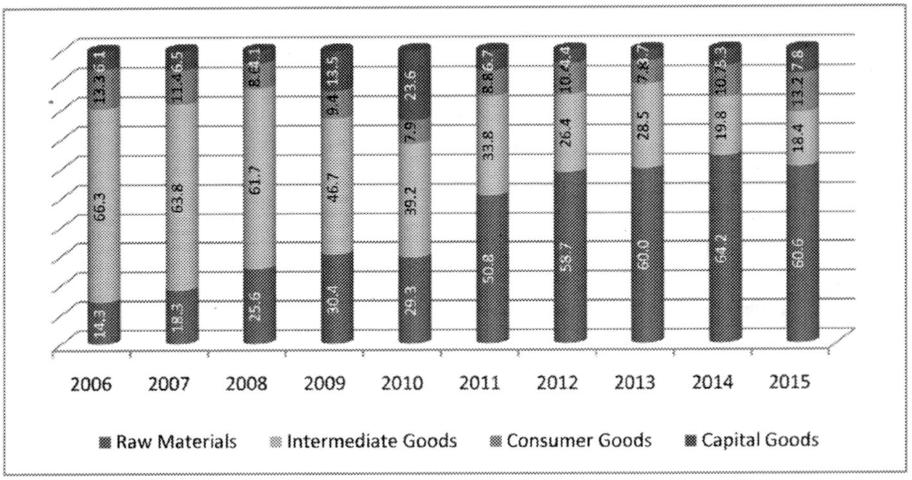

Source: WITS, World Bank.

Among the other import items from Vietnam to India in the raw material group, iron and steel figure prominently. As the Government of India is focusing on building physical infrastructure, it requires a huge supply of steel. Among agricultural commodities, dragon fruit has become very popular in India. Most dragon fruits also known as Pitaya are imported into India from Vietnam. According to the Vietnam Fruit and Vegetables Association, although India started importing Vietnamese dragon fruit only from early 2014, India offers a huge market for it.

India's Category-wise Imports from Vietnam

India's Top Trade Partners

Over the last twenty years, Vietnam's changing export patterns have been characterised by growing economic interdependence with United States and China specifically and East Asia more broadly. In 2015, United States was the biggest exporting partner of Vietnam with US$33.4 billion of exports having an export share of above 21 percent. China stood at 2nd rank with US $16.5 billion in total trade and a share of 10.2 percent. However, if we see India's ranking in Vietnam's trade, it is at 17th place with a miniscule trade of worth US $2.4 billion.

Figure 2: India's Category-wise Imports from Vietnam

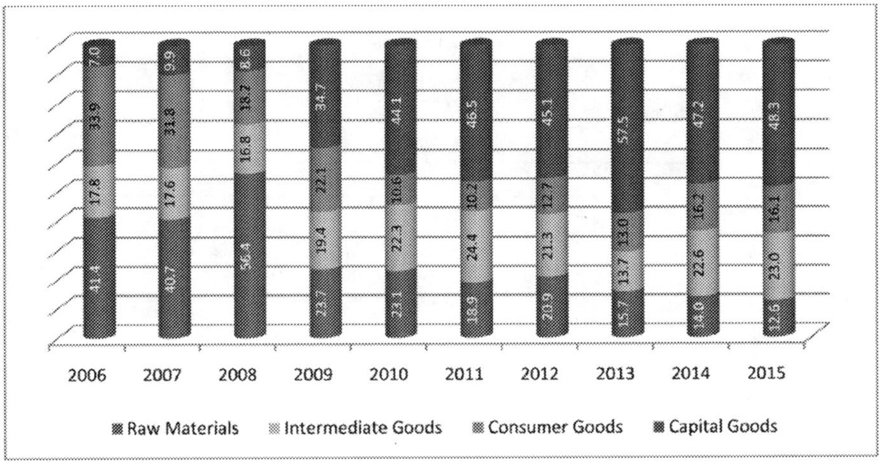

Source: WITS, World Bank.

Table 5: Vietnam's Top 10 Export Partners

Ranking	Exporters	Value exported in 2015 (USD thousand)	Trade balance 2015 (USD thousand)	Share in Vietnam's exports (%)
1	United States of America	33475029	25682522	20.7
2	China	16567686	-32873437	10.2
3	Japan	14100341	-81758	8.7
4	Korea, Republic of	8915384	-18663142	5.5
5	Hong Kong, China	6959274	5638912	4.3
6	Germany	5707416	2504683	3.5
7	United Arab Emirates	5690916	5169368	3.5
8	Netherlands	4759560	4069452	2.9
9	United Kingdom	4645220	3917387	2.9
10	Malaysia	3577077	-607658	2.2
17	India	2469722	-185441	1.5

Source: Authors own calculation, data taken from ITC.

Over the last twenty years, Vietnam's changing import patterns have been characterised by growing economic interdependence with China and Republic of Korea specifically, and also East Asia in a broad manner. In 2015, China was the biggest trading partner of Vietnam with US$49.4 billion of imports and import share of above 29.8 percent in Vietnam's imports from the world. Korea was Vietnam's 2nd most important trading partner with US $27.5 billion in total imports and a share of 16.6 percent. However, if we see India's ranking in Vietnam's imports, it stood at 11th place with value of US $2.6 billion.

Table 6: Vietnam's Top 10 Import Partners

Ranking	Importers	Value imported in 2015 (USD thousand)	Trade balance 2015 (USD thousand)	Share in Viet Nam's imports (%)
1	China	49441123	-32873437	29.8
2	Korea, Republic of	27578526	-18663142	16.6
3	Japan	14182099	-81758	8.6
4	Taipei, Chinese	10943323	-8866898	6.6
5	Thailand	8269567	-5091901	5
6	United States of America	7792507	25682522	4.7
7	Singapore	6030809	-2774202	3.6
8	Malaysia	4184735	-607658	2.5
9	Germany	3202733	2504683	1.9
10	Indonesia	2738492	109115	1.7
11	India	2655163	-185441	1.6

Source: Authors own calculation, data taken from ITC.

India-Vietnam Bilateral Trade Analysis and Interpretation

Import Penetration (IP) Rate

Import Penetration (IP) Rate examines the degree of domestic demand which (the difference between GDP and net exports) is satisfied by imports. It is also termed as self-sufficiency ratio at the sectoral level. At bilateral level, it is the ratio of total imports from trade partner to domestic demand, as a percentage. It provides a broad scenario of the degree of vulnerability to certain types of shocks in the partner's economy. IP rate lies between 0 (no imports) to 100 percent[13] (when all domestic demand is satisfied by imports only), a case of no-domestic production.

Based on the import penetration chart, India's penetration in Vietnam's economy is comparatively higher than Vietnam's penetration in Indian economy. However, Vietnam's import penetration in India has witnessed a surge in the recent few years. India's penetration rate in Vietnam has hovered in the range of 1.3-1.8 percent over the last ten years.

Figure 3: Import Penetration Rate

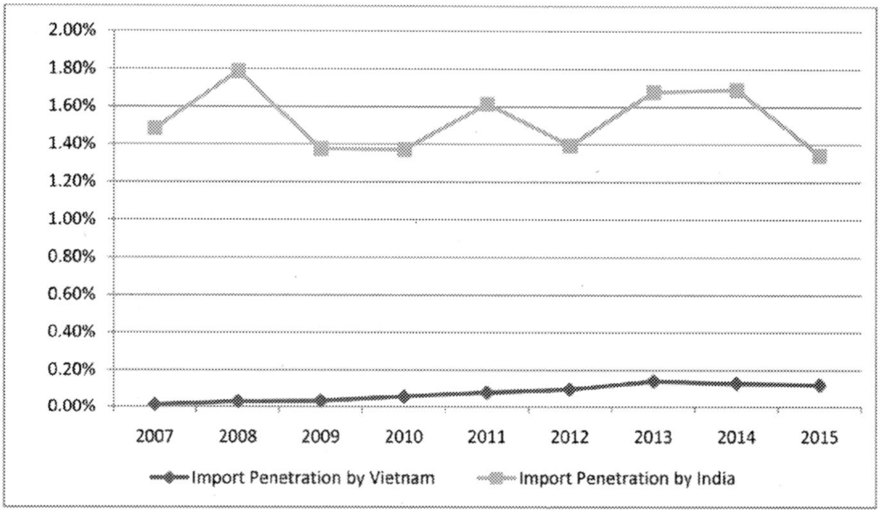

Source: Authors own calculation, data taken from ITC.

Trade Intensity Index (TII)

It is a uniform export share that describes the number of average exports of a country to a destination than to other countries of the world. TII value greater than 1 indicates an intense trade relationship, or significant presence of exporter nation in importer's market. It is quite clear from the chart below that India's presence in Vietnam is relatively lower than Korea and China. Even other top exporters in Vietnam such as Japan and US, are not able to create a significant presence in Vietnam. Notwithstanding, India's TII has been gradually and consistently improving over the years.

Figure 4: Vietnam's Trade Intensity Index with its major Trade Partners

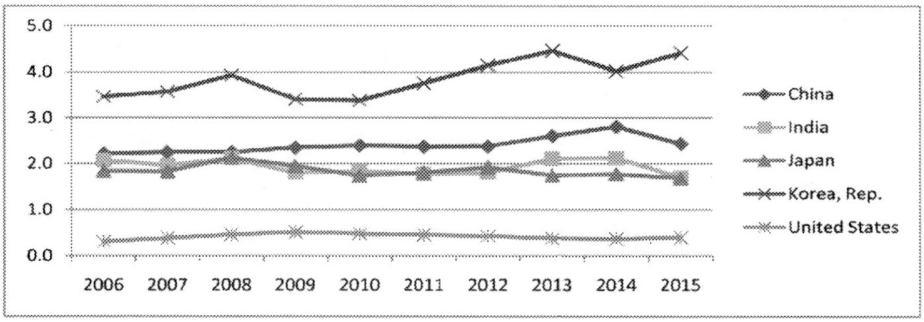

Source: WITS, World Bank.

India's Trade Complementarily Index with Vietnam

It is a nuanced overlap index wherein the index exhibits the degree of alignment of export pattern of one country with the import pattern of its partner's country. A high degree of TCI assumed to indicate more favourable prospects for a successful trade arrangement. It is quite evident from the table below that although India's trade complimentarily with Vietnam has observed a decreasing trend, but keeping in view of the higher import penetration rate of India's exports to Vietnam, it has the potential to go higher. In case of lower trade barriers with full implementation of India-ASEAN FTA, Indian exports to Vietnam have the potential to register significant growth in the coming years.

Figure 5: Sectoral Hirschman Index (SHI)

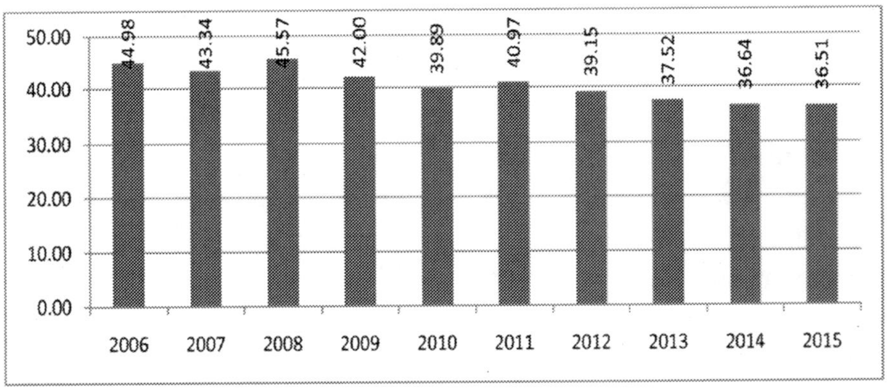

Source: Authors own calculation, data taken from ITC

Sectoral Hirschman Index (SHI)

It indicates the sectoral concentration of a country's exports. It describes the degree to which a nation's exports are dispersed across different economic activities. SHI lie between 0 and 1 wherein value closer to 1 indicates that exports are concentrated in fewer sectors. Compared to exports to Vietnam, India's imports are more diversified. Although both imports and exports from Vietnam are on the lower plane for degree of concentration, exports witnessed a plummet in diversification in the basket of products to Vietnam. Thus, exports to Vietnam are relatively more focused on fewer products than India's imports from Vietnam.

The crux of the above trade analysis suggests that there lies huge potential of growth in trade between India and Vietnam, on the back of rising intensity, penetration and decrease in trade costs. To further trade prospects, a serious attempt must be made by both nations to develop intra-industry trade, viz. continuously trading of products from similar industries.

Figure 6: Sectoral Hirschman Index (SHI) between India and Vietnam

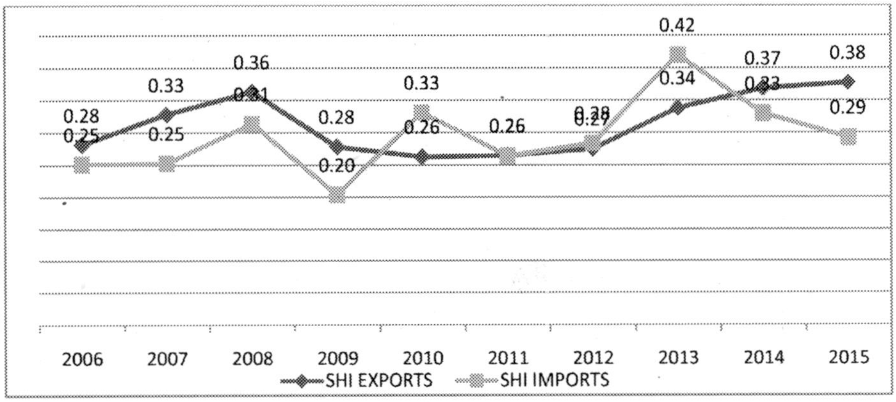

Source: Authors own calculation, data taken from ITC.

Grubel-Lloyd Index (GLI)

It is an indicator to measure the scale of intra-industry trade between nations. Nations can hugely benefit from intra-industry trade due to exploitation of economies of scale. GLI lie between 0 and 100 percent, wherein 0 indicates pure inter-industry trade and 100 percent indicates pure intra-industry trade. Adjustments are made if there are any total trade imbalances in a country.

Figure 7: Grubel-Lloyd Index (GLI)

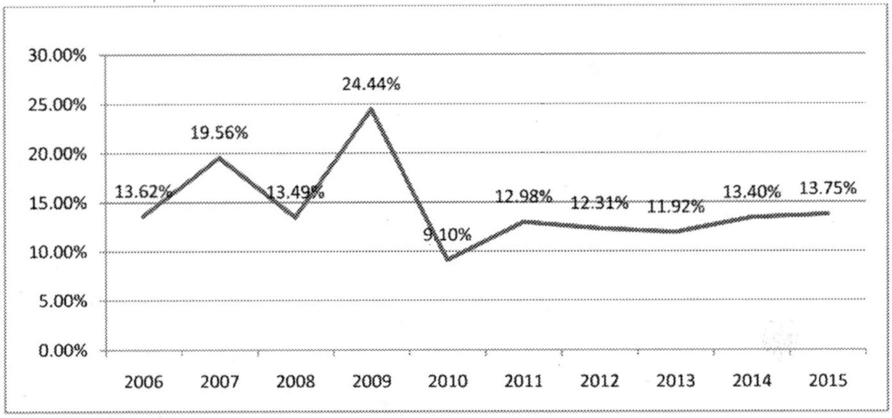

Source: Authors own calculation, data taken from ITC.

India and Vietnam's intra industry trade have remained on the moderate side. Although, mixed performance at IIT level, trend in adjusted GLI suggests a significant drop since 2009. Based on the adjusted GLI numbers, around 24.44 percent of the trade was intra-industry trade form in 2009. Intra-industry trade between India and Vietnam, however, witnessed a drop-in rate to 9.10 percent in 2010. To develop trade further, it is essential for both the nations to continuously indulge in high intra-industry trade to exploit the economies of scale.

Trade Cost of India and Vietnam with their Top Trading Partners

The analysis provides an optimal viewpoint to access the overall cost as a percentage of overall export, which is incurred during trade between two nations. Trade costs are the price equivalent of the reduction of international trade compared with the potential implied by domestic production and consumption in the origin and destination markets. Higher bilateral trade costs result in smaller bilateral trade flows.

The major advantage faced by Indian products is from the category of manufacturing products. In India's trade with Vietnam, the agricultural products faced a competitive 120 percent of trade cost in the year 2014. India's agricultural trade cost with Vietnam is lowest in comparison with India's top export partners. On the other side, exports of manufacturing products from India to Vietnam faced one of the lowest trade cost, viz. around 37.2 percent in the year 2012 which is also the lowest if comparison with India's top export destinations. In a nutshell, at an aggregate level, India's trade cost with Vietnam is at the lowest which could provide impetus to enhancement of trade relations with Vietnam.

India-Vietnam Investment Story

India has had some significant investments in Vietnam with the year 2007 marking a major shift in the pattern. Although Indian investments in Vietnam have remained constant at around US$1 billion as of now, these are expected to rise in the coming years. During 2015, Indian companies registered 23 new projects with a total capital of US$138.99 million in the areas of food processing, fertilizers, auto components and textile accessories etc. With these projects, India now has 132 projects with total investments of about US$1.07 billion. This includes Indian investment from third countries also. Major

Table 7: India's Trade Cost with its Major Trade Partners

Reporter Name	Partner Name	Sector	2005	2006	2007	2008	2009	2010	2011	2012	2013	2014
India	Vietnam	Agriculture	180.3	170.2	172.8	169.1	153.2	138.2	126.7	115.1	122.3	120.4
India	China	Agriculture	213.9	187.0	188.9	188.2	179.6	166.6	164.2	162.1	167.3	184.3
India	Hong Kong SAR, China	Agriculture	..	..	..	..	..	..	..	..	..	..
India	United Kingdom	Agriculture	206.8	200.0	205.1	197.7	193.7	197.1	188.4	192.6	198.7	200.8
India	United States	Agriculture	150.1	146.6	147.6	143.1	146.4	144.6	126.5	106.6	124.6	..
India	United Arab Emirates	Agriculture	181.1	176.5	172.0	146.4	146.0	145.7	145.3	144.9	131.6	140.5
India	Vietnam	Manufacturing	150.6	140.5	132.0	115.6	114.8	90.5	70.5	37.2	..	..
India	China	Manufacturing	112.1	107.4	108.2	111.3	107.4	98.6	99.9	102.7	93.7	..
India	Hong Kong SAR, China	Manufacturing	55.2	55.3	55.3	68.0	63.8	77.8	79.0	66.4	69.2	..
India	United Kingdom	Manufacturing	102.3	106.9	107.5	100.2	105.9	103.1	93.8	100.0	84.2	91.6
India	United States	Manufacturing	105.4	102.6	97.1	94.6	100.5	99.1	96.9	97.6	89.6	..
India	United Arab Emirates	Manufacturing	98.2	80.7	63.3	55.4	53.2	51.0	48.9	46.7	41.9	51.3

Source: World Development Indicators, World Bank.

sectors of investment are energy, mineral exploration, agro-processing, sugar manufacturing, agro-chemicals, IT and auto components. Some of the major Indian investors in Vietnam are OVL, Essar Exploration and Production Ltd, Nagarjuna Ltd, KCP Industries Limited, Ngon Coffee Manufacturing, Venkateswara Hatcheries, Philips Carbon and McLeod Russell and CGL.

Tata Power plans to develop the US$1.8 billion Long Phu-II Thermal Power Plant in Soc Trang. An MOU was signed between Tata Power and Vietnamese Ministry of Industry and Trade despite strong competition from Korean and Russian companies.[14] More recently in March 2015, Tata Power announced plans to continue to invest more with the project Long Phu 3 thermal power plant under BOT (Build–Operate–Transfer), and expressed a desire to invest in wind power projects in the province.[15]

ONGC, one of the biggest Indian companies, in fact, is one of the first foreign oil and gas companies that invested in Vietnam beginning in 1988, by securing a licence of investment because of the open policy in the economy and the passing of the Foreign Investment Law in Vietnam in September 1987. On 28 October 2014, ONGC Videsh Limited of India and PetroVietnam, in the presence of the Indian Prime Minister Narendra Modi and his Vietnamese counterpart Nguyen Tan Dung, signed a cooperation agreement on the exploration of two blocks off the coast of Vietnam. These are two of the five petroleum blocks for which Vietnam invited Indian partners to take part in the exploration process.[16]

In recent years, Vietnam has introduced favourable policies for investors and has implemented the policy of "one stop shop" for licensing. Vietnam encourages investment from India in specific areas of expertise such as infrastructure (rail), power generation and distribution, information technology, education, research and production of pharmaceuticals, and agricultural products. Vietnam also supports Indian presence in national projects in oil exploration, power, science and technology and agriculture. In the field of IT training, NIIT, APTECH and Tata Infotech have so far opened more than 80 franchised centres spread across Vietnam.[17]

India's Investment in Vietnam

Indian investments in Vietnam reached its highest level at US$76.11 million in 2010 and the lowest level in the year 2012 at US$2.39 million due to lower GDP growth rate and macroeconomic instability which led the outward foreign investments down. Indian investments started reviving from 2013 before coming down to US$9.44 million in the year 2015 respectively.

Figure 8: India's Outward FDI in Vietnam

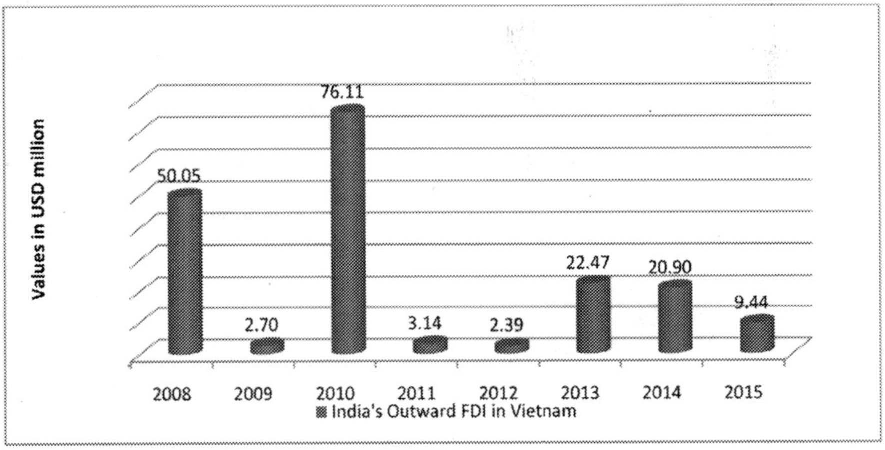

Source: RBI data on India's Outward Investments.

India's Sector-wise Investments in Vietnam

Indian projects mostly from the field of industrial processing and manufacturing with 41 projects amounting to a total investment of US$211.62 million, accounts for 55.8 percent of invested capital. The mining sector has three projects with a total investment of US$86 million, accounting for 22.67 percent of the total invested capital. This is followed by the wholesale and retail trade sector with 19 projects with a total investment of US$51.08 million, accounting for 13.73 percent of the invested capital[18] respectively.

India's Form of Investment in Vietnam

Most Indian investment is in the form of wholly owned subsidiaries while the rest are in Joint Ventures. During the year 2015, around 67 percent of the investments, based on the control and business structure were in wholly owned Subsidiary while 33 percent were in Joint Venture. The form of Joint Venture investment has undergone a significant shift from 63 percent in the year 2008 to 33 percent in the year 2015, whereas there has been a significant growth in the wholly owned subsidiaries from 37 percent in the year 2008 to 67 percent in the year 2015 respectively.

Figure 9: Type of India's Outward FDI in Vietnam

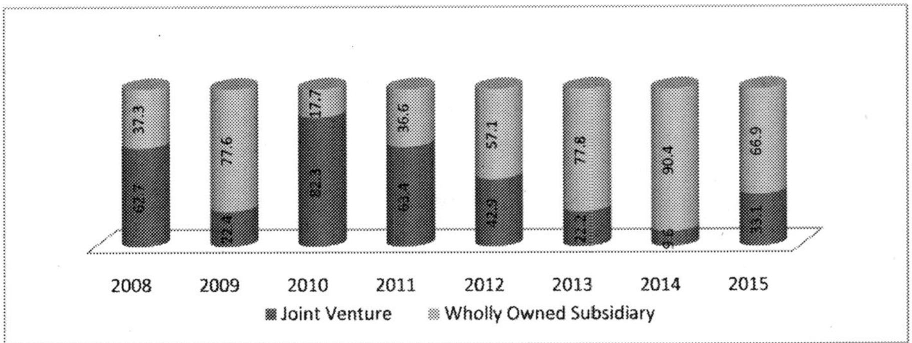

Source: RBI data on India's Outward Investments.

Investments in Vietnam by Area

India has invested in 22 local areas over 63 provinces (including five municipalities) of Vietnam, in which Ho Chi Minh city has 36 projects with a total investment of US$54.9 million, followed by Tuyen Quang province with three projects and a total investment of US$45 million, and BacNinh province with two projects with a total investment of US$40.5 million. While Hanoi and Ho Chi Mihn City offer infrastructure and agglomeration advantages, a secondary option for Indian investors lies in Vietnam's specialised economic zones of which Industrial Zones (IZs) are usually located next to ports, and benefit from tax incentives, improved infrastructure, and streamlined registration procedures.

India's Investment in Vietnam in Comparison to Top Investors in Vietnam

The most notable source of capital flows in Vietnam is from ASEAN countries. Although Vietnam is a choice destination for all within the economic bloc, based on the Vietnamese economy's low production costs, lowered trade barriers, in conjunction with the predictable government treatment and lucrative tax arrangements found within their respective home markets, the key investors in Vietnam are Malaysia and Singapore – accounting for 18 and 22 percent of Vietnam's inward FDI inflows respectively. The investments in Vietnam from Singapore and Malaysia, however, contrast sharply with that of traditional investors within the region such as China, Hong Kong, and Korea which has seen a decelerating trend in recent years.

While having an overall view, we find that, Indian investors are only ranked 30th out of 101 countries and territories investing in Vietnam. This is not commensurate with the potential for economic cooperation between the two countries. While constituting a small portion of FDI within Vietnam, India would likely become increasingly important investor in Vietnam evidenced by strong growth in recent years. Companies based in India have been exponentially increasing investments over the past three years reaching a 4 percent share of FDI as of January 2016 which is up 400 percent over last year's average. These investments have increased cooperation on issues of security as well as complimentary production of goods such as textiles and pharmaceuticals.

From the Vietnamese side, its investors have become stronger in recent years. Currently, Vietnam has five investment projects in India with a total investment of US$1.81 million. However, Vietnamase investments in India have reached US$0.45 million to date, which constitutes less than 1 percent share in India's FDI inflows. The areas in which the Vietnamese investors are interested, include distribution of products for animal feed, distribution and sale of building materials, import and export trade in cosmetics, computer products and small-scale hydropower.

Prospects of India-Vietnam Economic Ties

There is significant potential for development of India-Vietnam economic ties due to their traditional friendship and Vietnam's central location in ASEAN and Greater Mekong Sub-region which is important for India's relations with ASEAN and its "Act East Policy". India and Vietnam are also expected to play mutual beneficial role in one of the important upcoming regional economic frameworks, namely, the Regional Comprehensive Economic Partnership (RCEP) which was initiated in 2012 and signed in 2017. RCEP is a high-quality free trade agreement, aiming to form a comprehensive economic partnership between ASEAN and six partner countries, including China, Japan, Korea, Australia, New Zealand and India. The signing of RCEP can bring benefits and challenges to both the countries. For Vietnam, RCEP is expected to result in improving investment and export markets of ASEAN and other partners. This would also enable Vietnam to participate in the regional production and value chains'.

RCEP would bring about opportunities to connect India more strongly with large economies such as Japan and Korea (the countries which have had trade agreements with ASEAN). Besides, RCEP will also facilitate favourable conditions for India to take part in "the regional production chain" of Asia.

RCEP is expected to harmonise the rules of trade between India and ASEAN member countries, and attract FDI especially in export-oriented sectors. Moreover, India enjoys comparative advantages in areas of information technology, communications, activation services, professional services, healthcare and education. RCEP will also bring about opportunities for Indian companies to penetrate into new markets which would help India to strengthen its position in the region.

Vietnam is seeking ties and economic cooperation with India more closely to reduce its economic dependence on China, especially in the fields of textiles, agrochemicals, machinery, finance and information technology. However, it is a daunting task for India to take the place of China as it is the largest trade partner of Vietnam with a trade of over US$50 billion in the year 2014. However, the ASEAN-India Free trade agreement has opened vistas of cooperation for both the countries not only in trade but also in industry, oil and gas extraction, minerals, investment, science and technology, human resource development, infrastructure development, agro-processing, tourism, aviation, healthcare, and education. Through this Agreement, Vietnam's exports enjoy preferential import tariffs and in future it will be incumbent upon Vietnam to quickly take advantage of the reduction of import and export tariffs between Vietnam and India.

Despite great potential and many opportunities, both the countries face many other challenges like similar import/export products which is hindering the growth of trade between them. The list of similar products are garments, tea, rice, cashew nuts, footwear, pepper and sea products. While the AITIG in 2009 created favourable conditions for the development of bilateral cooperation, it also posed new challenges. According to the Agreement, many export items in which Vietnam has advantage belong to the list of India's sensitive goods, that is, goods with slow tariff reduction roadmap, such as textiles, footwear, plastic products, machinery and spare parts. Some other items, such as seafood, vegetables, processed foods and vehicles belong to the list of India's exclusive goods, that is, goods for which India has not committed to reduce tariffs. The other barriers are geographical distance, differences in customs, habits, tastes and business environments of both the countries.

Conclusion

Although bilateral trade between India and Vietnam has been growing at a fast rate, but Vietnam's share in India's total trade stands at a meagre

1.2 percent in 2015. In exports, Vietnam's share in India's total exports stands at a meagre 2 percent and in imports it is only 0.7 percent. Majority of exportable goods from India to Vietnam are focused in the raw material goods segments, viz. nearly 60.6 percent. The rest, viz. consumer goods, intermediate goods, and capital goods, comprised only 39.4 percent of the share.

Indian investments in Vietnam have also remained constant at around US$1 billion as of now, but are expected to rise in the coming years. During 2015, Indian companies registered 23 new projects with a total capital of US$138.99 million in the areas of food processing, fertilizers, auto components and textile accessories, etc. From the Vietnamese side, its investors have become stronger in recent years. Currently, Vietnam has five investment projects in India with a total investment of US$1.81 million.

Despite immense potential, India-Vietnam economic relations have also faced certain difficulties and challenges, such as the similarity in the structure of imports and exports of the two economies, geographical distance, difficulties in transport, and differences in tastes, habits and business environments. However, given that in any bilateral economic relations, there are always both opportunities and challenges; the expectation is that the challenges will be overcome with the determination and strong political will of both the countries. Going ahead, it is essential for both the sides to become proactive and engage in discussions related to mitigating bilateral trade issues and enhancing investments.

NOTES

1. Ministry of Commerce, International Trade, Government of India.
2. Ministry of External Affairs, Outgoing visits, Government of India. Web Access: http://mea.gov.in/outoging-visit-detail.htm?27363/Press+Statement+by+Prime+ Minister+ during+his+visit+to+Vietnam+September+03+2016.
3. Ministry of Statistics and Policy Implementation, Government of India.
4. DIPP, FDI Statistics, Ministry of Commerce and Industry, Government of India.
5. Central Statistical Office, MOSPI, Government of India.
6. Ministry of Commerce and Industry, Government of India.
7. Office of the Economic Adviser, Ministry of Commerce & Industry, Government of India.
8. The Đổi Mới aims to increase economic growth and development by liberating the economy within Vietnam and increasing Vietnam's contribution to the global economic community.
9. IMF, World Economic Outlook 2016.
10. GSO, Vietnam. Online access: https://www.gso.gov.vn/default_en.aspx?tabid=775.
11. Ministry of External Affairs, Government of India.
12. Vietnam Chamber of Commerce and Industry 2012
13. During application, Index can go beyond 100% if re-exports are not accounted for.

14. Vietnam Energy 2014.
15. Vietnam News Agency 2014, Government of Vietnam.
16. Vietnam News Agency 2014, Government of Vietnam.
17. Brief of India's bilateral relations with Vietnam, Ministry of External Affairs, Government of India, accessed on 2 January 217.
18. Foreign Investment Agency 2015, Ministry of Planning and Investment, Government of Vietnam.

10

Solutions to Promote Economic Relations between Vietnam and India

Nguyen Van Lich and *Nguyen Minh Trang*

The Current Status of Economic Relations

Vietnam and India have a traditional and friendly relationship which was built by President Ho Chi Minh and Prime Minister Jawaharlal Nehru in the 1950s. The two countries have preserved, nurtured and promoted the relationship to new heights. Many leaders of the state have visited each other in the recent past. In September 2016, the two countries unanimously upgraded the relationship to Comprehensive Strategic Partner, in which economic (especially trade) was identified as a key pillar of bilateral relations.

The two sides have great potential for trade: Vietnam is an important partner in the relationship between the two countries in particular, and India-ASEAN in general. Trade relations between the two countries have made significant progress. The turnover has increased five times from US $1 billion in 2006 to over US $5 billion in 2015 (Expected US $15 billion by 2020).[1] With a population of over 1.2 billion people, India is a potential market for Vietnam's exports.

India identifies Vietnam as one of the markets that need to be promoted, according to the country's flagship program. Therefore, exporters of key commodities such as pharmaceuticals, synthetic fibres, high-value plastic products, etc. will enjoy the privileges.

Both countries are stepping up economic reforms, opening up for regional and international integration. India and Vietnam have been achieving high economic growth for a long time and both are in need of expanding markets and attracting foreign investment to maintain high growth. This is an opportunity and a favourable condition for the two countries to step up the co-operative relations with the aim of expanding export markets, attracting investment, exchanging and sharing experiences on reforms to be undertaken.

India is one of the inputs-supplying centres for quality production in the world with a diversified economic structure and large-scale production. Meanwhile, the diversification of input-supply is highly appreciated by many Vietnamese enterprises. This is one of the bases for increasing trade with India. At the same time, cooperation between the two sides is increasingly effective. The two countries have agreed to promote cooperation in information supply, market access, removal of trade barriers, investment facilitation, co-operation in oil and gas, energy, agricultural products, garments.

There is a common legal basis between the two countries, which is the ASEAN-India Bilateral Trade in Goods Agreement (AITIG), with effect from 1 June 2010. According to AITIG, Vietnam has decreased tariffs more than five years earlier than ASEAN and India. Despite the longer roadmap, Vietnam still enjoys full benefits from tariff reduction commitments of India and other ASEAN countries. Meanwhile, India pledged to cut tariffs on many exports, such as garments, footwear, wood and wood products, seafood, coal, rubber and steel. In addition, at the request of Vietnam, India agreed to reduce tariffs on coffee, black tea and pepper. AITIG also has a positive impact for Vietnam in attracting FDI from India as well as from the world.

In addition to AITIG, Vietnam and India also entered into an Agreement on Trade in Services and Investment Agreement within the Framework Agreement on ASEAN-India Comprehensive Economic Cooperation. The two countries are also participating in the negotiations on the Comprehensive Economic Partnership Agreement (RCEP) between ASEAN and six ASEAN FTA partners (including India). These are also important factors for promoting bilateral trade.

The two countries have agreed on the viewpoint of development. The rapid rise of India, along with the construction of the East-West Economic Corridor, linking Mawlamyine Port located in the Indian Ocean of Myanmar to Da Nang, will contribute to boost Vietnam-India trade in future. India is now pursuing a Act East Policy, which seeks to establish more profound economic ties.

Difficulties and limitations in Economic Relations between Vietnam and India

Although the economic cooperation between Vietnam and India has continued to grow in recent years, the results have been modest compared to the potential and desires of both sides. Trade and investment relations are not commensurate with political relations. In trade, the noteworthy point is that the balance is on the side of India. Vietnam exports are mainly focused on raw materials; trading via intermediaries especially when exported in large quantities. Therefore, export turnover is not as high as the potential.

India imposes high tariffs on some of Vietnam's major exports such as pepper, cashew nuts, coffee and tea which are on the exclusion list. During the AITIG negotiation, India only agreed to reduce import tariffs on coffee and black tea to 45 percent, and pepper to 50 percent by 2018.[2] According to AITIG commitments, many exports of Vietnam's strength are in the sensitive category of India, which has a slow path of tariff cuts, such as textiles, footwear, plastics, machinery, equipment and spare parts.

Currently, the average tariff rate in India is 34.9 percent, much higher than the average applied tariff rate of 16.4 percent. According to the WTO, for agricultural products, India's WTO tariff rate is among the highest in the world. In addition to tariff, there are other trade barriers in India, such as poor infrastructure, poor management, conservative dispute resolution, high production costs, and widespread corruption.

India has a strong policy of protecting domestic production. India is one of the countries conducting anti-dumping investigations, applying the most trade remedies with exports related to Vietnam (5 cases of anti-dumping and 4 cases of self-defence). The products under investigation are relatively diversified from DVD, fluorescent to fibre – one of the important export products of Vietnam to India. In recent times, India has increases difficulties for Vietnam's exports, such as increased import duties on cashew kernels; self-defence investigation for cold rolled steel, plastic processing machines, laminated resin products.

India's legal system is relatively complex, making it difficult for business partners to proceed. The procedures required to enter the market, such as representative office procedures, branches and companies are very complicated and it requires many documents, consulting costs, time as well as effort.

In terms of investment, both Vietnam and India are developing countries, moving towards a market economy. Though there is a great demand for capital, markets and technology, complementarily there is no active promotion of relations and exploration of the market. Though the two sides are aware of the weaknesses, cooperation between sectors and businesses of the two countries is not effective.

In terms of mechanism and organisation: while a large number of Indian businesses are pro-active in Vietnam, the number of Vietnamese businesses in India is limited. Indian businesses have established Indian Business Offices in Vietnam and have more than 100 representative offices of Indian companies. Meanwhile, there is no representative office of Vietnamese enterprises in India. Vietnamese enterprises have not really paid much attention to the Indian market; Less proactive market survey, less participation in exhibitions to reach out to customers; the knowledge of market, competitiveness of products, consumption tastes in India is limited. The possibility of negotiating foreign trade contracts of Vietnamese enterprises is low. In addition, the qualifications of Vietnamese businessmen, especially private enterprises, are not high and lack professionalism in international competition, so they are often disadvantaged when dealing with Indian businesses.

Solutions to Promote Economic Relations between Vietnam and India

Economic and Political Solutions

Both parties should maintain regular high-level meetings at least once a year. Besides this the two sides should strengthen the exchange of delegations at ministerial, sectoral and local levels to find and evaluate the potential of partnership. In meetings and workplaces, it is necessary to create opportunities for enterprises to interact with each other, by increasing the number of enterprises, especially those with business needs and capabilities to join the official delegation.

On the other hand, India and Vietnam need to intensify propaganda and raise mutual understanding of each other. Vietnam needs to thoroughly grasp the Ministries, branches and localities: strengthening the relations and cooperation in many aspects with India is very necessary and strategic.

On the Side of the State

There is a need to reiterate that the two sides need to foster substantive and effective cooperation. Therefore, the state must play a leading role in promoting economic relations between the two countries. The state must have a major responsibility in promoting, disseminating and sharing information. The two countries should focus on the removal of trade barriers on the basis of signed FTAs. In the long run, the two countries would have to sign a Free Trade Agreement.

India and Vietnam need to promote connectivity, including infrastructure, such as aviation, maritime, road connectivity, digital connectivity, information collaboration, telecommunication and data sharing. This is an important condition for businesses to increase mutual investment. Both sides should continue to cooperate in exploration and exploitation of oil and gas. This activity will strengthen both economic relations and political relations.

On the Governance front the two countries should strengthen cooperation between their Chambers of Commerce and Industry to support the private sectors; organise trade fairs and workshops at regular intervals to exchange information on experience, trade opportunities, business and investment environment.

On the Business Side

Businesses should use existing channels to provide information related to each other's business and investment environment opportunities. At present, there are important information channels such as embassies, trade missions, fairs, exhibitions, seminars and exchanges. Vietnamese enterprises should actively study the Indian market in terms of demand, tastes, prices, consumption habits, distribution systems and international cooperation. At the same time, Vietnam participates in fairs and exhibitions, sales at supermarkets, advertises products on the mass media, etc., and launch campaigns to directly advertise Vietnamese goods to Indian consumers. On the other hand, Vietnam needs to enlist Indian programs such as "Make in India",[3] "Digital India", "Skill India",[4] etc. to invest in this country.

Indian businesses need to continue and increase investments in Vietnam in areas such as petroleum exploration, exploitation and processing, petrochemicals, mineral processing, textiles and garments, tea, coffee processing, energy, infrastructure, information technology, etc. to exploit the Vietnamese market and create export sources back to India, contributing to narrowing the trade balance between the two countries. India should also consider the establishment of SEZs in Vietnam (India has a lot of experience and capacity in this area).[5]

Enterprises of each country must proactively diversify their exports. At the same time, they should improve the competitiveness of each export product in terms of price, design and quality to further enhance the role of business associations and business partnerships.

Co-operation in other Economic Sectors

Together with the above bilateral cooperation, the two countries should pay attention to the exploitation of multilateral mechanisms such as India-ASEAN relations. While bilateral relations are difficult, strengthening multilateral cooperation is a means to improve the effectiveness of each party's activities. While cooperation between central agencies is still difficult, the two countries need to strengthen cooperation among localities, such as the establishment of relations between the provinces of Vietnam and the Indian states. It is noteworthy that the two countries can and should focus on tourism in general, spiritual tourism in particular.

Education-Training: India has a good education environment, at a suitable cost for Vietnam. Meanwhile, Vietnam has a great demand for studying abroad. Therefore, in addition to maintaining help for Vietnam with implementation of the signed agreements, India should further strengthen the promotion, introduction of education and training in Vietnam, to attract more Vietnamese students to study in India. On the Vietnamese side, it is necessary to create favourable conditions for Indian universities to build training facilities in Vietnam.

About the defence industry: India has many strengths in this field, while Vietnam has great demand. Therefore, there should be cooperation between the two countries in the defence sector to meet each other's demands and bring about economic efficiency.

NOTES

1. http://baotintuc.vn/thoi-su/thuc-day-moi-quan-he-sau-rong-viet-nam-an-do-20161206182602049.htm.

2. http://cis.org.vn/article/1078/development-of-vietnam-india-economic-trade-relations-the-barriers-and-outlook-part-3.html.
3. https://en.wikipedia.org/wiki/Make_in_India.
4. http://viisas.vass.gov.vn/noidung/tintuc/Lists/DiemNhan/View_Detail.aspx?ItemID=361.
5. http://sezindia.nic.in/about-introduction.asp.

REFERENCES

Development of Vietnam-India Economic Trade Relations: The Barriers And Outlook http://cis.org.vn/article/1078/development-of-vietnam-india-economic-trade-relations-the-barriers-and-outlook-part-3.html.

Đại sứ Ấn Độ tại Việt Nam Harish Parvathaneni: Cam kết đưa quan hệ hợp tác Việt Nam - Ấn Độ lên tầm cao mới, http://www.mod.gov.vn/wps/portal/!ut/p/b1/vZPLjptA.

Make in India https://en.wikipedia.org/wiki/Make_in_India.

Quan hệ Việt Nam - Ấn Độ ngày càng phát triển sâu sắc và bền vững, http://baotintuc.vn/thoi-su/quan-he-viet-nam-an-do-ngay-cang-phat-trien-sau-sac-va-ben-vung-20150116184122020.htm.

Thúc đẩy mối quan hệ sâu rộng Việt Nam - Ấn Độ, http://baotintuc.vn/thoi-su/thuc-day-moi-quan-he-sau-rong-viet-nam-an-do-20161206182602049.htm.

11

China and India: Vietnam's Neighbourhood Issues in the New Regional Context

Nguyen Tran Tien

Vietnam-China Relations: Historical Perspectives

Chinese civilisation which is one of the oldest in the world is now becoming a big power not only in the East Asian region but also in the world. Each move and policy of China would receive attention from not only the big powers but also the small and medium countries, especially in the Southeast Asian region. While the big powers may have their own worries of a growing Chinese dominance, the ASEAN countries also have some fear of being dominated economically and politically. China's strategy of a "peaceful rise" and "peaceful development" may not fully ease this fear of these countries. From the perspective of the ASEAN, this fear is not completely unfounded. Vietnam plays an important role in ASEAN as the neighbouring country to China, with a legacy of protecting itself from China.

Vietnam and China share a land border of approximately of 1,300 km. In the past, Vietnam was subjected to Chinese domination resulting in conflicts for centuries. According to the common perception, Vietnamese history as we know it today could not exist without Chinese history. It can also be viewed in a Southeast Asian comparative context. However, the disparity in surviving evidence, the great differences in culture and politics, and the exceptional imperatives of the Sino-Vietnamese relationship are obstacles to meaningful comparisons.[1]

To review the history of China-Vietnam relations we find that two countries have interacted since the Chinese Warring States period and the Vietnamese Thuc Dynasty of the 3rd century BCE, as noted in *the Complete Annals of Đai Viet.* Between the 1st century BCE and 15th century CE, Vietnam was subject to four separate periods of imperial Chinese domination, although it successfully asserted a degree of independence following the Battle of Ngo Quyen in 938 CE. After the defeat of King An Duong Vuong in the resistance against Trieu Da (179 BC.), Vietnam was ruled, exploited and assimilated by Chinese feudal groups. For thousand years, the Vietnamese people struggled firmly to preserve cultural identity, a national language, received and Vietnamised elements of Han culture; rose simultaneously in more than hundred rebellions against aggressors in order to gain sovereignty with the first revolt of two Trung sisters (40-43 CE.D). In 938 CE., Ngo Quyen completely expelled the Chinese aggressor on the historical Bach Dang River and began the era of the freedom and independence of Vietnamese people.

After a long period of domination by the Chinese dynasty under various regimes in the 11th century, the Vietnamese desire for expansion and regional control became stronger than ever. The early Ly ruler sent troops to conquer northern Champa in 1044. The invasion was successful, and it strengthened the Ly court. The Northern Song, having depended on a long-standing vassal relationship with the Chams, suspected that the Vietnamese had a plan for the domination of regional trade in their campaign, and took direct steps to counter Vietnamese movements. Emperor Renzong of the Song (r. 1022-1063) ordered the Fiscal Commissioner Du Qi (1005-1050) to lead troops into the strategic passes in the region to erect defences. The Vietnamese did not try to attack the border. However, disturbances among the Tai-speaking inhabitants of the frontier, in particular, the Nuìng clan, became quite severe at this time. These inland disturbances would soon occupy the attention of both the Chinese and Vietnamese leadership, and this intense attention paid on the borderlands would be a catalyst for the border war of 1076-77, which ended with the negotiation of a political line of demarcation between the two polities that has very nearly remained the same down to the present day.[2]

In the late 14th century, the rise of the Ming dynasty fundamentally altered the strategic and cultural environment in eastern Asia. The Ming rulers redefined civilisation and the sphere of government while at the same time they sought to restore the borders and to equal the glories of the Han and Tang Empires. Early Ming policies are commonly considered to be conservative and expansionist aimed at erasing the humiliation of Mongol rule by reanimating the Han–Tang imperial legacy. The result was a centralising mobilisation of human and material resources that led to extending Ming rule over neighbouring regions. Le Quy Ly was the first Vietnamese leader to respond to the Ming challenge and to envision a new future for the Vietnamese government.

In the early 15th century, China dominated Vietnam, taking the national archives and some of the country's intellectuals back to Nanjing (the capital of Ming dynasty) – a loss that was to have a lasting impact on Vietnamese civilisation. Ming educational policies left a strong legacy among the Vietnamese. According to the *Complete Annals of Đai Viet*, compiled by Le Dynasty historians in 1415 that "Taxes were heavy, levies were substantial, and so the people had nothing from which to make a living." Nguyen Trai (1380-1442) wrote of this period: 'Were the waters of the Eastern Sea to be exhausted, the stains of their ignominy could not be washed away; all the bamboo of the Southern Mountains would not suffice to provide the paper for recording all their crimes.

In the 20th century, China's relationship with Vietnam often contained old and new motivations. In the fall of 1950, Viet Minh forces crushed the French garrisons stationed along the Chinese–Vietnamese border, marking the first major defeat of the French in the First Indochinese War. This victory opened up communications between the People's Republic of China (PRC) and the Democratic Republic of Vietnam (DRV), bringing increased military support. In 1954, however, with the fall of the French forces at Dien Bien Phu the PRC leadership was anxious about the next stage of inevitable US involvement in collaboration with southern Vietnamese authorities. At Geneva, Zhou EnLai had emphasised that US military bases in the region would not be tolerated and that he could foresee an indefinite French presence in Mainland Southeast Asia to keep the Americans out.[3] When the region could not be neutralised in this manner, and the US military presence lingered to support the newly established Republic of Vietnam, Beijing renewed support for Hanoi's effort to bring national reunification. In 1962, for example, Beijing supplied Hanoi with enough weapons for 230 infantry battalions to engage with the RVN forces.[4]

The Vietnam-China relations positively improved during the Vietnam War of 1954-1975 as China became the ally of North Vietnam against South Vietnam and its ally, the United States. However, the deterioration of this relationship had been gradual starting perhaps most dramatically with Nixon's 1972 visit to China (which Hanoi later called the beginning of China's betrayal to Vietnam), but in the mid-1970s the signs of an impending breakdown were barely discernible. Following the Vietnamese invasion and occupation of Cambodia in 1976, relations with Beijing deteriorated and in 1979 China invaded and fought a short but bloody war with Vietnam. Vietnam-China relations in the span of ten years after Ho Chí Minh's period was termed as one that "deteriorated from one of 'comradeship plus brotherhood' to one between 'the most direct and most dangerous enemies'."[5] In this context of heightened tensions, the fall of Saigon on April 30, 1975, both marked the end of the Second Indochinese War and one step closer to the third one, the short border conflict between China and Vietnam in February, 1979. The pre-modern era was no less complex and the fear of expanding regional influence for Vietnam led to aggressive behaviour from China.

Vietnam-China relations continuously deteriorated after Hanoi instituted a ban in March 1978 on private trade, which had a particularly large impact on southern Vietnam's ethnic Chinese community. Following Vietnam's December 1978 invasion of Cambodia and the expulsion of a significant number of Hoa (ethnic Chinese) from Vietnam, China in February 1979 launched a 3-week incursion over Vietnam's northern border. While Vietnam had not experienced war since its withdrawal from Cambodia, tensions have periodically flared between Vietnam and China, primarily over neighbouring issues. In 1991, Vietnam-China relations were re-normalised after many years of mutual hatred. During this time, there were different trends in both the nations regarding their opposite views of the comprehensive relations. Vietnamese optimists, whose arguments now no longer depend on the naïve belief of the shared ideologies, still hold on to theories and facts which can support their advocacy of the Vietnam-China relations, if not a sort of expected alignment. A border agreement was eventually signed in 1999 following border skirmishes throughout the 1980s.

In 2007, the building of the Hanoi-Kunming highway was announced that marked a significant improvement in their relations. While China has now become the second-largest trading partner and the largest source of imports for Vietnam, tensions over territorial issues were rekindled over the Spratly Island, an oil-rich area in the South China Sea (or "East Sea" as the Vietnamese term it). When Vietnam and China were able to agree to land borders in 1999, overlapping maritime claims in the South China Sea continue to increase bilateral tensions. Vietnam and China each assert claims to the Spratly and Paracel Islands, archipelagos in the potentially oil-rich area of the South China Sea. China has reasserted claims to roughly 90 percent of the South China Sea as its exclusive economic zone. Malaysia, the Philippines, Brunei, and Taiwan also claim all or part of the Spratly Islands. Over the years, conflicting claims have produced small-scale armed conflict in the area; in 1988, 70 Vietnamese sailors died in a confrontation with China in the Spratlys. China's assertion of "indisputable sovereignty" over the Spratly Islands and the entire South China Sea has become a great concern of Vietnam and its Southeast Asia neighbours. Tensions escalated in the latter half of 2007. China pressured foreign oil companies to abandon their oil and gas exploration contracts with Vietnam in the South China Sea. China's efforts in the summer of 2009 to strictly enforce its unilateral fishing ban in disputed waters led to the detention for several weeks of more than two dozen Vietnamese fishermen. In contrast, Vietnam has made significant progress with China in delineating its northern land border and the Gulf of Tonkin, pursuant to a Land Border Agreement signed in December 1999, and an Agreement on Borders in the Gulf of Tonkin signed in December 2000. The two sides completed demarcation of their land border in December 2008 and have reached understanding on maritime boundaries in the mouth of the Gulf of Tonkin.

Both of them place great emphasis on joint declarations, and the decision to characterise Vietnam's relationship with China as a "Comprehensive Strategic Partnership" at the conclusion of CPV General Secretary Nong Duc Manh's June 2008 visit to Beijing, which marked a significant upgrading of ties. The relationship was on a much better footing than it was even two-three years earlier. Both sides pointed to an acceleration of high-level government and Party meetings, including Manh's summit in Beijing, the visit to Vietnam of Guangdong Party Secretary and Politburo member Wang Yang in September 2008, and the visit to Beijing by PM Nguyen Tan Dung, at the end of 2008. Specific deliverables included demarcating the land border and agreement to establish a hotline, as well as cooperation on "less sensitive" matters such as disaster relief, typhoon and tsunami forecasting, and search and rescue. Positive signs emerged not only in the field of economic-trade, but also some political, diplomatic, cultural exchange such as: increasing trading volumes year by year, high official exchange visits, land and sea border demarcations being completed in 2009. Optimists inferred to some institutional and neo-classical perspectives to opine that mutual economic and inter-dependent interests would lead to and maintain political and security stability between Vietnam and China as well as in the new regional context. Furthermore, economic growth is now considered to be the unique political legitimacy for the ruling government in China. That is why Deng Xiaoping's focus on "peace for development" or "peaceful rising" is still expected to be the leading principle in the future. However, as later seen, even the optimists in Vietnam hold on such belief, as long as they are Vietnamese. One of the reasons leading them to this perspective is that they see the need to go with China to form a possible balance against the US in case the latter wants to refer to such values as democracy, humanism, religious freedom to interfere into Vietnam's sovereignty, the need to take advantage of an economically rising China as a promising market. In other words, there is now no longer the purely naïve belief in a long-lasting China-Vietnam friendship built on the shared ideology of communism.

The hidden risk of a military confrontation between China and Vietnam is rising. Although the two countries have enjoyed close party-to-party ties for decades, since 2011 they have both asserted conflicting claims to the South China Sea. China has repeatedly moved oil rigs into disputed areas, dredged and occupied parts of the disputed Paracel Islands, and constructed at least one and potentially multiple airstrips, possibly for military use, in the Spratly Islands. Vietnam has also tried to use oil explorations to claim disputed areas of the sea and reportedly has rammed Chinese vessels in disputed waters. Vietnam has cultivated close military ties to the United States, to other Southeast Asian nations like the Philippines, and to regional powers such as India, all to the consternation of China. Also, both signed an agreement on general guidelines for addressing maritime conflicts, but have not progressed beyond generalities in 2011. Although ASEAN could theoretically mediate a dispute, the organisation's mediation capabilities, housed in its Institute for Peace and Reconciliation, are limited and untested.

Vietnam and China generally enjoy close relations; but the conflict over sovereignty, territorial claims and maritime resources in the South China Sea is a persistent source of tension. While Vietnam cannot hope to match China in naval power, it can make any conflict over disputed claims a complex and risky proposition for China. Despite agreement on the final demarcation of their land border and progress settling the maritime boundary beyond the Gulf of Tonkin, Vietnam and China have made no evident progress in resolving the offshore sovereignty dispute in the South China Sea. The offshore dispute continues to entangle multiple multinational energy companies, including those from U.S., India etc.

The other trend in Vietnam-China relation, tacitly or implicitly, considered to be the most prevailing one in the country, not only for now but also along the history. This is the so-called Vietnamese historical perspective on China. Most Vietnamese do know that the history of Vietnam is that of wars, and that most of the wars come (not only came) from China. Along the history of two thousand years, there have been wars of invasion initiated by China to invade and dominate Vietnam. In the Vietnamese's mind, China is a symbol of nationalism, realism, chauvinism, expansionism, ethnocentrism, which are strongly culturally characterised, with certain different implications compared with those usually perceived by Western minds. Such differences may lead to the fact that the West is still holding on to their biased perceptions of China and can hardly understand what the Chinese think and plan to do regarding their political, diplomatic, military intentions.

What can the past tell us about the future of Vietnam-China relations? One lesson seems to be in order: The centrifugal forces of nationalism are far more powerful than the centripetal forces of communism. Just as Mao eventually broke with Stalin, so did Ho eventually turn his back on Mao. Scratch a communist, and you will find a nationalist not far under the surface. As long as memories about "a thousand years of Chinese rule" remain fresh in the Vietnamese collective consciousness, Beijing's promise of peaceful rise would ring hollow, and ongoing tensions in the South China Sea would only make that promise even hollower. Hanoi would continue to seek support from third parties in order to prepare itself for an unpeaceful rise of China.

Vietnam–India: Traditional Relations

Geographically, Vietnam is located far away from India. India still shies away from coming out unequivocally in expressing its strategic preferences for countries which are vital or whose strategic partnerships are desirable for furthering India's national security interests. Along with Myanmar, in South

East Asia, India needs to build up a relationship of strategic partnership with Vietnam. Historically, what made India a good neighbour to Vietnam and different from other external influences was the fact that this relation was totally peaceful; they came through trade, culture, religion, and the philosophy of peaceful coexistence and non-violence. There was never any conflict, which is the most important feature of India-Vietnam relations. It is perhaps because of this firm foundation of peace between these two nations has endured in modern times and become even stronger.[6]

The former President Tran Duc Luong had proposed that "Vietnam treats India with strategic importance" to India's Foreign Minister Jaswant Singh during the latter visit to Vietnam in mid-November 2000 in connection with the 10th Indo-Vietnam Joint Commission meeting.[7] Since the establishment of official diplomatic relations in 1972, India and her most trusted neighbour and ally – Vietnam, have consistently stood together in resisting the external domination of Indo-China for 45 years. India also has been seeking to readjust the relationship to address not only China's growing economic and military power in ASEAN and beyond, but also India's own security ambitions in the region. In 1976, the two countries signed a bilateral Cultural Agreement. Since then, a series of successful cultural exchanges have taken place. In 1992, India and Vietnam established extensive economic ties, including oil exploration, agriculture and manufacturing. The relations between the two countries especially defence ties, benefited extensively from India's Look East Policy (LEP). In 2007, India and Vietnam signed the 'Strategic Partnership' agreement which was very important, with the aim of taking this relationship to higher level than before. To date, Vietnam and India have strongly cooperated in many fields of politics, national defence, security, trade and investment, culture, education and capacity building.

Over the years, India and Vietnam have created several institutional linkages for greater academic exchanges. India has also enhanced the cultural cooperation, people-to-people contact and linkages through education and training. Government leaders and decision makers on both sides who have grown up based on these linkages that were created early on in post-independence relations. During LEP-AEP, the two countries have tried to strengthen and widen the multi-faceted relations between them. Vietnam has become one of the largest recipients of training programmes under the Indian Technical and Economic Cooperation (ITEC) programme. Hundreds of

ITEC slots are being offered to Vietnam every year along with scholarships under the General Cultural Scholarship Scheme (GCSS), under the Educational Exchange Programme (EEP) and the MGC Scholarship Scheme. These scholarships are granted for short and medium term courses in various fields such as finance, banking, management, information technology, many engineering and water management related issues.

In 2012, India established the Entrepreneurship Development Centre in Hanoi as they negotiated with the People's Committee of Hanoi to inaugurate the Vietnam-India Advanced Resource Centre in Information and Communication Technology with a grant of $2 million. Besides, the Indian cultural diplomacy policy toward Vietnam has been promoted and Indian arts such as film, music and dance are popular in Vietnam. During Vietnamese Prime Minister Nguyen Tan Dung's visit to India in October 2014, it was agreed that the Archaeological Survey of India would help to renovate one of the temple complexes in My Son, which remains an enduring symbol of our ancient linkages. India has also announced a US$3 million project for conservation and restoration of temples at My Son. Moreover, we are also looking at the possibility of starting a research project between Vietnamese and Indian scholars on the links between the Cham civilisation and India. Many Vietnamese Buddhist scholars have gone to India for higher studies and conferences. In 2012, an international conference on Buddhism was organised in Hanoi. Within the same year, an important seminar, entitled 'Life and Legacy of Rabindranath Tagore' was organised on the occasion of Tagore's 150th birthday. Furthermore, the Indian government has also established a culture centre in Hanoi, aiming to promote Indian culture and education activities in Vietnam.

Under Modi's leadership, India's LEP has transformed into a proactive AEP that envisages accelerated across-the-board engagement between the two growth poles of a vibrant Asia. This has been reflected in a spate of two-way visits of the Modi government. President Pranab Mukherjee's landmark visit to Vietnam in September 2014 already resulted in some major cooperation agreements including an oil exploration deal in the East Sea,[8] followed by the visit of Vietnam's Prime Minister to New Delhi in October and the bilateral agenda would be seen as another strong assertion of India's interests in the South China Sea.[9] External Affairs Minister Sushma Swaraj has already visited Vietnam and Singapore and looks set to travel to most of other ASEAN countries in the months ahead. During her visit to Singapore, India's foreign minister articulated the need for an AEP forcefully: "Look East is no longer adequate; now we need Act East policy".[10]

The Indo-Vietnamese strategic relationship now upgraded, in nomenclature at least, to a 'strategic comprehensive partnership' is important, but its importance should not be overstated. In terms of substance, it is actually fairly modest, beginning with the MoU on defence cooperation that was signed by the defence ministers of the two countries in November 2009. India had offered a US$100 million line of credit to Vietnam to purchase four offshore patrol vessels that are currently being built in Indian yards. The two countries also have some unspecified cooperation in electronic intelligence in relation to Chinese naval activity in the seas of Vietnam. India has helped Vietnam train personnel who are operating its Kilo-class submarines, and New Delhi has offered to upgrade and maintain Russian-origin equipment with the Vietnamese forces such as tanks, fighter aircraft, helicopter and ships. So far, there is no reference to the Brahmos missile, though it is well known that India has been keen to sell the missile to Vietnam. Hanoi itself is likely to be cautious on such a deal which could be viewed as destabilising. The recent placement of a missile battery on the Chinese border in Arunachal was sharply criticized by China. The foundations of the political alliance between India and Vietnam and attempts since the turn of this 21st century to create a "strategic partnership" has significant security and economic dimensions.

Vietnam's Efforts to Solve her Neighbour Issues: Closer Ties with India and Awareness of not Interfering China's Rise

Despite living next to the giant neighbour for a thousand long years, it however, seems difficult for Vietnam to understand China. The experience Vietnam has had so far in her relations with China is inadequate in terms of the fact that Vietnam hardly holds an active role in such relations. Vietnam tries to understand China and its strategic intentions so as to balance its power. Protecting national security and sovereignty has always been a challenge to generations of all Vietnamese people on one hand and leaders and policymakers on the other. Therefore, to understand China and her diplomatic, political, military tricks, it is necessary for Vietnam to go deeply into their cultural, political and diplomatic tradition, to have some sense of their deep thoughts, to understand the Chinese black box of decision making. A recent example is the massive protests of Chinese people against Japan on the issues of Japanese historical textbook, and the two nations' conflict over some rocks in the East China Sea. These protests, which were politically controlled shows that Chinese nationalism now is as still an effective weapon in hands of Chinese politicians as it was hundred years ago. Regarding Vietnam, due to some particular historical reasons, especially the border war in 1979, there is no need for the Chinese government to mobilise the masses if they want to prepare for any political movements against Vietnam.

Vietnam is seeking to diversify its international relationships and enmesh itself in ASEAN; it is willing to do so only within a framework of public deference towards China. Accordingly, if India wishes to extend its role as a potential security provider in Southeast Asia, it would need to take proper account of regional security needs and historical relationships with China. China is the biggest long-term strategic threat to Vietnam, India and other countries and dealing with this threat would require a multi-faced scheme. The key component of that scheme should be to strategically obstruct China by keeping it mired in North and South East Asia; this would fall in line with the broader strategy for India to create a pan-Asian maritime security system (from Southeast Asia, to the Indian Ocean littoral states) with India is its centre. Vietnam is well placed to be the central thrust of such an effort due to a convergence of strategic interests with India. The China factor weighs heavily and figures prominently in the respective strategic calculus of both India and Vietnam. George Fernandes, India's Defence Minister was accurate when in 1998 he described China as a "major threat" to India. Prime Minister Vajpayee had also in 1998 mentioned the Chinese threat as an impulse for India's nuclear weaponisation.[11] Recently a Vietnamese Foreign Ministry official had remarked "we don't trust China";[12] in other words, Vietnam is suspicious of China and fearful of China's intentions.

Vietnam has reasons to come closer to India as both of them share long land borders with China and Vietnam shares sea borders. China has disputed the existing border with both. China launched punitive military attacks on India in 1962 and on Vietnam in 1979. India suffered badly because Nehru never suspected that China would attack India. China again attacked Vietnamese garrisons in the Spratly Islands group and forcibly occupied six of them. However, once again the Vietnamese Navy met Chinese aggression intensely. China's recent expressions professing friendship with both India and Vietnam respectively do not matchup with genuine efforts to settle border issues. China's perceived strategic concerns regarding India and Vietnam forced it to create strategic pressure points to destabilise these two countries. In the case of India, China created the Pakistani threat (nuclear and missile threat) and in the case of Vietnam, it posed proxy military challenges in Cambodia, besides direct military force on both land and sea borders. India and Vietnam, therefore, have a natural strategic congruence on how to restrain China from aggressive actions in future, while keeping it engaged diplomatically. India's strategic and national security interests demand that Vietnam emerges as a strong state. Relatively, India is better placed to contribute towards this aim in all fields – defence cooperation, political cooperation, economic and technical assistance and technology transfers.

Understanding the new regional context, India has recently strengthened its cooperation with Vietnam in various fields. India supports freedom of navigation as well as Vietnamese territorial claims in the South China Sea, both by patrols and port calls by Indian naval ships on Vietnam and by energy exploration (of ONGC Videsh Limited and PetroVietnam). The Indo-Vietnamese Defence Pact signed in 2014 formalised India's role in the South China Sea as a way to take on China's maritime aggression in that area. That this was aimed at China was clear – the captain of INS Airavat – an Indian amphibious assault ship also paid his respects to a Vietnamese general who had defeated the Chinese in a war when he arrived at Vietnam. On energy cooperation, India ignored Beijing's objections to start exploration by ONGC Videsh Limited of offshore energy blocks within Vietnamese claimed territory. Under capacity building of the Vietnamese military, India has trained Vietnamese submarine crew as well as Sukhoi-30 pilots. To build a limited presence for Indian forces in Vietnam, India has already stationed navy personnel at Cam Ranh with signals and electronic surveillance of Hainan. Hainan is not just the main naval base for China's South Sea forces, but also its centre for cyber-warfare, hence India having Cam Ranh as a post for both signals and electronic surveillance is quite significant. India also carried on transferring military technology and armaments. India seems ready to arm Vietnam with the Brahmos supersonic anti-ship cruise missiles and has transferred patrol vessels. These would be hugely benefited for Vietnam to challenge the South Sea fleet. India has stepped up joint exercises with the other naval powers in the region, ranging from Japan, the US, Australia and also Vietnam. This would help both navies develop ways to cooperate operationally.

Narendra Modi visited Vietnam, the first bilateral by an Indian Prime Minister since Atal Bihari Vajpayee in 2001. In today's hyper-nationalist times, Modi's visit assumes a larger-than-life form with some Modi 'bhakts' virtually seeing the feisty South-East Asian nation as an instrument of Indian geostrategy in the same way that Beijing uses Islamabad against New Delhi. This connection is underscored by the fact that Modi chose to visit Hanoi on his way to the G-20 summit in Guangzhou, where he was to meet Chinese leader Xi Jinping.[13] Vietnam, on the other hand, is a smart country which has a ruthless understanding of self interest; after all, confronted with a rising China, it has not hesitated to befriend the United States, the country that was responsible for the deaths of an estimated 1.5 million Vietnamese in the 1960s and 1970s. Given these reasons, Vietnam could very well play the role of a linchpin for India in South East Asia, which is similar to the role that Pakistan plays for China vis-à-vis India in South Asia.

Following his meeting with Nguyen Xuan Phuc, Modi announced a new $500 million line of credit for defence products and a target of $15 billion for two-way trade (currently it is around $9 billion). The two sides also signed agreements in areas like health, cyber security, shipbuilding and naval information sharing. Indian investments are of the order of $1 billion in the area of food processing, fertilizers, sugar, auto components, information technology and agro-chemicals. Indian companies like ONGC Videsh have been active in Vietnam's oil exploration efforts since the late 1980s despite some offshore areas being contested by China.

The Indo-Vietnamese strategic relationship now upgraded, in nomenclature at least, to a 'strategic comprehensive partnership' – is important, but its importance should not be overstated. In terms of substance, it is actually fairly modest, beginning with the MoU on defence cooperation that was signed by the defence ministers of the two countries in November 2009. However, India has the capacity to deepen cooperation and help Vietnam become a far more significant threat to China. This, however, requires strategic boldness, vision as well as risk-taking which the Indian defence establishment has not shown traditionally. Building defence bases in Vietnam could be a bold move against China. India can build a much stronger and direct forward presence in the Vietnamese coast to confine China's South Sea Fleet on its base in Hainan. This could include actually building a foreign military base for Indian forces. The idea of India having foreign military bases may seem quite outlandish, but that may be our own timidity in contemplating the nature of the role that India can play in Asian security.

A foreign military base for India in Vietnam would be a bold move to counter China. The Vietnamese forces themselves are reported to have offered India exclusive use of the Nha Trang port, as well as docking rights in Cam Ranh. Both of these have significant strategic value: Nha Trang has direct line of sight to China's Hainan Island and is within its naval range; Cam Ranh is a deep water port, one of the few in this region, and has been refurbished by the Russians and is hence well setup for use. The other high-risk move would be to supplement the transfer of cruise missiles with actual lethal ballistic missile technology. This could be an alternative to actually developing a base itself as it would act as a check on China at relatively low cost to India. A really out of the box, high-risk manoeuvre would be to arm Vietnam with nuclear weapons, essentially as a tit-for-tat for China arming Pakistan. While this may seem irresponsible, the experience of Chinese proliferation to Pakistan and North Korea shows that the non-proliferation regime is anyway violable, and without significant costs.

Vietnam is a responsible power, with no possibility of conflict ever with India. With the transfer of ballistic missiles with nuclear warheads (naturally covertly) India may have plausible deniability, and still, change the game in the South China Sea and more broadly with China. Strategic analysts in India such as Bharat Karnad have advocated for such an aggressive move as part of a grand strategy for India to achieve "great power" status. The capacity for Indo-Vietnamese cooperation to achieve mutually beneficial strategic goals is significant and limited only by our imagination and capacity for risk-taking. India should treat this relationship with the attention it deserves.

Conclusion

In short, from the above analyses of the Vietnamese neighbouring issues in general and relations with China and India in particular, we can see that Vietnam and India are both geo-strategically important countries, vital to all major nations with a stake in the freedom of high seas. Both countries share disputed borders with China and both have been subjected to military aggression by China. Chinese nationalism, realism, chauvinism, expansionism, ethnocentrism, have been and still are the very challenges to not only Vietnam, India but to other regional countries. With its rising economic and military power, such challenges may become actual threats. The reason is that Vietnam is too close to China, and with China being a traditional "land imperialist" power (compared to the US as a "sea imperialist"), it is too risky for Vietnam to stand on the US side. It is more difficult for Vietnam, its academic community and policymaking elites to find a safe and balanced position.

The open question is whether Hanoi will take up the South China Sea issue through the UNCLOS arbitration system following the successful example of the Philippines. The likely answer at this juncture is 'no'. While Vietnam insists that peaceful settlement must be based on "equality" and respect for international law, China will be brazen and seek to strike a bilateral deal with Vietnam, after it has done so with the Philippines. At the end of the day, Vietnam will do what it considers best for its national interest. Indian policymakers would do well to understand that.

In such a strategic context, while making all efforts towards keeping China peacefully engaged in the Asia-Pacific, India and Vietnam should work towards building a comprehensive strategic partnership based on the current mutual interests.

NOTES

1. W.K. Taylor (2013). *History of the Vietnamese* (Cambridge: Cambridge University Press, 2013), 27.
2. James Anderson, *The Rebel Den of Nuỉng Trì Cao Loyalty and Identity Along the Sino-Vietnamese Frontier* (Seattle: University of Washington Press, 2007), 144.
3. Kuo-kang Shao, "Zhou Enlai's Diplomacy and the Neutralization of Indo-China, 1954-55," *China Quarterly*, no.107 (September 1986): 495-496.
4. Xiaoming Zhang, "The Vietnam War, 1964-1969: A Chinese Perspective," *The Journal of Military History* 60, no. 4 (Oct., 1996): 736-737.
5. Y.S. Cheng Joseph, "Sino-Vietnamese Relations in the Early Twenty-first Century: Economics in Command?" *Asian Survey* 51, No 2: 379.
6. Speech by Ambassador extraordinary and plenipotentiary of the Republic of India H. E. Ms. Preeti Saran at University of Social Sciences and Humanities, Vietnam National University, http://dongphuonghoc.org/article/71/phat-bieu-cua-ba-preeti-saran-dai-su-cong-hoa-an-do-tai-viet-nam-tai-vnu-ussh-ha-noi.html.
7. Prasamrajan. "Ahoy Hanoi: With India and Vietnam reviving old bonds, the chances of a strategic tie-up become stronger," *India Today*, New Delhi, November 20, 2000: 50.

8. Indian President visits Vietnam to boost ties, http://www.thanhniennews.com/politics/indian-president-visits-vietnam-to-boost-ties-31166.html.
9. Oil, defence top Vietnam PM's agenda, http://www.thehindu.com/news/national/vietnams-prime-minister-nguyen-tan-dung-twoday-visit-to-india/article6535542.ece.
10. Act East: India's ASEAN Journey, http://www.mea.gov.in/in-focus-article.htm?24216/Act+East+Indias+ASEAN+Journey.
11. J.N. Dixit, *Across Borders: Fifty years of India's Foreign Policy* (New Delhi: Picus Books, 1998), 408.
12. S. Prasamrajan "Ahoy Hanoi: With India and Vietnam reviving old bonds, the chances of a strategic tie-up become stronger," 50.
13. Vietnam Will Never Be for India What Pakistan is to China, https://thewire.in/63871/vietnam-will-never-india-pakistan-china/.

12

Mekong-Ganga Cooperation and India–Vietnam Relations through the Prism of Act East Policy

Bharti Chhibber

Introduction

The paper examines the shifting historical trajectory of India's Look East Policy (LEP) and existing contours of India's foreign policy which defines India's role in Southeast Asia. India's Look East Policy was envisioned during the period of Narasimha Rao Government in 1991 as a focused foreign policy approach towards the Asia-Pacific region particularly towards the Association of Southeast Asian Nations (ASEAN) region. At present the cooperation between India and ASEAN has gone beyond functional aspect to include political and security dimensions. Now Look East has been reinvigorated as Act East Policy comprising three 'Cs', commerce, culture and connectivity and Vietnam is the bedrock of India's foreign policy. Mekong-Ganga Cooperation (MGC) exemplifies all three 'Cs'. However, there are still some irritants like the policy of protectionism in the economic sphere and low people-to-people contact i.e. historical and cultural linkages can be truly invoked by actually facilitating human movement across the borders through enhanced infrastructural development.

This paper has two sections; the first section after a brief overview of

ASEAN traces the evolution of India's Look East Policy to the rejuvenated Act East Policy which defines India's role to counter China in Southeast Asia. Vietnam is a crucial factor in this Act East Policy. The second section, after a brief analyses of the historical association between India and Vietnam further explores the Mekong-Ganga initiative which is a symbol of inter-regional cooperation. In the final section, the paper reflects on the way ahead to augment the cooperative venture.

SECTION I

ASEAN as a Regional Organisation

Established in Bangkok in 1967, ASEAN was conceived as an organisation for economic, social and cultural cooperation. But it was clear from the very beginning that the real objectives were regional and national security. ASEAN emerged after the cessation of hostilities between Indonesia and Malaysia. Thus one of the most important regional security goals for the ASEAN states was to expand and institutionalise this process of reconciliation (Chhibber, 2004). At the first ASEAN Heads of State Summit at Bali (1976), Declaration of Concord and Treaty of Amity and Cooperation were signed. These were steps towards building a regional identity and solidarity. The Concord called upon member states to take joint approaches on economic issues in international multilateral fora. ASEAN concluded an agreement in 1992 for the establishment of a Free Trade Area.

At the 2003 ASEAN Summit in Bali, ASEAN leaders declared Bali Concord II calling for the establishment of an ASEAN Community comprising ASEAN Security Community, ASEAN Economic Community and ASEAN Socio-Cultural Community. In the post-Cold War period, ASEAN institutionalised cooperation in the security field through ASEAN Regional Forum (ARF) which is modelled on ASEAN Post-Ministerial Conferences with its dialogue partners. The establishment of the ASEAN Economic Community (AEC) in 2015 was a watershed moment. The AEC Blueprint 2025, adopted by the ASEAN Leaders at the 27th ASEAN Summit in November 2015 in Kuala Lumpur, Malaysia, provides broad directions for the AEC from 2016 to 2025. The ASEAN Political-Security Community (APSC) Blueprint 2025 and the ASEAN Socio-Cultural Community (ASCC) Blueprint 2025 also form part of 'ASEAN 2025: Forging Ahead Together'. The ASEAN Community Vision 2025 consist of 5 features (i) A Highly Integrated and Cohesive Economy; (ii) A Competitive, Innovative, and

Dynamic ASEAN; (iii) Enhanced Connectivity and Sectoral Cooperation; (iv) A Resilient, Inclusive, People-Oriented, and People-Centred ASEAN; and (v) A Global ASEAN. ASEAN Leaders further adopted the Master Plan on ASEAN Connectivity 2025 (MPAC 2025) in Vientiane in September 2016. The MPAC 2025 focuses on five strategic areas: sustainable infrastructure, digital innovation, seamless logistics, regulatory excellence and people mobility.

India-ASEAN Partnership: From Look East to Act East

India initially was seen as a champion of decolonisation in Southeast Asia during the 1950s and 1960s as head of the Non-Aligned Movement (Cohen, 2001). However, with the signing of an India-Soviet Peace and Friendship Cooperation Treaty in 1971, relations between India and ASEAN took a downturn. Ideological differences precluded close political ties from developing, throughout most of the Cold War. Further India's recognition of the People's Republic of Kampuchea regime was contrary to the ASEAN view which condemned the Kampuchean regime and this resulted in the worsening of relations between India and ASEAN (Acharya, 2001 and Zhao, 2006).

India's relationship with ASEAN is the foundation of its Look East Policy initiated in 1991. From 1980s onwards both domestic and international factors like India's balance of payment crisis and subsequent economic liberalisation, end of cold war and disintegration of Soviet Union, China's growing influence in East Asia and ASEAN's success as a regional organisation, drew India's attention toward Southeast Asia which resulted in India's 'Look East policy' under then Indian Prime Minister Narasimha Rao. 'The urgent imperative was to be a part of the region's new economic dynamism and rebuild political relations with the rest of Asia, frayed during the Cold War. Among all the sub-regions of Asia and the Indian Ocean littoral, Southeast Asia promised to be the most attractive in terms of the political and diplomatic opportunities' (Raja Mohan, 2008).

Geographical proximity played an important role in India's Look East Policy as the Southeast Asian states, especially along the Mekong River are also strategically important to China. With Myanmar joining ASEAN in 1997, India came to share a 1,500-kilometre contiguous border with ASEAN which added a strategic dimension to Indo-ASEAN relations. India has large economic potential with a huge market. ASEAN countries have realised that it is in their interest to include India in a regional cooperative effort to tap India's strength.

Further, with the withdrawal of US troops from strategic locations in the region following the collapse of the Soviet Union, the Southeast Asian countries deemed it appropriate to guard against Chinese influence. Accordingly, ASEAN countries justifiably perceive India, with the largest naval forces in the Indian Ocean and nuclear capabilities, a strategic partner to balance China's growing power in the region (Christophe, 2003).

India became a sectoral dialogue partner of ASEAN in 1992, which was upgraded to full dialogue partnership in 1996. The First Indo-ASEAN Summit in Phnom Penh in November 2002 institutionalised ASEAN-India relations. India-ASEAN functional cooperation deals with a diverse range of sectors including agriculture, culture, environment, human resource development, health and pharmaceuticals, information and communication technology, new and renewable energy, space science, science & technology, telecommunications, transport and infrastructure, tourism and trade. India has also signed bilateral free trade agreements with Singapore and Thailand and sub-regional initiatives like the MGC and the Bay of Bengal Initiative for Multi-Sectoral Technical and Economic Cooperation (BIMSTEC). ASEAN and India have also concluded an ASEAN-India Free Trade Agreement in Goods (AIFTA), which was concluded in May 2009. Trade between India and ASEAN was worth about $76 billion in 2014-15. Both sides have set a target of increasing this to $100 billion and double that by 2022. 'The ASEAN-India economic partnership is as much influenced by respective national interests to promote greater trade and business linkages as their concern over the growing influence of China in the region' (Yahya, 2003)

At the 4th India-ASEAN Tourism Ministers Meeting held in Vientiane in January 2013, a Protocol to amend the MoU on Strengthening Tourism Cooperation between ASEAN and India was signed. The facility of 'Visa on Arrival' was extended to 7 ASEAN countries – Cambodia, Indonesia, Lao, Myanmar, Singapore, the Philippines and Vietnam. India has established Centres for English Language Training (CELT) and Entrepreneurship Development Centres (EDC) in Cambodia, Lao PDR, Myanmar and Vietnam (CLMV countries).

Established in 2005, East Asia Summit (EAS) is another meeting point between India and ASEAN. It is a forum of 18 countries of the Asia-Pacific including 10 ASEAN countries + Japan, India, China, U.S., Russia, Australia, New Zealand and the Republic of Korea. It focuses on strategic political, security and economic issues in the region. ASEAN Defence Ministers Meeting Plus (ADMM+)[1] is a relatively new security initiative aiming at confidence building through dialogue and discussion. It reflects on significant matters like counterterrorism, coordination in the realm of humanitarian assistance and disaster relief, peacekeeping and maritime security.

However, India faltered on two major grounds during the earlier phase i.e. in the timely implementation of projects and lack of coordination among its various agencies & departments. With proactive Act East Policy Prime Minister Narendra Modi has taken note of these drawbacks. High-level visits in a short span of time to ASEAN states was a step in this direction. At the 12th ASEAN summit, Prime Minister Modi highlighted the importance of ASEAN in an era of economic development, trade, investments and industrialisation. The Indian government is also focussed on augmenting people-to-people relations. It is hoped that the Act East Policy will be successfully implemented culminating in desired results. The 3rd Plan of Action for the period 2016-20 was adopted by the ASEAN-India Foreign Ministers Meeting held in August 2015. Similarly, the Expanded ASEAN Maritime Forum (EAMF), a track 1.5 initiative which deals with maritime issues of common concern. India participated in the 4th EAMF held in Manado, Indonesia in September 2015.

'Swiftly changing regional security architecture can be cited as one of the most prominent reasons for India's proactive engagement with the region. India's rising bonhomie with Australia, Japan, South Korea and the U.S. paves its path for reinforcing its position in the Southeast Asian and the wider Asia-Pacific region' (Mishra, 2015) The importance India attaches to ASEAN is clear from a dedicated Mission to ASEAN and the EAS in Jakarta which was set up in April 2015 with an Ambassador to enhance commitment to ASEAN. With a Commemorative Summit on the theme 'Shared Values, Common Destiny' in 2017, India and ASEAN are celebrating 25 years of their Dialogue Partnership, 15 years of Summit Level interaction and 5 years of Strategic Partnership.[2]

'Under the AEP, India aims to gain a degree of pre-eminence in the Indian Ocean, and with this, it also wants to contain China's growing hegemony in the South China Sea. Complete control over South China Sea by Chinese maritime forces would bring these forces to the Strait of Malacca choke point, which looks out onto the Indian Ocean. This is a strategic point of entry into India's backyard, and New Delhi would never like China to reach to the point of controlling the waters (Jawli, 2016). With Commerce, Culture and Connectivity as three important dimensions of Act East Policy, northeastern states are India's entrance to Southeast Asia through land connectivity.

'However, poor infrastructure and insurgency have been hindrances to road connectivity in the region. Despite this, India's trade with Myanmar through the northeast corridor has increased by 86 percent between 2013-14 and 2015-16' (Sahasrabuddhe and Mallapur, 2017).

SECTION II

India-Vietnam Relations: Cornerstone of Act East Policy

Sharing historical, cultural and economic ties, India-Vietnam relations have grown over the years into a deep comprehensive collaboration in diverse fields of traditional and non-traditional security areas. Although India and Vietnam share a long relationship, it was only in the early 1990s that Vietnam started taking ASEAN more seriously. Vietnam finally signed Treaty of Amity and Cooperation in 1992.[3] ASEAN and India have both found each other useful when facing the strategic challenge posed by the rise of China in Asia. 'Vietnam's increasingly tense relationship with China and its dominant geostrategic position in Indochina and the South China Sea makes Vietnam a natural partner' (Rajendram, 2014).

'Signalling a break from the over-cautiousness of the past, Delhi now seems candid about its intention to strengthen defence ties with Hanoi... Southeast Asia has long sought greater Indian maritime presence, but the fear of angering Beijing had pushed Delhi's much-touted defence diplomacy into inertia... Defence and maritime cooperation between India and Vietnam, extended to much of Southeast Asia, will maintain freedom of navigation in the sea lines of communication, ensuring the South China Sea remains a global commons' (The Indian Express, 2014). A strong Vietnam is critical not only for the stability of the region but also for protecting India's economic and strategic interests.

Historically India has shared close relations with Vietnam due to a common struggle for freedom from foreign rule. India welcomed Vietnam's independence from France and later supported Vietnam during the Cambodian crisis. 'Vietnam acquired importance for India for several reasons. India's foreign policy at its most general was non-alignment [which] involved, inter alia, anti-colonialism, opposition to racialism, and an extension of the area of peace by undercutting and eliminating the bloc system. On all three counts, India would throughout be opposed to the Western cause in Vietnam (Thakur, 1979). Jawaharlal Nehru visited Vietnam in 1954. In 1979, the then Minister of External Affairs, Atal Bihari Vajpayee cut short his China visit in protest when China launched a military offensive against Vietnam. In 1995, India was one of the first countries to welcome the accession of Vietnam to ASEAN. With the renewed engagement with ASEAN, then Indian Prime Minister Vajpayee also visited Vietnam in July 2001.

Similarly, Vietnam supported India during India-Pakistan War of 1971 and the 1999 Kargil conflict. Vietnam also supported India's membership to the East Asia Summit (EAS) despite Chinese opposition. Vietnam also supports India's claim to a permanent seat in United Nations Security Council.

Significant developments have happened in the economic, energy security and defence spheres. Other chapters in this book have gone into the details. Suffice to say that what has been achieved is still modest while the potential is immense. However, the relationship is poised to attain new heights.

Inter-regional Cooperation through Mekong-Ganga Initiative

One of the reasons behind India's Look East Policy was to manage China's interests in ASEAN's riparian states along the Mekong River including Cambodia, Laos, Myanmar, Thailand, and Vietnam. In this background geographical proximity influenced India's Look East Policy because the Southeast Asian states, especially those along the Mekong River, are also strategically important to China.

India played a crucial role in setting up of the Mekong-Ganga Cooperation Project in 2000 which includes India and the five ASEAN countries including the four newer ASEAN members – Vietnam, Lao, Cambodia, Myanmar and Thailand. India's cultural and civilisational links with the Southeast Asian states provide it with immense opportunity to make sub-regional initiatives a huge success. As Zhao argued, MGC 'underline cooperation in tourism, culture, education, and language training, emphasising the 'natural connectivity' between India and mainland Southeast Asia based on cultural and historical similarities. The MGC has not only boosted regional trade, especially between Vietnam and India... In September 2004, Vajpayee declared in New Delhi that India would cooperate with ASEAN to build a railway from New Delhi to Hanoi, cutting through Myanmar, Thailand, Laos, and Cambodia. Some Chinese analysts considered this as India's response to China's proposal to build a 'Pan-Asian Railway'. Obviously, India's intention is to open up a new trade corridor in the Mekong sub-region, thereby enhancing its clout in the Mekong sub-regional economic cooperation and competition' (Zhao, 2008)

In the field of tourism, MGC idea was to go in for joint marketing, launch the Mekong-Ganga Tourism Investment Guide, develop people to people contact, expand multi-modal communication and transportation links to enhance travel and tourism and promote cultural-religious package tours. The MGC agreed to encourage networking among universities in the region, and translate classics of MGC countries into other MGC languages.

The 2nd MGC Ministerial Meeting in 2001 adopted the Hanoi Programme of Action (HPA), a detailed Work Programme for six years – July 2001 to July 2007. The 3rd MGC Ministerial Meeting in 2003 reviewed the progress of HPA. Cambodia noted that 'the progress was slow and much remains to be done to translate the idea to be reality'. It adopted the Phnom Penh Roadmap and gave a political push to the initiative. In 2006, India had also set up Entrepreneurship Development Centres in Cambodia and Vietnam. India and Vietnam are two strong pillars of this initiative. India is engaging with Vietnam both bilaterally and multilaterally. There are bilateral cooperation agreements in science and technology with Laos and Vietnam.

The 6th MGC Ministerial Meeting in 2012 was held in India. Apart from four existing areas of cooperation i.e. tourism, culture, education, and transport & communications, it was decided to collaborate in fields like SME cooperation, conservation of Rice Germplasm, setting up a Working Group on Health, establishment of a Common Archival Resource Centre (CARC) at the Nalanda University, and India–Cambodia Laos Myanmar Vietnam Quick Impact Projects. India has been cooperating with Mekong countries in health and pharmaceutics.

In the 7th MGC Ministerial Meeting held in Vientiane in 2016, India announced 50 new ITEC scholarships for MGC countries in areas of culture, tourism, engineering, management, teachers training, film directing, sound, lighting and stage management in addition to 900 scholarships already given every year. Prime Minister Modi, at the 14th ASEAN-India Summit held in September 2016 in Vientiane, proposed a Joint Task Force on Connectivity to carry forward the exploratory work on the extension of India-Myanmar-Thailand Trilateral Highway to Cambodia, Laos and Vietnam. He said that 'Seamless digital connectivity between India and Southeast Asia is our shared objective...For this, we have already shared several proposals, involving setting up of a regional high-capacity fibre-optic network, supplemented by a national rural broadband network and digital villages in remote areas' (MEA, GOI. 2016). He further proposed a project for mapping of Indian inscriptions along the Mekong River, as well as a project to capture the cultural symbols of our diversity. India has already set up Centres of Excellence in Software Development, English Language and IT Training in Cambodia, Laos, Myanmar and Vietnam. India is also working with Vietnam to establish the India-ASEAN ground station to provide Indian remote-sensing satellite data for the entire ASEAN region.

Through inter-regional collaboration, member states can move ahead on a common path of economic growth, infrastructure development, better means of transportation among states and enhanced people to people contact. This will further have a positive impact on politico-strategic relations among the partner states. However, there are certain critical issues affecting India-Vietnam relations in MGC which need to be addressed like facilitation of trade, expansion of trilateral highway which at present only include India, Myanmar and Thailand, reduction of transaction costs and interconnectivity of goods and labour market. 'India should focus on renovating and reinvigorating existing sub-regional initiatives that have not lived up to their promise. Despite some early successes, the Mekong-Ganga Cooperation Initiative (MGCI)... has been bogged down by multi-year meeting delays, petty arguments over acronyms and ad hoc projects that lack any sort of vision' (Singh, 2007).

At the 7th Mekong Ganga Cooperation Finance Ministers Meeting, held in late July 2016 in Lao PDR, India's representative, Minister for State for External Affairs, General V K Singh mentioned that India has a plan to extend the India-Myanmar-Thailand Trilateral Highway to Lao PDR, Vietnam and Cambodia.

Way Ahead

India should further facilitate economic engagement with ASEAN to develop its north-eastern states. India and ASEAN agreed in November 2012 at Phnom Penh to develop a new India-Myanmar-Laos-Vietnam-Cambodia Highway, and extend the much-delayed India-Myanmar-Thailand Trilateral Highway to Laos and Cambodia. The present low status of people to people contact need to change. Historical and cultural linkages can only be truly accessed by wider human movement across the borders between the north-eastern region of India and Southeast states of Asia.

'ASEAN may view India as a potential counterweight to China's influence in the region, or simply widening its options, but this allows India a role in the region. For India, this is real progress from being 'bottled up' with purely strategic preoccupations in South Asia. India's economic engagement in Southeast Asia has both geostrategic and trade implications. For example, the bilateral cooperation between India's infrastructure sector in the road, bridge and railway development among the CMLV states has strategic significance but also earns India kudos from fellow Asian developing countries' (Yahya, 2003).

India and ASEAN signed the FTA in services and investments on September 8, 2014. The final agreement was signed two years after the conclusion of detailed negotiations on the pact. The FTA in services is expected to boost India's trade and investment relations with ASEAN. The ASEAN-India Agreements on Trade in Service and Investments came into force on 1 July 2015. ASEAN and India should also cooperate in the sharing of intelligence and technologies as enshrined in the 2003 ASEAN-India Joint Declaration on Cooperation to Combat International Terrorism. India announced a Line of Credit of US$ 1 billion to promote projects that support physical and digital connectivity between India and ASEAN and a Project Development Fund with a corpus of INR 500 crores to develop manufacturing hubs in CLMV countries at the 13th ASEAN India Summit held in Malaysia in November 2015 (MEA, GOI, 2017).

As Swaran Singh has argued, 'The MGCI intends building bridges with least developed countries where India's presence had become weak over the years. This also wishes to underline the social responsibility of private sector and to emphasise how this may rebound in the long run. Some of them, like Thailand and Vietnam, have been catching up rapidly in recent years. In that sense, MGC presents an opportunity for Indian companies, which can provide world standard products at competitive prices to GMS countries. This will also assist Indian companies in enhancing their competitiveness on global basis' (Singh, 2007).

Further, it is also the time that instead of ad hoc measures, India should not only recognise but be willing to take charge as a leader in the region. 'A security provider not necessarily needs stronger security presence all the time but requires to have leadership vision and presence. To attain this status of security provider, India needs to take along all ASEAN members seriously along with the Association itself...As regards the maritime politics in the South China Sea, India must emphasise more on network building and thrust its emphasis on both bilateral and multilateral interactions (Panda, 2015).

Conclusion

Free movement of people and connectivity is the major issue and MGC focuses on strengthening connectivity among member states. MGCI now deals with a vast arena of issues from cultural to economic to geostrategic and military. It aims at building infrastructural connections and enhancing people to people contacts. As both Ganga and Mekong are civilisational rivers, the MGC's objective is to facilitate accessibility and contacts among the member states. Although positive outcomes like the construction of MGC Textiles Museum by India to promote tourism and funding of projects in Vietnam under India-CLMV Quick Impacts Projects Fund need to be appreciated, there are some challenges to cooperation within MGC which require attention. It is imperative to further strengthen ties within MGC in areas of food security, agriculture, health and education to take the partnership between India and Vietnam forward for it to be called truly comprehensive in nature. India is not only a security partner for regional states but is emerging as a security provider. With a common strategic understanding, shared concerns, India-Vietnam interests converge in Asia. To appreciate the dynamics of India-Vietnam relationship, instead of seeing it only through the narrow prism of bilateral relations, one needs to employ the multilateral perspective.

NOTES

1. The ASEAN Defence Ministers' Meeting (ADMM) is the highest defence consultative and cooperative mechanism in ASEAN. The ADMM+ brings together Defence Ministers from the 10 ASEAN nations plus Australia, China, India, Japan, New Zealand, Republic of Korea, Russia, and the United States on a biannual basis.
2. Earlier in 2012, India and ASEAN celebrated the 20th anniversary of dialogue-level partnership and the 10th anniversary of Summit-level partnership with a Commemorative Summit in New Delhi under the theme 'ASEAN-India Partnership for Peace and Shared Prosperity'.
3. During the Cold War, Vietnam looked at ASEAN as an imperialist organisation backed by the US. For details see Chhibber, Bharti (2004). Regional security and regional cooperation: A comparative study of ASEAN and SAARC New Delhi: New Century.

REFERENCES

"Act east: New candour in ties with Vietnam could pave the way for a more forthright engagement with Southeast Asia," *The Indian Express*, Oct. 31, 2014.

Acharya, Amitav, *Constructing a security community in Southeast Asia* (Oxford: Routledge Press, 2001).

ASEAN, *ASEAN Economic Community 2009* (Jakarta: ASEAN Secretariat, 2009).

ASEAN, *Declaration of ASEAN Concord 1976* (Bali, Jakarta: ASEAN Secretariat, 1976).

ASEAN, *Declaration of ASEAN Concord II* (Bali, Jakarta: ASEAN Secretariat, 2003).

ASEAN, *Treaty of Amity and Cooperation in South East Asia* (Bali, Jakarta: ASEAN Secretariat, 1976).

Baruah, Amit, "Consensus in ASEAN for summit with India," *The Hindu,* January 10, 2001.

Chhibber, Bharti, *Regional security and regional cooperation: A comparative study of ASEAN and SAARC* (New Delhi: New Century, 2004).

Cohen, Stephen Philip, *India: emerging power* (Washington, D.C.: Brookings Institution Press, 2001).

Government of India, Ministry of External Affairs, *ASEAN-India relations*," 2017, http://www.mea.gov.in/aseanindia/20-years.htm. (accessed on June 5, 2017).

Government of India, Ministry of External Affairs, *Prime Minister's remarks at the 14th ASEAN Summit*, 2016, https://www.mea.gov.in/aseanindia/SpeechStatement EAS.htm?dtl/22612/Main+Remarks+by+Prime+Minister+ at+ the+14th+ASEANIndia+Summit+held+ on+8+September+2016+in+Vientiane+Lao+PDR (accessed on May 20, 2017).

Jawli, Nandini, "South China sea and India's geopolitical interests," *Indian Journal of Asian Affairs* 29, nos. 1-2 (2016): 85-100.

Mishra, Rahul, "Security engagement in Southeast Asia," In *Asian strategic review 2015: India as a security provider*, edited by S D Muni and Vivek Chadha, 193-212. New Delhi: Pentagon Press, 2015.

Panda, Jagannath, "India in East Asia: reviewing the role of a security provider," in *Asian strategic review 2015: India as a security provider,* edited byS D Muni and Vivek Chadha, 213-230. New Delhi: Pentagon Press, 2015.

Raja Mohan, C., "India's geopolitics and Southeast Asian security," *Southeast Asian Affairs,* (2008): 43-60.

Rajendram, Danielle, "India's new Asia-Pacific strategy: Modi acts East," *The Lowy Institute for International Policy*, 2014, http://www.lowyinstitute.org/files/indias-new-asia-pacific-strategy-modi-acts-east.pdf.

Sahasrabuddhe, Uttarra and Chaitanya Mallapur, "Modi's Strategic Foreign Policy Vision: A Glass Half Full," *The Diplomat*, May 17, 2017, http://thediplomat.com/2017/05/modis-strategic-foreign-policy-vision-a-glass-half-full/ (accessed on May 28, 2017).

Singh, Swaran, "Mekong-Ganga Cooperation Initiative: Analysis and Assessment of India's Engagement with Greater Mekong Sub-region," *IRASEC*, 2007.

Thakur, Ramesh, "India's Vietnam Policy 1946-79," *Asian Survey* 19, no. 10 (1979): 957-976.

Yahya, Faizal, "India and Southeast Asia revisited," *Contemporary Southeast Asia*, 25, no. 1 (2003): 79-103.

Zhao, Hong, "China and India: Competing for good relations with Myanmar," *Journal of East Asian Affairs*, 22, no. 1 (2008): 175-194.

Zhao, Hong, "India's changing relations with ASEAN: From China's perspective," *East Asian Institute Working Paper No. 133*, (2006).

13

India–Vietnam Cooperation on Non-Traditional Security Issues

Do Thu Ha

Joining ASEAN had crucial social, political, economic and security implications for Vietnam. Vietnam's membership of the grouping integrated its security with the whole of South-East Asia and created a favourable environment for economic development. This, in turn, raised Vietnam's global image, leading to increased cooperation with multiple players in the region and greater bargaining clout with superpowers like the United States, India and China. The co-operative relation between Vietnam and India is challenged by a number of non-traditional security issues including the energy nexus, terrorism, environment, health, trans-national organised crimes and economic performance. This paper categorises and clarifies some key emerging issues between the two countries and looks at their interconnectedness and implications but focuses more on Vietnam's side.

Non-traditional Security – A Global Issue to both Indian and Vietnam

The historic end of the Cold War and the rising tide of globalisation have significantly changed the nature of threats and security discourses in Asia. There is a notable shift of attention from military power as the core determinant of national security to several non-traditional sectors with a much-enhanced role of economic, political, and societal forces. Non-traditional security issues – such as climate change, natural disasters, trans-national crimes, and terrorism – require both policymakers and military strategists to deal with security threats in a more comprehensive manner. Increasing interdependence among states also magnifies the impacts of these threats, urging Asian countries to forge regional cooperation in multilateral forums such as ASEAN, EAS, APEC, and ARF. Though these efforts are commendable, their effectiveness in tackling such a wide canvass of threats is still open to question.[1]

What is more worrying about Asia is the resurgence of border disputes and nationalism. Territorial and maritime disputes in the South China Sea have "doubled" the risks for several Asian countries, including Vietnam and India. Having been troubled by the global economic meltdown and the creeping effects of climate change, Vietnam must confront the rising challenges of conflicting claims in the South China Sea and water security in the Mekong region.[2] This paper aims to analyse how Vietnamese official perceptions of national security challenges have changed over the last few years, identify the three most daunting security challenges to Vietnam in the year 2017, and study its implications for the defence sector and for the future of regional cooperation.

Official Perceptions of Vietnam's National Security Challenges

1. Although official perceptions of the most challenging security threats and the priorities attached to them were largely shaped by the external environment and internal situation, there are four major security challenges that Vietnam has confronted since the end of Cold War. They are the economic weakness, regime security, territorial sovereignty, and non-traditional security issues.
2. The Defence White Paper in 2004 and especially the Defence White Paper, 2009 highlighted "diversified and complicated security challenges" Vietnam is facing, as follows: (i) Economy has been in danger of further lagging behind due to insufficient resilience while coping with the serious impact of the global financial crisis and economic recession, (ii) Democratic freedom, religious freedom, and human rights have been abused by hostile forces in order to undermine the great national solidarity, and to incite violence and separatism in some areas of the country, (iii) Disputes over sovereignty, sovereign rights, and jurisdiction in the East Sea[3] has "seriously affected many activities and the maritime economic

development of Vietnam," (iv) Non-traditional security issues such as illegal trafficking of weapons and drugs, piracy, organised transnational crimes, terrorism, illegal migration and immigration, environmental degradation, climate change, and epidemics continue to concern Vietnam.[4]

The 11th National Party Congress adopted a resolution in January 2011 that "The Asia-Pacific, including Southeast Asia, will contain many factors possibly leading to instabilities. More territorial, sea and island disputes will occur." For Vietnam, the Resolution identified "major and inter-twined challenges" that Vietnam will face in the next five years, namely economic weakness and regime security. Regarding economic weakness, the Resolution stated that Vietnam is at "risk of lagging behind in economic development with other countries." For regime security, there are both internal and external challenges. Internally, "the degradation in political ideology, thought, morality and lifestyle of a number of cadres and Party members who are involved in bureaucracy, corruption and waste will still be serious, lowering the people's confidence in the Party and State." Externally, "hostile forces will continue implementing the 'peaceful evolution' scheme, causing disturbances and using the so-called 'democracy' and 'human rights' in order to change the political system in Vietnam".[5]

The Political Report adopted at the 11th Party Congress in 2011 defined major defence and security objectives, and tasks relating to three of the four aforementioned challenges. They are: (i) protecting national independence, sovereignty, territorial integrity, (ii) protecting the Party, State, people, and the regime, ensuring political stability, social order and security, as well as actively preventing and defeating any hostile attempts and activities to damage the state, and (iii) readily responding to global non-traditional security challenges.[6]

Among non-traditional security threats, the issue of water resources has become increasingly important for Vietnam in recent years. Construction of dams by China and Laos on the mainstream of the Mekong River will have a major impact on the Mekong Delta of Vietnam. On September 29, 2012, Vietnam's President Truong Tan Sang delivered a speech at the meeting with business leaders on the sidelines of the Asia-Pacific Economic Cooperation (APEC) summit in Russia, warning that tensions over water resources were not only threatening economic growth, but also presenting a new source of conflict. He believed that the management and utilisation of water resources in the Mekong River are developing into a "pressing issue with direct and unfavourable bearing" on Vietnam, especially on rice production.[7] Water resources in the Mekong River are transnational in nature – therefore Vietnam needs to engage in international cooperation to ensure water security.

Official Perceptions of Vietnam's Non-traditional Threats

Documents of Vietnam's Communist Party mention recent non-traditional security threats with some special characteristics as follows:

1. Vietnam's Communist Party has always put non-traditional security threats alongside traditional ones, with the former though having potential and manifest in different forms and levels, mainly follow peaceful trend while non-traditional security threats have fiercely emerged;
2. Complicated non-traditional security challenges are developing due to the negative side of globalisation, market economy, the use of science-technology;
3. Forms of non-traditional security threats are human security, financial security, energy security, food security, climate change, natural disasters, and epidemics. The scale of non-traditional security threats would expand in a complex manner requiring continued monitoring, research and timely supplement;
4. Non-traditional security threats are not specific to Vietnam but are global in nature;
5. A number of non-traditional security threats can transform into traditional ones, such as ethnic conflict, religious conflict, terrorism, and political unrest.

On the basis of the Party's viewpoints, it is necessary to make the political system, and stakeholders responsible for the administration of non-traditional security threats, business community and the entire people to be fully aware of the challenges, impacts and effects of these to human life, community and national security.

In the domain of human security, non-traditional security threats have impacts on the physical and mental health of human beings, such as spreading of an epidemic, trafficking and use of drugs, trafficking in people (children, women, illegal immigrants). In the domain of community security and national security, non-traditional security emerges due to threats of food shortages, water resources and energy shortages and disputes, high-tech and cyber security crimes, financial speculation and security. In the domain of national sovereignty, non-tradition security issues create a direct threat, capable of transforming into the traditional security threats. In the domain of global security, the issues of maritime and aviation security, energy security, financial security, cross-border migration, dangerous diseases transmitted in human and plants are transnational and no single country can solve on their own.

Prompted by that understanding, each stakeholder with their responsibility must be prepared to proactively prevent and respond to non-tradition security challenges. Many non-traditional security problems arise from artificial factors, i.e. accidentally or intentionally caused by people, and in its turn pose threats to human security, community security, national security and the broader human security. Therefore, prevention of non-tradition security threats is a very basic task, which is done by raising awareness and responsibility of each individual and society, through specific actions in everyday life, such as heightening sense of responsibility to protect the ecological environment, adopting sober attitude before negative impacts of the market economy and globalisation, making wise choice of scientific and technological advances, respecting different values and shared interests between community groups with different levels of living standards. On the basis of enhanced awareness, effective response to non-traditional security threats can be made by building synchronous institutions, mechanisms, policies, apparatus in Vietnam.

Another issue of importance in raising awareness about non-traditional security challenges in Vietnam is to make people reflect on threats to human security, public security, national security and human security. For human security, the non-traditional security threats affect adult healthy maturity guaranteed by security and welfare, meaning they threaten the right to development of human beings in the modern world. For public security, the non-traditional security threats endanger stability and development of the community, even degrade or disintegrate the whole community due to separation, conflict, epidemic, injury, death, lack of minimum security conditions for development, the impact of environmental hazards, terrorism, ethnic and religious conflicts. For national security, non-traditional security issues either at a low or high level, directly or indirectly threaten the national security, from environment security, energy security, cyber security, food security, maritime security, cultural security to ethnic issue, a religious issue, terrorism, financial security, and cross-border migration.

That is why Vietnam's Communist Party believes that raising awareness among different components of society on non-tradition security threats can be made in many different ways. First is through *the media* including radio and television, print and the internet to raise public awareness. *The second form* is to integrate education and raising awareness of people and businesses on non-traditional security issues into programmes, and projects on economic, cultural, social development and protection of the environment.

Dynamic Elements of India-Vietnam Relations in Current Context of Non-traditional Security

"Non-traditional security threats are very diverse and found in many areas of socio-economic life; causes to these threats are complex, including natural and artificial threats; have the ability to spread quickly in a large scale and transnational impacts. Some non-traditional security threats can transform into traditional ones if there is lack of security threat control, administration and coordination mechanism for action among nations."[8]

It is from the above characteristics, for each non-traditional security threat there must be corresponding solutions to organise force, resources, working methods and implementation. It is difficult to apply specific measures of prevention, response and control of one non-traditional security threat to other. This part of the paper would only mention common solutions to prevent, control and respond to non-traditional security threats in the specific conditions of Vietnam and in the context of cooperation with India.

At different periods of history, the relations between India and Vietnam have had different characteristics and levels. However, in the last 10 years, efforts have been made to strengthen and widen the multi-faceted relations. The turning point came in 2007 when during the state visit of Vietnam's Prime Minister Nguyen Tan Dung to India, Vietnam and India agreed to upgrade the comprehensive cooperation established in 2003 between the two countries to a strategic partnership. The strategic partnership encompasses bilateral relations in the political, economic, security, defence, cultural, scientific and technological dimensions and steers their cooperation in regional and multilateral fora.

From the context of the relationship between India and Vietnam as well as the viewpoints of Vietnam's Communist Party, the author believes that the two countries need to expand and strengthen their international cooperation in preventing, controlling and responding to non-tradition security threats.

Some Common Aims in the same Directions

First of all, fully grasp the viewpoints of Vietnam: proactively and actively cooperate with other countries and regional and international organisations in coping with challenges to non-traditional security, especially in climate change; improve the effectiveness of external activities, continue to deepen international relations on the basis of maintaining independence, autonomy and maximize internal resources, preservation and promotion of national identity; actively prevent and mitigate negative effects of international integration. Join bilateral and multilateral security cooperation mechanisms on the basis of maximizing the protection of national interests, while respecting fundamental principles of international law.

Second, unifying awareness, build trust and complete institutional framework between the two countries on non-traditional security – the basis for effective international cooperation. Despite debates among scholars and political circles, until now understanding viewpoints of non-traditional security are widely different, some countries include it in the list of non-traditional security but other countries do not agree. Therefore, regional organisations and international organisations of the two countries should soon agree on a definition and propose a list of priorities for multilateral cooperation to prevent and respond to non-traditional security challenges. After reaching a common understanding, our countries and international organisations should collaborate to shape regulatory institutional framework and legislation in order to bind the countries in preventing and responding to non-traditional to overcoming the practice of issuing statements and less effectiveness in real life.

Third, being the proactive and active member in international integration, including cooperation on preventing and responding to non-tradition security threats through mechanisms and multilayer, diverse, flexible methods. That is, a mechanism for cooperation in the framework of the United Nations of which Vietnam is an active and responsible member, and has signed many international treaties on different fields, especially the commitments to implement the Millennium Development Goals (MDGs); mechanism for regional cooperation in the framework of ASEAN or ASEAN and its partners (called ASEAN+) on non-tradition security issues arise in areas which Vietnam has signed or agreed in joint statements of the organisation; bilateral cooperation between Vietnam and other developed countries to take advantage of financial resources, science-technology, human resource training, experience sharing in institutional building policies to prevent and respond to non-traditional security threats; *cooperate with neighbouring countries* to tackle drug trafficking, illegal migration, maritime and aviation security, water security, quarantine of animal and plants, anti-money laundering and transnational crime trafficking in women and children.

Fourth, strengthening information sharing between Vietnam and India on each of the non-tradition security threats through specific and effective cooperation mechanisms. Non-traditional security is transnational, so there is a need to set up mechanism to share information at national level, between the specialised agencies of countries in various fields, such as information, data on global climate change; forecast and warnings on potential environmental disasters in different areas; data of water resources, and energy in the world; information about transnational crimes which can potentially penetrate any other country from money laundering, drug production and trafficking, trafficking in women and children, high-tech crime, and terrorism. If there are good coordination mechanisms in bilateral relations or international organisations (such as Interpol, ASEANPOL), the information would help detect threats early and thereby prevention and response will be more effective. Reality shows that it is not easy for one country to share information with other countries if it does not have any benefit from it. Thus, the establishment of the information-sharing mechanism must be based on full awareness of their own and common interests when responding to each concrete non-traditional security threat.

Fifth, expanding international cooperation on sharing scientific-technological achievements, training of human resources and mobilising financial resources for prevention and response to non-traditional security threats. One of the extremely important areas in international cooperation is the prevention, control and response to non-traditional security challenges. First and foremost is cooperation and exchange of scientific-technology achievements and modern means capable of coping effectively with the non-traditional security challenges that any sector needs, such as assessment, forecast and warning and response to environmental change; prevention and control of high-tech crimes, financial crimes, drug trafficking; prevention and control of infectious diseases in humans and animals; and prevention of terrorism. To make use of scientific and technological resources from developed countries to constantly strengthen national scientific-technological capacity for non-traditional security management. Forms of cooperation can be a transfer of technology through training or through direct purchase.

The Dangerous Nexus of Non-traditional Security Threats: The Mekong Case and the role of India in the Mekong-Ganga Cooperation (MGC)

Vietnam is one of the several countries most adversely affected by climate change, and this has been confirmed in many studies by the World Bank, UNDP, and the UN Intergovernmental Panel on Climate Change (IPCC). In 2009, an assessment report by the Institute of Strategy and Policy on Natural Resources and Environment (within Vietnam's Ministry of Natural Resources and Environment) revealed that during the 1958-2007 period, Vietnam's annual average surface temperature has increased by approximately 0.5–0.7°C, while the sea level along its coastline has risen by approximately 20 cm.[9] It is estimated that if the sea level rises by 1 meter, 22 million Vietnamese people will be homeless. Climate change has resulted in more severe and/or frequent occurrences of natural disasters, such as cyclonic storms, floods, and droughts. From 2001 to 2010, extreme patterns of weather in Vietnam killed 9,500 people with a total property loss equivalent to 1.5 percent GDP per year.[10]

What seems more alarming is that the catastrophic impact of climate change can "spill over" to other sectors such as agricultural production and water resources. It is estimated that if the temperature increases by 1°C, the rice yield will decrease by 10 percent.[11] Large cultivation areas in the Mekong and Red River Deltas are likely to be affected by saltwater intrusion due to sea level rise. Climate change is also likely to result in increasing extinction of biodiversity and affect people's health, as increasing temperatures facilitate the growth of various viruses and disease carriers. Here, the "evil" nexus between climate change, food/water security, and other aspects of human security unfolds and the region most vulnerable to these complex threats is the Mekong River Delta.

According to the IPCC, 1 meter of sea level rise in Vietnam would lead to the flooding of up to 20,000 km^2 of the Mekong River Delta, and more than 1 million people in this region would be directly affected. 1.77 million ha of land will be salinized, accounting for 45 percent of the total land. A sea level rise of 30 centimetres (a scenario for 2050) would increase the salinity of the main tributaries of the Mekong River as far as 10 kilometres inland. Inundation and the resulting loss of land and saline water intrusion in the Mekong Delta and parts of the Red River Delta, the country's most important agricultural areas, will pose serious threats to farmers as well as to agricultural exports such as rice (of which Vietnam is the second largest exporter in the world), and possibly to national food security.

Added to the existing problems is China's massive cascade of dams on the Upper Mekong in Yunnan province and the dams proposed on the Lower Mekong Basin's mainstream in Laos, Cambodia, and on the Thai-Lao border. Vietnam is greatly concerned about these projects, at least for following reasons. *First,* dams in China and in the lower mainstream (with total reservoir storage capacity of about 40 billion m^3) will trap a big portion of the Mekong's sediment that the river should naturally transport to the Delta. The fertility of the Delta, vital for rice cultivation, will suffer and productivity will decline.[12] *Second,* most of the dams in China and all of 12 dams in the mainstream of Lower Mekong basin are "run-of-river dams," but they are designed for daily regulation to meet changing power demand, mainly during the dry season. This poses a risk to downstream water levels, especially during the dry season and gives way to salinity intrusion in the Mekong Delta. *Third,* Laos' recent decision to move ahead with the construction of Xayaburi can be followed by the development of another 11 dams on the Mekong mainstream. However, the cumulative downstream impacts of Xayaburi and the 11 other dams have not yet been adequately studied. The real possibility might be distant, but should there be a dam failure, whether due to human error or natural factors (disasters) like earthquakes, it will leave huge negative impacts on Vietnam, as well as other countries affected by dams on the Mekong River. While the complex vested interests of states in this region make it harder to coordinate actions, the Mekong River Commission is only an advisory body that cannot alone impose or enforce any binding agreements on plans to develop the water resources of the Mekong basin.

It can be seen that the Mekong Delta of Vietnam is expected to suffer greatly under the "double impacts" of both upstream dam development and global climate change. The interfaces of between environment, development, and security in the Mekong Delta will pose a direct threat to the country as the region is now home to nearly 18 million people, and the source of half of Vietnam's national rice production.

The Mekong-Ganga Cooperation (MGC) is an initiative by six countries – India and five ASEAN countries, namely, Cambodia, Lao PDR, Myanmar, Thailand and Vietnam for cooperation in tourism, culture, education, as well as transport and communications. It was launched in 2000 at Vientiane, Lao PDR. Both the Ganga and the Mekong are civilisational rivers, and the MGC initiative aims to facilitate closer contacts among the people inhabiting these two major river basins.

Map 1: Mekong Mainstream Dams

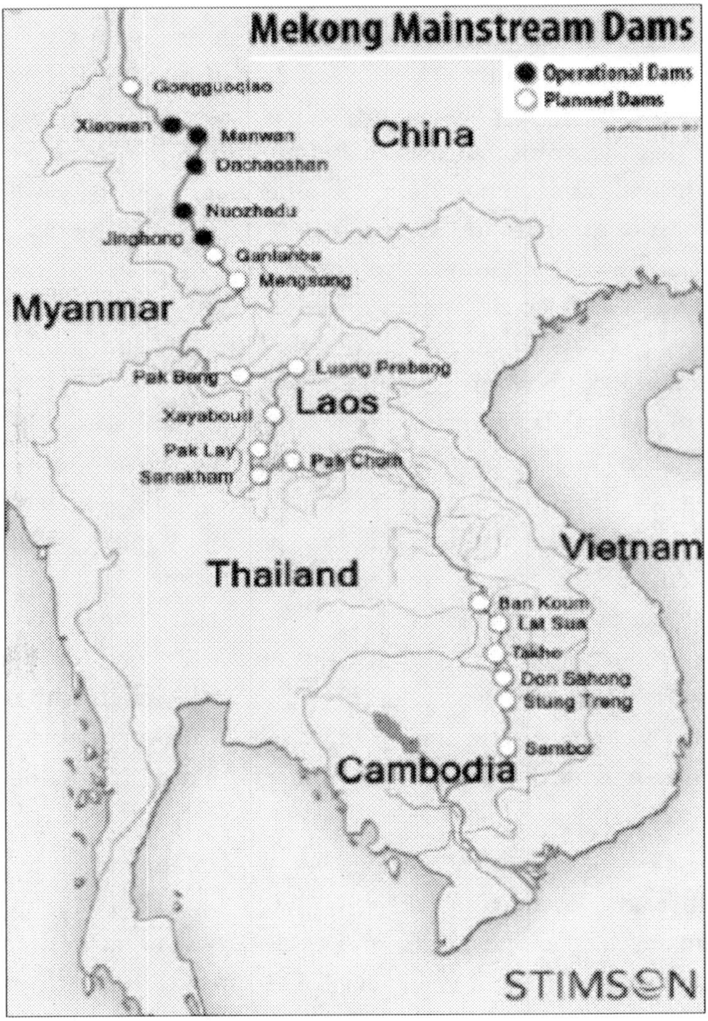

Source: Richard Cronin and Timothy Hamlin, "Mekong Turning Point: Shared River for a Shared Future", Stimson Center, January 2012.[13]

Acknowledging that the importance of Mekong to the survival of all the countries in MGC, that rice is the most important crop in MGC countries and rice production continues to face many challenges despite significant progress, the Mekong-Ganga Cooperation in general and India, in particular, should have got a more important role in:

- Exploring mutually beneficial cooperation in rice production techniques and downstream processing projects and conserving of Rice Germ Plasm project.
- Supporting connectivity corridors especially the concept of the East-West corridors connecting India to the Mekong region by taking substantial commitment in the development of the India-Myanmar-Thailand Trilateral Highway, which connects Moreh in India to Mae Sot in Thailand. CLMV countries would like India to commit to the extension of the Trilateral Highway to Cambodia and Lao PDR and also a new highway linking Viet Nam.
- Realising a Joint Working Group on Maritime Connectivity between India, Thailand, Cambodia, Myanmar and Viet Nam to explore Maritime Cargo route/ Coastal Shipping services between these countries.
- During the 6th MGC Meeting, in order to strengthen the region's capacity to respond to the menace of drug-resistant malaria and other such emerging public health threats, India had suggested that Health Ministries in MGC countries consider setting up a Working Group for undertaking health research relevant to the MGC region and share information and expertise on pandemics management. The Ministers of MGC agreed to recommend that MGC Health authorities consider the formation of a Working Group on the threat of drug-resistant malaria, which is emerging as a major public health issue in MGC Countries.
- Last but not least, the drug smuggling from Africa to Vietnam via India (Bangalore especially) is now a real threat, regardless of the terrorists' fleeing back from IS groups recently. Vietnam and India should develop close cooperation to solve those hot issues.

Modi's Act East Policy as New Setting for India-Vietnam Relations in Non-traditional Security

It is undeniable that Modi's Vietnam visit was timely and crucial for several reasons. *First*, Vietnam lies at the heart of India's vision for South-East Asia as also its 'Act East' policy. India also wants to boost its defence exports to friendly countries. And it is looking to increase trade between the two countries. *Second*, Vietnam is India's country coordinator for the Association of South East Asian Nations (ASEAN) till 2018. Therefore, for further strengthening relations with ASEAN, it is vital for India to focus on bilateral relations with Vietnam too. *Third*, India is in the process of boosting its defence exports to friendly countries. As stated by Secretary (East) Preeti Saran on 1st September in a press briefing, "Vietnam is an important strategic partner to India and a central pillar of the Act East Policy."[14]

India and Vietnam on 03/09/2016 signed 12 agreements in a wide range of areas covering defence, IT, space, double taxation and sharing white shipping information, signalling a strong upward push in their strategic ties.

MoU between Vietnamese Academy of Social Science and Indian Council of World Affairs, and MoU between BIS and STAMEQ for mutual recognition took place in the aftermath of the much-debated ruling on the South China Sea dispute by the Permanent Court of Arbitration at The Hague. The ruling turned out to be in the favour of the Philippines discarding China's so-called 'historic rights' on the sea. Though India's stand on the issue of the South China Sea has been consistent, Vietnam along with the Philippines desire India to play a bigger role.

Conclusion

Globalisation has essentially made collective security an essential element of national security and vice-versa. Relevant stakeholders, both in and out of this region, should be able to realise this truth and collaborate to build a more predictable future of their own. The value of such a shared commitment toward peace and stability lies in what UN Secretary General Ban Ki Moon once said: "We should not let our future generations suffer because of our failure to do the right thing".[15]

NOTES

1. Eddie Walsh, "Non-traditional security threats in Asia: Finding a regional way forward," *East Asia Forum*, June 4, 2011, http://www.eastasiaforum.org/2011/06/04/non-traditional-security-threats-in-asia-finding-a-regionalway-forward/ (accessed on January 10, 2013).
2. Tran Truong Thuy & Nguyen Minh Ngoc, Research Fellows at the Institute for East Sea Studies, Diplomatic Academy of Vietnam *about Vietnam's Security Challenges: Priorities, Policy Implications and Prospects for Regional Cooperation.*

3. The South China Sea is translated in Vietnamese as East Sea (or Biển Đông). For the purpose of academic discussion, the author will use "the South China Sea" in this article.
4. *Defence White Paper 2004* http://admm.org.vn/sites/eng/Pages/vietnam-snationaldefenseintheearly-nd-14441.html?cid=236. *Defence White Paper 2009*, pp 17-18. http://admm.org.vn/sites/eng/Pages/vietnamnationaldefence%28vietnam whitepapers-nd-14440.html?cid=236.
5. "Resolution of the 11th National Party Congress," http://www.nhandan.com.vn/cmlink/nhandan-online/ homepage/politics/11th-party-congress/coverage-on-the-party-congress/resolution-of-the-11th-party-nationalcongress-1.282810.
6. "Political Report of the 11th National Party Congress."
7. Address by President of Viet Nam Truong Tan Sang at the plenary session on "Water: A New Global Strategic Resource" at APEC 20, 2012, http://www.mofa.gov.vn/en/nr040807104143/nr040807105001/ns120908003447.
8. Doan Minh Huan, *Alternate member of the Party Central Committee, Deputy Editor in chief (in charge) of the Communist Review in his speech of 26/1/2017.*
9. "Vietnam Assessment Report on Climate Change," *Institute of Strategy and Policy on Natural Resources and Environment*, Hanoi, 2009. www.unep.org/pdf/dtie/VTN_ASS_REP_CC.pdf (accessed January 11, 2013). "Fighting climate change: Human solidarity in a divided world," *Human Development Report 2007/8 UNDP*, 105, http://hdr.undp.org/en/reports/global/hdr2007-8/ (accessed January 11, 2013). "Economics of Adaptation to Climate Change," *World Bank*, 2010. http://climatechange.worldbank.org/sites/ default/files/documents/EACC_Vietnam.pdf (accessed January 11, 2013).
10. Vietnam's National Strategy on Climate Change, issued by Prime Minister Nguyen Tan Dung in Decision 2139 /QĐ-TTg on December 05, 2011, p.6, http://www.chinhphu.vn/portal/page/portal/English/strategies/strat egies details? categoryId=30&articleId=10051283 (accessed January 11, 2013).
11. "The Economics of Climate Change in Southeast Asia: A Regional Review," *ADB*, 2009, pp.4-6. http://www. adb.org/publications/economics-climate-change-southeast-asia-regional-review (accessed January 11, 2013). "Climate Change 2007: Impacts, Adaptation, and Vulnerability," *Contribution of Working Group II to the Fourth Assessment Report of the Intergovernmental Panel of Climate Change,* Cambridge University Press.
12. Dao Trong Tu, "A Vietnamese Perspective on Proposed Mainstream Mekong Dams, *"Stimson*, December 8, 2011, http://www.stimson.org/summaries/a-vietnamese-perspective-on-proposed-mainstream-mekong-dams/ (accessed January 11, 2013).
13. See more at http://www.stimson.org/spotlight/new-publication-mekong-turning-point/.
14. *Press Briefing*, www.Rediff.com. 2nd September 2016.
15. United Nations Secretary-General on Climate Action [as delivered on 30 May 2017].

REFERENCES

Address by President of Viet Nam Truong Tan Sang at the plenary session on "Water: A New Global Strategic Resource" at *APEC* 20, 2012, http://www.mofa.gov.vn/en/nr040807104143/nr040807105001/ns120908003447.

"Climate Change 2007: Impacts, Adaptation, and Vulnerability," *Contribution of Working Group II to the Fourth Assessment Report of the Intergovernmental Panel of Climate Change*, Cambridge University Press.

Defence White Paper 2004. http://admm.org.vn/sites/eng/Pages/vietnam-snationaldefenseintheearly-nd-14441.html?cid=236.

Defence White Paper 2009, pp 17-18. http://admm.org.vn/sites/eng/Pages/vietnamnational defence%28vietnamwhitepapers-nd-14440.html?cid=236.

Doan Minh Huan, *Alternate member of the Party Central Committee, Deputy Editor in chief (in charge) of the Communist Review in his speech of 26/1/2017.*

Eddie Walsh, "Non-traditional security threats in Asia: Finding a regional way forward," *East Asia Forum*, June 4, 2011. http://www.eastasiaforum.org/2011/06/04/non-traditional-security-threats-in-asia-finding-a-regionalway-forward/ (accessed January 10, 2013).

"Economics of Adaptation to Climate Change," *World Bank*, 2010, http://climatechange.worldbank.org/sites/default/files/documents/EACC_Vietnam.pdf (accessed on January 11, 2013).

"Fighting climate change: Human solidarity in a divided world," *Human Development Report 2007/8 UNDP,* p. 105. http://hdr.undp.org/en/reports/global/hdr2007-8/. (accessed on January 11, 2013).

"*Political Report of the 11th National Party Congress.*"

Press Briefing, www.Rediff.com, 2nd September 2016.

"Resolution of the 11th National Party Congress." http://www.nhandan.com.vn/cmlink/nhandan-online/homepage/politics/11th-party-congress/coverage-on-the-party-congress/resolution-of-the-11th-party-nationalcongress-1.282810.

"The Economics of Climate Change in Southeast Asia: A Regional Review," *ADB*, 2009, pp. 4-6. http://www.adb.org/publications/economics-climate-change-southeast-asia-regional-review (accessed January 11, 2013).

Tran Truong Thuy & Nguyen Minh Ngoc, Research Fellows at the Institute for East Sea Studies, Diplomatic Academy of Vietnam, *Vietnam's Security Challenges: Priorities, Policy Implications and Prospects for Regional Cooperation*, in *Security Outlook of the Asia Pacific Countries and Its Implications for the Defense Sector.*

Tu, Dao Trong. "A Vietnamese Perspective on Proposed Mainstream Mekong Dams." *Stimson*, December 8, 2011. http://www.stimson.org/summaries/a-vietnamese-perspective-on-proposed-mainstream-mekong-dams/ (accessed on January 11, 2013). See more at http://www.stimson.org/spotlight/new-publication-mekong-turning-point/.

United Nations Secretary-General on Climate Action [as delivered on 30 May 2017].

"Vietnam Assessment Report on Climate Change," *Institute of Strategy and Policy on Natural Resources and Environment,* Hanoi, 2009, www.unep.org/pdf/dtie/VTN_ASS_REP_CC.pdf (accessed January 11, 2013).

Vietnam's National Strategy on Climate Change, issued by Prime Minister Nguyen Tan Dung in Decision 2139 /QĐ-TTg on December 05, 2011, p.6, http://www.chinhphu.vn/portal/page/portal/English/strategies/strategiesdetails?CategoryId=30&articleId=10051283 (accessed January 11, 2013).

14

Disaster Preparedness and Resilience: Providing Scientific and Technical Safety to Vietnam

Athira Anand

Introduction

Linda (1997), Lingling (2001), Damrey (2005), Xangsane (2006), Lekima (2007), Kammuri (2008), Ketsana (2009), Kai-Tak (2012), Haiyan (2013), Hagupit (2014) and Mirinae (2016) – the names of typhoons that brought huge loss to the land of Vietnam. Vietnam is not only vulnerable to typhoons but also to a greater extent to floods, droughts, landslides etc., of which floods and typhoons are the most terrific onslaughts. The topography of Vietnam makes it a mix of all sorts of landscapes – plains, plateau, slopes, mountains and coastal areas. As a stretch of land in South East Asia with the whole of its eastern side bordering the sea it becomes more vulnerable to natural hazards. In the North, Vietnam shares the borders with the People's Republic of China and in the West with the Democratic Republic of Laos and Cambodia. Each year Vietnamese social and economic sphere gets challenged with natural hazards and it is necessary that they should deal better with disaster preparedness and resilience. This paper focuses on scientific and technological safety measures to be initiated for disaster preparedness and resilience in Vietnam with an international outlook when Indo-Vietnam relationship widens to new horizons. When it comes to science and technology (S&T), disaster is not solely related to nature but to a wider scope incorporating the economic, social and managerial defects.

What is Disaster and Resilience?

Disaster is described as a complex mix of natural and human action. 'For many people, a disaster is not a single, discrete event. All over the world, but especially in LDCs (Least Developed Countries), vulnerable people often suffer repeated, multiple, mutually reinforcing, and sometimes simultaneous shocks to their families, their settlements and their livelihoods' (Wisner, Gaillard, & Kelman, 2012). Here in this paper too disaster is treated as an entity which is not solely natural in essence but also socially and economically initiated. The causative agents of disaster in Vietnam are not only the climatic change and topography but also the lack of diligence in governance, in which includes the resilience measures. The United Nations Office for Disaster Risk Reduction, UNISDR (United Nations International Strategy for Disaster Reduction) Terminology and Disaster Risk Reduction defined Resilience as ability of a system, community or society exposed to hazards to resist, absorb, accommodate to and recover from the effects of a hazard in a timely and efficient manner, including through the preservation and restoration of its essential basic structures and functions (Geneva, 2009). As disaster is natural, social and economic in existence the resilience of a particular area thus, depends on the socio-economic and geographical aspects. This paper deals with the disaster preparedness and resilience in Vietnam in which the role of science and technology (S&T) is discussed as it can help to a large extent in managing disaster risks.

Table 1: Vietnam – An Overview

Area (sq. km)	330,957.6
Average Population (Thous. pers)	87840
Population Density (per sq.km)	265
Average Urban population (Thous. pers)	27888.2
GDP growth rate	5.89

Source: *General Statistics Office of Vietnam* (2011 details).

Even though the economy in Vietnam keeps a satisfactory growth rate, science and technology has to keep pace with the growing needs. The rampant occurrence of disaster hampers Vietnamese environmental, economic and social system. 'Vulnerability and exposure to disasters are increasing as more people and assets locate areas of high risk. Since 1970, the world's population has grown by 87 percent. During the same time, the proportion of people living in flood-prone river basins increased by 114 percent and on cyclone-exposed coastlines by 192 percent. More than half of the world's large cities, with populations ranging from 2 to 15 million, are located in areas of high earthquake risk. Rapid urbanisation will increase exposure to natural hazards, especially in coastal zones' (UN Task Team on the Post-2015 UN Development Agenda, 2012). The 2009 Population and Housing Census estimate say that between 1999 and 2009, the average annual growth rate of the urban population in Vietnam was 3.4 percent per year, while that of the rural population was only 0.4 percent per year (The 2009 Population and Housing Census). The rapid growth of the urban population is mainly attributed to migration and urbanisation. The large coastal areas of Vietnam are also densely populated like the urban areas (Map 1). These densely populated area are prone to severe damage to life and property, thus making urban and coastal areas the hotspots of disaster risk. The Red River delta in the north and Mekong delta in the south are also highly vulnerable to disasters (Map 2). Alteration of the natural landscape leads to hazards and even the landscape itself can become the instigator of disaster as in the case of Vietnam. The social and economic inadequacies disrupt the mitigation processes, thereby increases the risk of disaster.

Resilience determines the impact of the disaster in an area, better the resilience less will be the risk involved in a disaster. Disaster preparedness and resilience are now an internationally acclaimed topic of discussion, particularly for the Least Developed Nations (LSDs) where the disaster is caused by natural, economic and social reasons. In Vietnam, the issue becomes more of a matter of scientific and technological innovations and better governance.

Science, Technology and Resilient Governance

The larger part of disasters in Vietnam is initiated through challenges posed by topography and climatic change which can be mitigated through good governance and advanced science and technology, which is at a blooming stage. The role of science and technology (S&T) in the management of structures and processes like settlement and housing can lessen the impact of disasters. S&T advancement has to be such that it is capable of reducing

Map 1: Population Distribution

www.middlebury.edu/~scs Source: Agroviet.gov.vn, 2004.

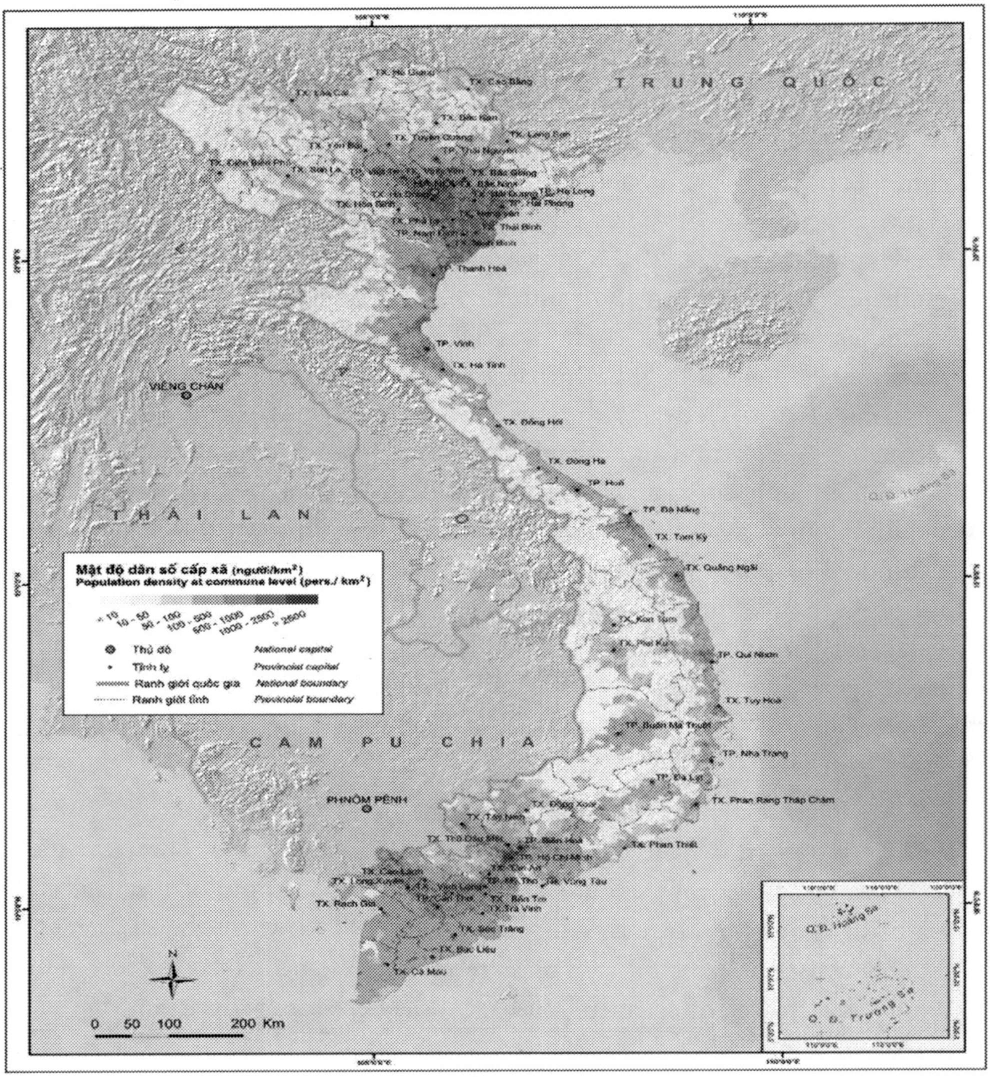

Source: *National Report on Disaster Reduction in Vietnam*, 2004.

disaster risk rather than considering it merely as a GDP growth enhancer. As Vietnam continues with its high growth trajectory, it is worth mentioning that the recurrent disasters that take place in Vietnam causes huge economic loss. When hazards like flood and drought come to pass, a great loss to society and economy also supervene those disasters. Neil Adgar opines that the transition of Vietnam from centralised economy undermined the collective

Map 2: Vulnerability Map of Vietnam

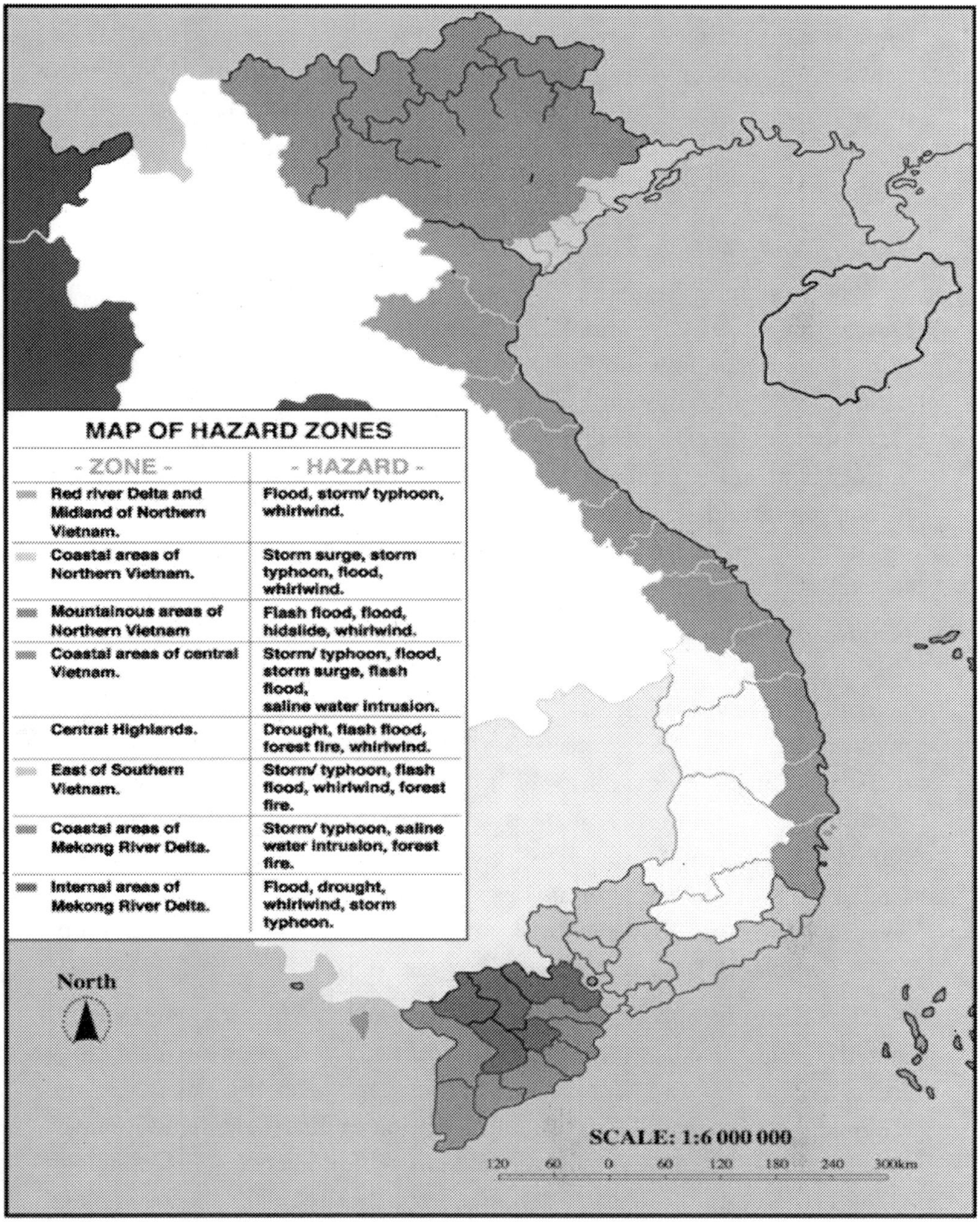

Source: *National Report on Disaster Reduction in Vietnam*, 2004.

action to ameliorate flood hazards associated with coastal storms (Adgar, 2000). Actually transition demands collective action in S&T innovations for safety and the matter to be rectified due to the weakness in governance. The transition process envisages the role of private enterprises in dealing with disaster risks as governance become weak in its approach. The aspects that are to be given great concern in governance for assuring technical safety to Vietnam are discussed below.

Research and Development (R&D) Initiatives

The combined report by Organisation of Economic Cooperation and Development (OECD) and World Bank states that the current science, technology and innovation (STI) capabilities in Vietnam are weak and the national innovation system is in a nascent, fragmented state. Research and Development (R&D) is still a peripheral activity in Vietnam, both in the business and in the public sector (OECD/ World Bank, 2014). The R&D initiatives should be widened to incorporate disaster preparedness and resilience for making scientific tools in managing disaster risk.

To define the critical role played by S&T in disaster reduction, the National Science and Technology Council's subcommittee identified six grand challenges-providing hazard and disaster information where and when it is needed, understanding natural processes that produce hazards (for making predictions), developing strategies and technologies reducing the impact of disaster, reducing vulnerability of infrastructure, developing standardised methods for communities to measure and assess disaster resilience across multiple hazards and to promote risk-averse behaviour (Applegate, 2008). Creating risk-averse behaviour involves the task of making Vietnamese people aware about the risk hidden areas as it incorporates a large coastal area (about 3000 km), floodplains and other risky areas.

The State Agency for Technology Innovation (SATI), Vietnam Science and Technology Evaluation Centre and the National Agency for Technology Entrepreneurship and Commercialisation have been formed under the Vietnamese Ministry of Science and Technology for the enhancement of Science and Technology. The National Council for Science and Technology Policy can directly advise Prime Minister on National Science and Technology Policy. But those initiatives could not yet foster better disaster management tools in Vietnam. High death tolls and property loss in Vietnam each year signals enhancing research initiatives in tackling disaster risks.

The National Centre for Natural Science and Technology (NCNST) was established in 1993 forging its mission as to conduct fundamental and applied research. But, now NCNST extensively relies on contract research and consultancy because of lack of funding. The total budget from the central government is less than US$ 8 million and its total staffs is more than 2000 (Bezanson, 1999: 47). The lack of appropriate funds and research equipment force many R&D institutions like NCNST to depart from their foundational objectives and to rely on contract research and providing technical services to customers. The National Technology Innovation Foundation (NATIF) which was established in Vietnam in 2011 is not yet ready for full operation (OECD/ World Bank 2014). NATIF enhance private sector innovations in S&T which gets stagnated with a delay in governance. The role of governance is to ensure R&D initiatives to be more disaster risk reductive and resilient in nature.

Disaster Risk Reduction and Resilience

Disaster risk reduction is the concept and practice of reducing disaster risks through systematic efforts to analyse and manage the causal factors of disasters, including through reduced exposure to hazards, lessened vulnerability of people and property, wise management of land and the environment, and improved preparedness for adverse events (Geneva, 2004). The topography and climate of Vietnam are such that most of the areas are disaster risk-ridden and it needs more environmental professionals which include planners, designers, surveyors etc. Vietnam occupies 8th position in Global Climatic Risk Index (prepared by Greenwatch) with 0.621 percent GDP loss. R&D initiative in disaster risk reduction and resilience is needed as part of resilience in governance.

Analysing Vietnam's demographic details the urban and coastal areas are densely populated making them most vulnerable to disasters. The housing and settlement in the coastal and urban area need more scientific adaptation in reducing disaster risk. Thus, R&D initiative promoting resilience in housing and settlement becomes a great concern in the governance of coastal and urban area. The Asian Disaster Preparedness Centre conducted a workshop on safer shelter in Vietnam in collaboration with the Ministry of Construction (MoC), Vietnam Red Cross and International Federation of Red Cross and Red Crescent Societies on September 2004 in Hanoi which gathered suggestions, inputs and ideas to urban disaster mitigation programme. Along with the establishment of safer shelters, managing safer settlements is also necessary. High-risk area and impact of the disaster are to be identified in preventing population agglomeration in such areas. Combined research initiatives in Science and Technology from International, state-owned and private enterprises can ensure resilience.

International, State Owned and Private Enterprises

Vietnam is characterised by Multinational Enterprises (MNEs) operating as a joint venture with State-owned Enterprises (SoEs) and the parallel emergence of small-scale private enterprises (OECD/World Bank, 2014). Earlier it was centrally planned economy which was later transformed into the socialist oriented market economy by adopting open economy/*Doi Moi* reforms (the 1980s). The Doi Moi reforms initiated private enterprises within business and trade which needs to be expanded to research, planning and innovation in disaster management. Vietnam receives assistance from international enterprises like United States Agency for International Development (USAID), The Asia Foundation, and United Nations International Strategy for Disaster Reduction (UNISDR). With the support from USAID, The Asia Foundation initiated a project for strengthening public-private partnership in disaster risk management and community resilience in Vietnam from 2011 to 2015. This project primarily mainly focuses on the involvement of Small and Medium Enterprises (SMEs) and public-private partnerships (PPPs) in disaster management. The disaster risk management initiated by World Bank in 2010 in Vietnam covered 12 areas to build flood and storm mitigation infrastructure projects which include constructing river dykes, evacuation routes, safe harbour and drainage pumping stations. The international enterprises assist in the governance of disaster management and in the same way the governance need to empower the private enterprises.

International enterprises play the major part in bringing forward Small and Medium-sized Enterprises (SMEs) to form resiliency and disaster preparedness. The SMEs compose 90 percent of Vietnamese businesses but 46 percent of SMEs have not yet developed a plan for disaster risk management. The first pro-SME development document emerged only in November 2001 in the form of Government Decree 90/2001/ND-CP provides the official definition of SME as "a business establishment with registered capital of no more than Vietnam dong (VND) 10 billion (equivalent to USD 630,000) or with an workforce of no more than 300 regular employees." Majority of the large enterprises are State Owned Enterprises (SOEs) and Foreign Invested Enterprises (FIEs), hence the SMEs constitute the most part with non-state actors (Tran, T.C., X.S. Le and K.A. Nguyen, 2008). The Ministry of Planning and Investment introduced the Small and Medium Enterprises Development Fund which gives more hope for SMEs participation in disaster risk reduction. The weakness in the governance of disaster risk from the part of the State is to be tackled so as to enhance better cooperation between international, state and private run enterprises.

Diplomatic Resilience – India and Vietnam

When the discussions surrounding disaster preparedness and resilience are taken to the international scenario, it is essential that such discussions need to be incorporated into diplomatic relationships which give rise to 'diplomatic resilience'. The diplomatic relationship between India and Vietnam is currently drawing the attention of international onlookers. It does not matter what the attitude of India towards ASEAN is or vice versa, the Indo-Vietnam bilateral relationship is entering into new heights. Vietnam and India signed seven agreements in 2014 strengthening their bilateral cooperation with a focus on politics, defence and security cooperation, economic cooperation, science and technology, culture and people to people links, technical cooperation and multilateral and regional cooperation (*The Hindu*, 2014). India and Vietnam have always had close and cordial relationship in the past too. India's first Prime Minister Jawaharlal Nehru (1954) and President Rajendra Prasad (1959) visited Vietnam. The diplomatic relationship between India-Vietnam was enriched with the establishment of full diplomatic relations in January 1972.

Vu Quang Diem, the former Ambassador of the Republic of Vietnam to India noted that the last few decades have seen the strongest surge and development of bilateral relations. Indian assistance in credit, education, training, science and technology, and many other fields contributes practically to the cause of 'renewal' (Doi Moi) of Vietnam and the striving for modernisation, industrialisation, and active international integration. Vietnam supports India's claim for UN membership and also India's 'Look East Policy'. Diem hoped for widening the bilateral relationship with India and looked forward in expanding cooperation in economic, trade, science and technology, education and tourism. But there is a new horizon that needs to be added to this bilateral relationship. This is assistance and cooperation in disaster preparedness, and India can act as a significant international actor assisting Vietnam in enhancing disaster preparedness and resilience.

A Sustainable Development View

Sustainable development, a paradigm shift in approach towards the concept of Development, is given due importance in forging domestic and international policies and programmes. The publication of 'Our Common Future' also known as Brundtland Report in 1987 (by World Commission on Environment and Development) established sustainable development as a global agenda. International Strategy for Disaster Reduction (ISDR) came out with the observance of International Decade for Natural Disaster Reduction in 1999. Sussane Wymann and Fani Kakriti outlined the aims of ISDR as 'building disaster-resilient communities by promoting increased awareness of the importance of disaster reduction as an integral component of sustainable development, with the goal of reducing human, social, economic and environmental losses due to natural hazards and related technological and environmental disasters' (*Mountain Research and Development* 2004). The World Summit on Sustainable Development (WSSD), 2002 in Johannesburg reaffirmed the idea of disaster risk reduction within the scope of sustainable development. The political statement adopted by Heads of State at the WSSD acknowledged that the impacts of natural disasters are more frequent and more devastating, with developing countries more vulnerable to hazards than ever before. The result was that UN system task team was created to formulate post-2015 Sustainable Development Goals agenda succeeding the Millennium Development Goals which undoubtedly incorporated disaster risk and resilience to the sustainable development initiatives.

The sustainable development view attributes international recognition to disaster preparedness and resilience in providing security to the future generation. The inclusion of disaster risk reduction to post-2015 global development agenda stresses this view which also gives prior importance to sustainable development. In the case of Vietnam too, the disaster preparedness and resilience need to be sustainable in nature as the vulnerability rate is so high in Vietnam. Considering the emerging horizons of Indo-Vietnam relationship, they can foster their bond by adding cooperation in disaster risk reduction in addition of having already a strong commercial bond.

Conclusion

The concept of Disaster Preparedness and Resilience is globally recognised developmental target and a seriously debated matter of concern in Vietnam. The role science and technology in achieving this developmental target has been discussed in this paper at a time when Indo-Vietnam relationship is climbing to new heights. Resilient governance needs equal participation of international, state-owned and private enterprises in tackling disaster risk as the State performs weakly in Vietnam. Innovations in S&T and efficiency in governance is necessary in the case of Vietnam. The emerging trend in Indo-Vietnam relationship, with its focus on trade and business, needs to be expanded adding disaster preparedness and resilience which is a part of sustainable development. The emerging generation needs to be in a safer shelter and riskless surrounding as Vietnam is rampantly prone to disasters.

REFERENCES

Adgar, Neil W., "Adaptation to Environmental Risk under the Transition in Vietnam." *Annals of the Association of American Geographers* 90, no. 4 (2000): 738-758.

Applegate, D., "Challenges to Building a Disaster-Resilient Nation." *Science News* 173, no. 19 (2008): 32, http://www.jstor.org/stable/20465527. (accessed on May 22, 2017).

Bezanson, A. Keith, *Vietnam at the Crossroads: The Role of Science and Technology.* Cananda: International Development Research centre, 1999.

Diem, V.Q., "Vietnam and India: Scaling new Heights." *The Hindu*, Jan. 5, 2007, http://www.thehindu.com/todays-paper/tp-opinion/Vietnam-and-India-scaling-new-heights/article14701844.ece.

Mehra, P., "India-Vietnam for Access to South China Sea." *The Hindu,* April 20, 2016, http://thehindu.com/news/national/india-vietnam-ink-seven-agreements/article6412345.ece.

National Report on Disaster Reduction in Vietnam, Hanoi: Socialist Republic of Vietnam, 2004.

Science, Technology and Innovation in Vietnam, OECD/ The World Bank: OECD Publishing, 2014, 323-364, http: //dx.doi.org/10.1789/8789 264213-500-en.

The 2009 Population and Housing Census (2010, July 22), http://www.gso.gov.vn. (accessed on June 10, 2017).

Tran, T.C.X.S. Le and K.A. Nguyen (2008), "Vietnam's Small and Medium Sized Enterprises Development: Characteristics, Constraints and Policy Recommendations." In *SME in Asia and Globalization, ERIA Research Project Report 2007-5, Living with risk: a global review of disaster reduction initiatives, edited by H. Lim. New York: United Nations, 2004.*

UN DESA | DPAD | UNTT | UN Task Team on the Post-2015 UN Development Agenda. (n.d.), http://www.un.org/en/development/desa/policy/untaskteam_undf/. (accessed on June 1, 2017).

Von, S. W. Dach, & Enz, F.K., "Websites on Hazards and Resilience." *Mountain Research and Development*, 24, no.1 (2004): 88-99.

Wisner, B.J. Gaillard C. & I. Kelman, *The routledge handbook of hazards and disaster risk reduction.* London: Routledge, Taylor and Francis Group, 2012.

15

Emerging Research Horizons of Indo–Vietnamese Shared Cultural Heritage

Shubham Singh

Introduction

India and Vietnam have had strong cultural and socio-economic links which date back to the 2nd century. Indian culture has left an impact on Vietnam and the signs of the same can still be seen in the country's geographical boundaries. India, owing to a common motive of a struggle for freedom from colonial powers, supported Vietnam's independence from France and actively stood for the unification of Vietnam. The relationship between the two nations was strengthened further after India's outright condemnation of the role of the United States in the Vietnam War. Thereafter, India's "Look East" policy which was developed and fostered with a view to building up widespread economic and strategic relations between Southeast Asian nations so as to structure itself as a significant regional power, also gave impetus to closer ties with Vietnam. India shares not just economic and strategic defence ties but also a cultural legacy with Vietnam which has remained unstressed for long.

There are diverse areas of possible research into relations between India and Vietnam. Since the two nations have witnessed similar conditions prior to Independence and have struggled to free themselves of colonial rule, with

India playing a strong advocate for Vietnam's freedom, the ties between the two sovereign states have gradually grown deeper and elaborate. This paper attempts to highlight fresh areas of probable research into India and Vietnam's shared historical heritage that chalks out ways for a more mutually interactive future. The broad research horizons that may open up with dedicated effort in this direction include a study of the shared architecture and religious structures, the organisation of towns, the religious influences and practices, a shared culture, the ancient Hindu kingdoms, the degree of assimilation of the people of the two civilisations, parameters of caste and gender, the ancient inscriptions, the art and historical artifacts, and the ancient languages of the two civilisations. How the two nations bear similarity and interdependence in terms of these broad factors is the central discussion point of this paper.

The Ancient Champa Kingdom: Shared Cultural Heritage

The Cham or the Champa Kingdom is a testimony to this common heritage with its Champa Towers, which is a local name for the Hindu temples built in Central Vietnam. Hinduism has left its impact on Vietnam in the form of the Champa people, and the discovery of the temple towers, the sculptures of various Hindu deities, the red brick temples in Vietnam attest to the same fact. The first Hindu kingdom in Central Vietnam was named "Amaravati" and the first king to establish the Champa kingdom in Amaravati was Bhadravarman. The first Hindu king to rule this region was Srimara. The people of the two countries had congenial interactions in the distant past and several Hindu people who travelled to Vietnam, took their cultural attributes along with them, the traces of which are perceptible even to this day. Regarding the origin of the term "Champa", Gitesh Sharma explains:

> The term Champa has its origin in Pauranic mythological literature in Sanskrit and Pali wherein it is mentioned as Champa, Champapuri, Champa Nagar, Champa Malini, etc. According to Pauranic literature Champa was the name of the son of Pritulaksha, a descendant of Anu, who had founded the city of Champapuri. Champa was also the capital of Emperor Bimbisara (544-493 B.C.), who expanded his flourishing Magadh Empire from Champa to Varanasi. Champa also happens to be the name of a fragrant flower that was treated as sacred and finds mention in Pauranic literature. Even in various Buddhist and Jain texts one finds its mention. (Sharma, 2009, p. 45)

This shows that naming of the city itself was inspired by classical Indian texts. For the people in the Champa kingdom, Sanskrit was adopted as a scholarly language, and Hinduism, especially Shaivism, was declared to be the religion of the state.

The Indian Perspective on the Shared Cultural Attributes

Prior to making sense of the scope for researchers of the shared cultural heritage of India and Vietnam, it becomes imperative to briefly cast a look at the outlook which have fostered the view of certain commonly shared cultural attributes between the people of two nations. There are several perspectives through which the study of the Champa kingdom in Vietnam is visualised and the one that most concerns us is the one which motivated even the colonial French researchers and that is analyzing the history of the Cham people through its linkage with the Indian culture. Although intermittent attempts at carrying out a complete study of the Champa kingdom have followed since the beginning of colonial reign in Vietnam, it is quite recently – specifically in the past decade – that some genuine interest in studying the Cham civilisation and culture has sparked. But, what is even more problematic is that the Cham people are not known to be indigenous to Vietnam and have been understood to have come under the country's societal setup as a result of the expansion of Vietnam, and also via a process of widespread cultural assimilation of people of considerably different ethnicities. Bruce M. Lockhart observes in this regard:

> Champa and its history pose a thorny and awkward problem for Vietnamese scholars. The kingdom of Champa no longer exists, and its disappearance is the direct consequence of Vietnamese expansion and colonisation. Although evidence of an ancient Cham presence has been found as far north as Quang Bình province, the group's present numbers in Vietnam are confined to small areas along the south-central coast (Bình Thuan and Ninh Thuan) and the Cambodian border. This situation is the result of gradual ethnic and cultural assimilation rather than any sort of genocide, but the fact remains that the present-day Cham are a mere remnant of what was once a regional power. (Lockhart, 2011, p. 1-2)

Therefore, the study of the Cham people and their cultural and geographic past is a part of Vietnam's relations with its neighbouring states, one of the key ones of which is India. The early colonial French scholars, while studying the cultural and architectural origins of the Cham people, were faced by obvious barriers such as, the lack of knowledge of the Cham language and so they were largely dependent on inscriptions found in the Sanskrit language for gaining insight into the civilisation's past. This also led them to connect these people to be influenced by Indian culture to a considerable extent.

The Indian perspective stated that the Champa people were of Malay origin and hence were outsiders to Vietnam. But they had come to acquire much of their religion and customs from India and so it would be inevitable to make a complete sense of their civilisation by making sincere attempts to relate them to the Indian civilisation which they were greatly influenced by. Although the colonial French scholarship was preoccupied with finding Indian on the arts, religion and architecture of the Champa people, this was basically owing to an inability to understand their indigenous roots and their native language. Even a celebrated French Indologist and Sanskrit scholar Abel Bergaigne, who was himself a comparative linguist, was continually informed by the "Indian-centric approach" as Lockhart terms it, to the Cham civilisation. Not only that, he goes on to find the connecting links between the two cultures to such an extent that he seems to be consciously negating the indigenous cultural traits of the people of the Cham kingdom. This is why his critical discussions were centred solely on the worship of Buddha, and the Hindu deities. Lockhart makes assertive comments in this regard:

> The famous temple at Nha Trang dedicated to the important Cham goddess Po Nagar, for instance, is mentioned only in terms of the worship of Uma, Siva's consort. That this veneration of Uma was in fact the worship of the indigenous deity in another form seems to have escaped Bergaigne, who only saw the Hindu exterior and not the Cham substratum in the Uma cult. He goes on to mention a "Po Nagar inscription" near a different "Vietnamese" temple further down the coast but apparently fails to recognise the connection with the major religious centre at Nha Trang. (Lockhart, 2011, p. 5)

Hence, much of the dedication of the scholars seem to have been concentrated on establishing connections between the religious practices of the inhabitants of India and Vietnam rather than delving more deeper into their original influences. They were so consumed by the belief that the Indian culture has impacted Vietnam and its Champa civilisation in its bare essence that they comfortably overlooked the point of indigenous religious worship of the Cham people. It is these primordial traditional practices that a modern researcher working on Indo-Vietnam shared cultural and religious ties has the responsibility to discover and bring them to the attention of the world at large so that, a proper historical and literary perspective of the two civilisations could be put up.

The Religious Influence of India and Shared Religious Practices

The Construction of Temples and Idol Worship of Hindu Deities

It is a fact commonly agreed by researchers that Vietnam does show signs of the considerable religious influence of the Indian civilisation. Hindus and Buddhists have been known to have migrated from India to Vietnam for centuries. It is an accepted point that Buddhism reached Vietnam directly through India. Similarly, the Hindus who migrated to Vietnam brought with them not just their arts, culture and religion but also fully assimilated with the natives and established a kingdom of their own, the signs of which are still perceptible in the ruins of the temples found scattered at different locations within the country. After the heyday of the Hindu kingdom in Vietnam was over, these people became Vietnamized without any tension or battle. This attests to the fact of the long-standing harmonious relations between the people of the two sovereign republics of India and Vietnam. The early Hindu or Indian settlers in Vietnam established temples and installed statues of their gods and goddesses. This is the main reason we perceive signs of Indian artistry on the temples and sculptures of Vietnam, even to this day. Gitesh Sharma makes a significantly corroborative statement in this regard when he says:

> Among the various carvings and inscriptions recovered through excavations one is amazed to find various carvings depicting Hindu mythological characters like Rama setting the strings of his bow; marriage ceremony of Rama and Sita; Rama's army of monkeys; Krishna playing flute under a tree; Indra flocked by dancing apsaras, Garuda devouring snake; Mahishasurmardini Durga killing buffalo headed demon; four headed Brahma; Vishnu reclining over Sheshnag; Saraswati; Lakshmi; Shiva Linga and Yoni etc. (Sharma, 2009, p. 26)

Some of these idols can still be seen in temples in Vietnam and these are a proof of the religious interaction that the native culture of the place underwent with the Indian tradition. This reinforces the idea proposed by the critic Raymond Williams who famously proposed: "Culture is ordinary, in every society and in every mind." (Williams 93) The local people of Vietnam imbibed the cultural traits from early settlers coming from India and over time these practices became an integral part of their culture. Therefore, the cultural interaction of the two civilisations did not occur as a refined activity comprising of the high and mighty people of the society, but the commonplace people with their routine activities such as worship in temples. In recent times, when the respective governments of India and Vietnam have taken considerable and determined measures to widen the range of their co-operation and work with solidarity to foster a better and secured future for the citizens of the two nations, the foundation of the same is provided by such religious intermixing in a distant yet shared past.

Restoration of Cultural Art and Heritage Sites: An Opportunity for Practical Research

The aspect of the shared cultural legacy of the two nations centres on the Cham people who came to be influenced by Hinduism in the 4th century. The Champa people still retain and preserve their Hindu customs and festivals, although some of them are now followers of Buddhism. The Balamon Cham people are the only living followers of Hinduism in Vietnam today, but for a great part of its history, the nation has been home to a dominant and beautiful Hindu culture. Even though UNESCO declared the remaining Hindu temples in My Son area of Vietnam as World Cultural Heritage Sites, Indian government or scholars hardly took any real interest in the restoration and study of these as part of a step to understand more about our shared cultural past. This highlights new horizons for research about the shared cultural heritage of India and Vietnam which, coupled with the ongoing socio-economic partnership, would provide a holistic form to the harmonious relations between the people of the two nations. Historical documents claim that My Son was the first city of Vietnam where Hindu temples were built. The construction of the Champa Temple Towers or the Hindu temples began during the reign of Bhadravarman, who was the king from 349 to 361 A.D. These temple towers were firstly made of wood but soon they got destroyed and the new towers were built from bricks. As soon as these temples came into existence, the statues of Hindu deities, some of whom have been listed above, were placed in them and gradually, they came to be regularly worshipped. Even the architecture of these temple towers resembles those of the temples in South India and this is an important avenue of research for scholars working on the architecture of the ruins of these temple towers to establish their links to Indian cultural heritage. Gitesh Sharma makes a keen observation in his book, *Traces of Indian Culture in Vietnam,* in this regard:

> The architecture of Hindu Temples of Vietnam shows a noticeable influence of the architecture of the temples in Orissa and South India. Indeed, it will not be an exaggeration to say that most of the temples of Vietnam are to some extent replica of the style of South Indian temples. The statues of Hindu gods and goddesses as well as the carvings on stone, unearthed during excavations, are influenced by the sculptures of Mathura, Gandhar, Amaravati (Andhra Pradesh), and Kalinga (Orissa). In view of these facts, it can be said that it must have been done on such a large scale by the artisans and craftsmen who had migrated from India, of course, with the assistance of local artisans and craftsmen. (Sharma, 2009, p. 27)

Not just this, he even remarks that the terracotta art found in Vietnam and that in Bishnupur region of West Bengal evince such similarity that it can be safely concluded that this art form must have reached Vietnam from India through the skilled Indian craftsmen. It is significant to observe Williams' idea of the ordinary culture being manifest here:

> A culture has two aspects: the known meanings and directions, which its members are trained to; the new observations and meanings, which are offered and tested. These are the ordinary processes of human societies and human minds, and we see through them the nature of a culture: that it is always both traditional and creative; that it is both the most ordinary common meanings and the finest individual meanings. (Williams, 2001, p. 93)

The ordinary, day-to-day assimilation of the people of two civilisations over a long period brought about a new hybrid culture. There is a traditional aspect of culture at work here, as also the new directions that have come up under the influence of the migrant Hindu settlers. Moreover, Vietnamese people learnt the art of brick-making through these craftsmen from India and went on to build beautiful architectural constructs of their own. Although the temples in South India are predominantly made of stone, unlike their Vietnamese counterparts, which are made of bricks, there are several temples in Orissa, West Bengal and other regions of southern India that are made of brick and they used a particular adhesive made from rice-bran to conjoin the bricks. It is believed that this is the technology which the Vietnamese architects would have adopted to join the bricks in a flawless manner. This entire technology of brick-making and fixing is also an interesting area of research for scholars to establish the interdependence and interaction between the two countries since the ancient times.

The Dominant Hindu Religious Sects in Antiquity

During the Champa period, the Shaivas or Shivaites were a predominant group and this is attested by two major points. Firstly, king Bhadravarman, who was the progenitor of the trend of construction of the Hindu temples in Vietnam, installed a Shiv Linga in the very first temple that was built as per his commands. Secondly, a vast number of temple towers in Vietnam, depict Shiva in various forms, including the symbolic Shiva Linga and the Yoni and their numbers are much more than those devoted to other deities. But, when Prakash dharma took the charge in the year 653, the Vaishnava sect gained predominance over the Shaiva and as such, he built the first Vishnu temple in Vietnam and installed an idol of Lord Vishnu into it. Later on, with the ascent of King Indravarman in the year 854, Buddhism came into prominence and the first Buddhist monastery in Vietnam came into existence during his tenure in 875, that too, in the Champa area. The influence of Hinduism in Vietnam is so deep and pristine that even before Champa kingdoms were established in the country, there already existed "Hindu kingdoms in Suvaranadvipa that comprised Malaya, Sumatra, Java, Bali, Borneo and other islands of East Indies." The oldest Hindu kingdom that was established in the lower valley of the Mekong, was the famous Funan empire. Tradition has it, that it was built by a Brahmin named Kaundinya from India, sometime in the first century. Sharma further notes:

> The rulers professing Hinduism or Buddhism set up a socio-political structure on the ancient Pauranic-Brahmanical and Buddhist Indian Model and patronized Indian learning, art and architecture. Although the rulers considered themselves to be a part and parcel of the native soil, yet the Indian culture dominated in every sphere of life. Later on, however, the Indian culture got completely submerged in the local culture. (Sharma, 2009, p. 25)

The Hindu kings and migrants never imposed their supremacy over the natives; they did not reach Vietnam and settled there by means of strife, battle or force. There was a peaceful and willing assimilation of two great civilisations which is quite a rare phenomenon in much of the world's history dominated by bloody wars of annexation and encounters. The Hindus came to Vietnam not as conquerors but as settlers and fellow brethren and this is the main reason why there has always been a strong co-operative and cordial bond between the two countries for their long and glorious past and which also enables them to develop even more trustworthy and valuable strategic socio-economic ties in the present.

Societal Set-up and Establishment of Hindu Kingdoms in Vietnam: a Society Rooted in Equality

Since the knowledge of the societal organisation of a particular community is a pivotal factor in making a thorough sense of its structuring and its originating influences, it becomes an engaging and interesting domain of research for modern researchers to study the entire fabric of the social categorisation and the class system of the Vietnamese Champa people and thereafter, to evaluate and make sense of the extent to which these are influenced by the class hierarchy and caste system in their Hindu counterparts. This would also help the researchers to cast a keen look at the way their social conditioning has taken shape over the centuries and how have they come to develop a particular pattern of thinking and action. The migrant Hindu settlers in Vietnam did not choose to bring the disagreeable caste system of their Hindu counterparts in India to this one. They rather preferred a society rooted in equality, free from the discriminating tenets of untouchability:

> The immigrant Hindus were, in fact, quite liberal than their counterpart in India and so the inhuman casteism by birth could never find its roots in Vietnam. There were mainly three castes among the Chams in Vietnam viz. Brahmin, Kshatriya and Vaishya. There is no mention anywhere of the Shudras. The slaves contributed manual labour. Besides sharing the power, marital alliance between the Brahmins and the Kshatriyas was quite common. (Sharma, 2009, p. 31)

Similarly, discrimination on the basis of gender was also something essentially unknown to the Vietnamese Hindu people. Women were accorded a status equal to men in the family. Neither were they revered like goddesses, nor were they mistreated. This implies that unlike the traditional Indian household, the women were not placed on a pedestal and referred to as a superhuman goddess thereby divesting them of their humanity. They were treated with respect and worth as a male member of the family and which in itself presents an image of a utopian society. Even though Hinduism lost ground with the passage of time and blended with the native culture of the place, its signs are still perceptible in the current society of Vietnam and what is even more fortunate is that the government of Vietnam has given it its due credit and recognised the impact it has had on the traditional Vietnamese culture. Not only this, but the government of Vietnam has given much emphasis on the restoration and preservation of the historical relics that were discovered at various sites in the country during excavations and the ancient temples and other heritage structures which were doomed to ruins.

Indebtedness at the Level of Architectural Technique

A particular focus on the architectural technique of the Cham people, without doubt, reveals an Indian influence but what is more characteristic to their religious architecture is the use of corbel technique in which baked bricks are "stacked in a slightly offset manner and are used on the spire to support the roof" (Phuong, 2011, p. 278). As of present-day Vietnam, there still exist some prime Hindu temples that bear close resemblances with those in Southern India. One such temple is the Mariamman Temple in Vietnam's Ho Chi Minh City which is dedicated to the Hindu goddess Mariamman, who is believed to be the South Indian goddess of rain. Festivities are carried out to appease her during the summer and autumn seasons so as to bring rains. This temple was built in the late 19th century by traders from Tamil Nadu known as Nagarathar or Nattukkottai Chettiar who followed Shaivism. Similarly, quite famous are the temple ruins found in the My Son area of Vietnam that were constructed by the Champa kings over a period of several centuries. These are primarily dedicated to the worship of Lord Shiva which has already been stated to be the prime deity of Hindus residing in Vietnam. It is one of the most significant heritage sites in Vietnam comparable to the Angkor Wat of Cambodia. Its significance is such that the UNESCO recognised it as a world heritage site in the year 1999. It was in 1937 that the French scholars began the restoration work of the temple towers in the My Son region. Restoration of such ancient heritage sites is one of the key steps involved in making a genuine and complete analysis of not just the architecture and sculpture of a region but also its religious adherence. This is one of the prime areas of research in which modern scholarship of Indo-Vietnam shared cultural heritage would have to rigorously strive to establish some determined conclusions in the common religious influences of the two grand civilisations. Many historical monuments in the country were damaged during the infamous Vietnam War. Carpet bombing by the USA left deep craters in the region which are clearly perceptible even to this day. The architectural genius of the people is evinced by the fact that many of the temple ruins are still existent as it is, although they have grown weaker and are vulnerable to collapse. The significance of the temples at this site is also made clear by the fact that many of the statues in the region have been safely shifted to historical museums built specifically for the purpose of their preservation. Moreover, the serious intent of the government of Vietnam is visible in that its Ministry of Culture assigned a huge sum of 440,000 USD during 2002-2004 for their efficient preservation and maintenance. Another famous temple in Vietnam is that of Po Nagar in the modern-day Nha Trang, in Vietnam, which is devoted to Yan Po Nagar, the goddess who came to be identified with the Hindu goddesses Bhagavati and Mahishasuramardini Durga, and who is called Thiên Y Thánh Mâu in the Vietnamese tongue. The temple is situated on the Cù Lao Mountain and consists of three levels. Goddess Durga is represented on the pediment above the entrance to the temple. The central sculpture of the temple is that of goddess Yan Po Nagar sitting cross-legged with ten hands holding several religiously symbolic items. According to a Vietnamese scholar Ngô Van Doanh, these sitting postures and the symbolic pieces bear quite close resemblance to the Hindu goddess Durga and hence the influence of the Indian civilisation cannot be overstated.

The Ancient Inscriptions and Cultural Assimilation

The Inscriptions in Sanskrit

Inscriptions are another valuable resource of comprehending the historical culture and way of life of the Vietnamese people and to suggest how Indian influence was pervasive among the general aspects of their day to day lives. In this regard, it has already been strongly claimed that the Champa people maintained records in the Sanskrit language apart from their own native Cham language. They engraved inscriptions on large biodegradable leaves as well as in stone and the scripts for the same were Indian in origin. Many of the Cham's most significant inscriptions have been found on steles or slabs of stone crafted specifically for the purpose of representing these inscriptions. What they profess is basically the perspective of the rulers who built them and are generally structured as their offering to their gods. They also serve as an important source of the names of the kingdoms and cities of the then Vietnam. Some of them also assume a narrative role and describe significant historical events. The building techniques of the temple ruins and these steles is still not deeply understood by the researchers and so this provides a great opportunity for fresh researchers to come together to study not just the structure and subject-matter of these sites but also the techniques which were normally used by these people in their construction and particularly what aspects of their art of construction were borrowed or inspired by the styles of temple constructions in India. For example, we already know that many of these temple towers were made of red brick in contrast to those of South India but issues such as the firing of the bricks to harden them and the resins used to stick the bricks together are still to be discovered. Equally crucial is the factor that how and at what points the carvings on the temple walls was done. Were the bricks carved prior to structuring or were the walls carved after the construction had been done? Although, as the carvings done on these ruins reveal such efficient finesse that the scholars have generally concluded that the architects carved directly onto the constructed brick walls. Still, it is a fact that needs to be corroborated by fresh research and modern scholars need to go into the depth of the construction techniques of these people and their borrowings from India.

Peaceful Cultural Assimilation

Raymond Williams thinks of culture as "customary difference" implying that the culture of a society is to which they are habitual but other societies or their inhabitants may be unaware or unaccustomed to. There are customary aspects of both civilisations that have remained but their differences have also been at play. This is the reason why the influence of Indian architecture, religion and culture took roots in Vietnam. It is not only the Hindu religion that reached Vietnam through India but Islam too, spread to Vietnam through India via Malaysia and Indonesia. A small section of the Champa community adopted Islam, even though they continued to practice certain Hindu traditions as well. They continued idol worship, dance, music, funeral processions with music bands, all of which are not permissible under Islam. The Cham people do not perform the burial rites of their dead, rather they prefer to cremate the dead and preserve the ashes to be worshipped later. This forms the basis of a genuinely religiously tolerant Vietnamese society which had the capacity to evolve and improve as and when required. Despite their different faiths these people continue to live in harmony and peace. This brings a core issue of discussion to the forefront – that of cultural assimilation. With great skill, the Champa people have Vietnamised their Indian traits and they have also mixed with the indigenous Vietnamese people to such a degree that today, it is hard to distinguish between the two. Another important feature that may be mentioned here is the celebration of the Champa festival of *Kate*, which seems to be of Hindu origin because its ceremonies are carried out in temples in which the Cham Hindus as well as Muslims participate and the chants refer to Hindu deities such as Shiva and Vishnu. The festival is celebrated at the beginning of the month of July to express people's gratefulness to their gods. The Cham Brahmins perform all the rituals and the younger generation of the Cham people too participates in them with fervour. This factor of peaceful cultural assimilation of the people of different communities and the degree to which they have adapted and accepted each other is an intriguing area of research for the modern scholarship. What is even more crucial is to find out those dwindling numbers of the population which have maintained their identity to this day and still practice their own indigenous customs.

Research Opportunities in the Fields of Literature, Music and Arts

A disappointing factor, as well as a workable opportunity for research, is the lack of sufficient literature, both religious and secular, of the Cham people of Vietnam. Sharma comments in this regard:

> Literature is, usually, the spiritual food for all classes but due to lack of proper preservation and maintenance not many of the ancient Cham literary manuscripts could be preserved. Moreover, there seems to be less enthusiasm among the younger generation towards the preservation of their ancestors' legacy and this is also another reason for the rarity of Cham literary manuscripts. However, realising the danger ahead, there are committed people like Inrasara, who have taken up the challenge of editing the new literature of Champa under the title "Collection of Champa Literature" in 10 volumes. (Sharma, 2009, p. 49)

The onus lies on fresh researchers to not only procure whatever ancient literary material they can and to restore them with proper care but to reassess the documents and manuscripts available to fill in the gaps and to bring out a clear unambiguous perspective of the people. Since the very naming of the cities and towns as well as the whole way of their traditional life has been influenced and inspired by the ancient Hindu Pauranic texts, efforts must also be continually made to determine the extent of Indian influence on the literary corpus of the Vietnamese Cham people.

Music and dance have always been a great source of cross-cultural interaction between different civilisations and so are the case between India and the Vietnamese Champa people. The researchers may find the motivation to study the music of the Cham Brahmins and relate it to the cultural music of other ethnic groups in India. That the music of the Cham people, like other parameters of culture, had been influenced by Indian tradition is a recognised fact. Gitesh Sharma observes in this context:

> The book titled Music in the Brahmin by Van Thu Bich has unique characteristics, which have just been discovered, of the Cham Brahmin music performed in their traditional ceremonies as well as its cultural/musical exchange and interaction with other ethnic groups so as to propose several measures to protect and preserve the Cham Brahmin music. Many traditional music instruments of the Chams are quite identical to Indian music instruments viz. Mridang, Dholak, Shehnai, Flute, Tanpura, etc. (Sharma, 2009, p. 49-50)

This provides a wonderful chance to the researchers to identify the inherent characteristics of the Cham Brahmin music and to state how its musical exchange has impacted people of other communities. It also enables them to find out how the interdependence of traditional Indian culture and the Cham people has created music that has strengthened the bonds between the people of the two nations. Dance too, is an integral part of the cultural life of the Cham people and most of their dances have an Indian origin. This also becomes a happy arena of cross-cultural exchange and mutual give and take. Sharma asserts in his book:

> Their colourful dances form an integral part of their festivals that attract both the local Vietnamese as well as the foreign tourists. Traditional musical instruments e.g. Ginang (Mridang), Baranung (drum), Ceng (gong), Xaranai (horn, identical to Indian Shehnai), Grong (tintinnabulum) provide the dance its rhythm. (Sharma, 2009, p. 50)

Therefore in the matters pertaining to music and dance, the influence of Indian culture on the traditional Vietnamese culture is clearly discernible.

Preserved Ancient Artifacts as Source of Research

The signs and symbols of cross-cultural exchange between India and Vietnam in the distant past have been adequately preserved and showcased in several of the country's museums. Therefore, these museums spread across

Vietnam could serve as resourceful sites for the modern researchers who may be used the artefacts stored in them for an in-depth study of the glorious past of the two civilisations. It will be interesting to mention here that the jewellery of the Champa people was closely identical to the Indian jewellery. An artisan Vu Kim Loc who owns a museum which houses plenty of stuff such as jewellery and pottery related to Cham art and culture has written a book on the ancient artefacts of the Cham people and their indebtedness to the Indian art and craft in this regard:

> Very recently this gentleman has written a book with the help of his friend Le Xuan Diem titled *Ancient Artifacts of Champa* after years of his research on the Cham art and culture. The book highlights the Indian connection with the Cham jewellery and also explains that the import of jewellery from India had already started since initially, the merchants and traders from India had carried the jewellery with them and subsequently, the traders took along trained artisans with them to Vietnam, who later settled there. (Sharma, 2009, p. 51)

It is this connection and transfer of skilled craftsmen which is a possible area of research and evaluation for current scholars. This also provides ample scope to connect with people who have a deep knowledge of the jewellery of ancient India and that of Vietnam in order to find exactly in what ways and to what extent the Indian influence in the making of jewellery has impacted the Chams. This museum owner, in fact, claims that some of the artefacts that were discovered in various excavations in Vietnam were actually imported through India. Moreover, when the artisans of jewellery, pottery, utensils and other such domestic stuff settled permanently in Vietnam, they began to develop such artefacts locally in the same style as the Indian artefacts were made. They even made certain changes in accordance with the local style and thus gave birth to a new hybrid variety of jewellery specific to Vietnam. The Indian influence becomes more clearly pronounced with the discovery of pots and vases bearing inscriptions in Sanskrit. The Champa people also knew the art of making gold and silver ornaments and readily adopted the methods of the making of Indian ornaments to diversify the scope of their craft. Sharma observes that even in the current times the designs of gold and silver ornaments in Vietnam are 'quite identical' to the ones made in India.

Since architectural art is an important factor in assessing the cultural interdependence of any two civilisations, it is important to note the comments of Dr. R.C. Majumdar who claims in his book, *Champa, History and Culture of an Indian Colonial Kingdom in the Far East, 2nd-16th century A.D.*, that there is great similarity between the Indian and Cham architecture which the European scholars have conveniently disregarded:

> ...As regards Cham sculpture and iconography, their striking agreements with the Indian style in both essential and nonessential elements have been shown in the preceding pages, and nobody has doubted or can possibly doubt their Indian origin. As to the relative excellence of the two, opinions might, of course, differ. Both were dominated by religious ideas and the aesthetic sense of the artists in both countries has to be sacrificed in a considerable degree to his religious preconceptions. (Sharma, 2009, p. 53)

Therefore, this is a key area where lies much scope of research as to how the architecture and sculpture of the Chams came to be influenced and shaped by that of India and in what manner.

Similarity in the Structures of Languages

Ultimately, one of the most common parameters of similarity that can be established between the cultures of two ancient civilisations is that of their languages. So, it is an even more plausible field of research for the scholars to find out the essential similarities between the basics of the language of the Cham people and Sanskrit. The native language of the Chams belongs to the family of the Sanskrit language. The vowels and consonants used in the Cham language have been found to be identical to those in Sanskrit and Hindi. The way these are pronounced and articulated also is closely similar. The language has undergone only minor changes in script and dialect in the course of time but the essential elements have remained almost homogeneous. This provides huge scope for linguists as well as scholars and historians of Indo-Vietnamese culture to research and establishes the Indian origin of the language of Vietnam's Cham people:

> The most astonishing part, however, is that the remarkable similarity that Sanskrit and Champa language had, escaped the attention of Indian historians and linguists. Know not why? Why no material regarding the Champa community, its language and traditions are available in India? Why has no serious research work regarding the Champa community of Vietnam and its Indian origin yet been undertaken in India? (Sharma, 2009, p. 57)

The possibility of a detailed analysis of the common characteristics of Sanskrit and the native Champa language wields immense opportunity for the establishment of a shared historical past and future interdependence of the two nations.

Conclusion

Hence, all the above-discussed parameters bear solid scope of research for establishing strong historical, cultural and strategic links between India and Vietnam. With the support of organisations such as the UNESCO and a little will of the respective governments to take measures in this regard, the scholars desirous of working on the shared cultural heritage of India and Vietnam have immense opportunities to study and analyse factors such as the architecture of the ruins of the temple towers in Vietnam, the historical accounts and manuscripts available, the languages of the two civilisations, the current cultural and strategic ties and interactions, the administration and societal set up of the kingdoms of the Cham people, and other valuable artefacts. Thereafter, the interdependence and mutual co-operation between India and Vietnam would gain a firm foothold and the bond that the nations share would become stronger than ever.

REFERENCES

Chon, Kaye Sung and Arthur Asa Berger, *Vietnam Tourism*, Binghamton: The Haworth Hospitality Press, 2005.

"Culture is Ordinary", in *The Everyday Life Reader,* edited by Ben Highmore, 91-100. London: Routledge, 2001.

Galla, Amareswar, "Culture and Heritage in Development," *Humanities Research IX*, no. 1 (2002): 63-76. Retrieved from https://openresearch repository.anu.edu.au.

Kalman, Bobbie, *Vietnam: The culture*, New York: Crabtree Publishing Company, 2002.

McLeod, Mark W. and Thi Dieu Nguyen, *Culture and Customs of Vietnam,* Westport: Greenwood Press, 2001.

Phuong Tran Ky and Bruce Lockhart, *The Cham of Vietnam: History, Society and Art*, Singapore: NUS Press, 2011.

Power, Paul F. (1967), "India and Vietnam," *Asian Survey* 7, no. 10 (1967): 740-751, doi: 10.2307/2642422.

Sharma, Geetesh, *Traces of Indian Culture in Vietnam*, New Delhi: Banyan Tree Books Pvt. Ltd, 2009.

Srinivasan, K.R., *Temples of South India*, New Delhi: National Book Trust, 1979.

Thakur, Ramesh (1979), "India's Vietnam Policy, 1946-1979," *Asian Survey,* 19, no. 10 (1979): 957-976.doi: 10.2307/2643848.

Thắng, Đặng Văn (2017), "Hindu Temples in Go Thap Dong Thap Province, Vietnam," *ASRJETS*, 30, no. 1 (2017): 85-398, http://asrjetsjournal.org/index.php/American_Scientific_Journal.

Thi, Le Lien, "Hindu Deities in Southern Vietnam: Image on Small Archaeological Artifacts," in *Early Interactions Between South and Southeast Asia: Reflections on Cross-Cultural Exchange*, edited by Pierre-Yves Manguin, A. Mani, & Geoff Wade, 407-431, Pasir Panjang, Singapore: Institute of Southeast Asian Studies, 2011.

White, Christine Pelzer, "State, Culture and Gender: Continuity and Change in Women's Position in Rural Vietnam," in *Women, State and Ideology*, edited by Haleh Afshar, 226-234, Albany: State University of New York Press, 1987, https://link.springer.com.

Williams, Raymond, *Culture and Society: 1780-1950*, New York: Columbia University Press, 1983.

16

Buddhist Female Iconography in the Art of Ancient Vietnam: A Study of the Interrelationships of Indian and Southeast Asian Art

Abira Bhattacharya

Introduction

Vietnam marked its emergence as one of the earliest and leading centers of the international trade and commerce in the early first-millennium on the global map, which immensely promoted sharing of new ideologies and cross-cultural assimilation of religious and cultural traits, coming from different polities, while appearing as a common interface to all the major Asian civilisations, including – India, China, Cambodia, Indonesia, Thailand, Burma and Sri Lanka. This was made possible due to its strategic and prime geographic location on the international maritime network and its close proximity to the extended Silk Route, which could be deduced from its long coastline stretching over a large span, linking China in the north and insular Southeast Asia in the south, while the fertile river basins and deltas, Red River Delta in the north and in the Mekong Delta in the far south, acting as linkages between the overland and the oceanic routes of Southeast Asia. Similar to other Southeast Asian kingdoms, Vietnam also became an integral part of the unprecedented global wave of acculturation and process of transmission of Indic conceptual models of linguistics, literature, ideals of kingship, statecraft and religious order, which led to the shaping of its statehood and cultural framework. This was a glorious phase which witnessed remarkable signs of growing rapprochement between India and Southeast Asian polities. This led to the formation of a broader cultural matrix through global diaspora with the expansion of ideas, life, culture and societal values.

The wave of cultural transmission was heightened by the increased movement and resettlement of Indian merchants and Indian religious proselytizing delegations, which extensively traversed for economic gains and propagating the faiths, Hinduism and Buddhism, respectively. A common dialogue was built up, strengthening the cultural and religious alliances with Indian traditions. The rich Indian mercantile class got relocated in the newly formed polities through inter-ethnic martial alliances, thereby attaining high status in their society, while the Brahmins played a pivotal role in the kingship and administrative structuring, and accrued immense wealth by serving the ritualistic services in the local royal courts. Thus, the importance of the religious missionaries lays in their connection to the propagation of the ritualistic practices, religious imageries and wide circulation of textual sources. During this time, Vietnam became familiar with the Brahmanical and Buddhist practices.

As a result, Indian commercial settlement sprang up in different parts of Southeast Asia, leading to the formation of principal kingdoms of early Southeast Asia. Likewise, Vietnam also underwent the same process of "Indianisation" or "Hinduisation" sometime after the 4th or 5th century CE, and came to closer contact of India which led to the establishment of two major neighbouring political realms – firstly, the Oc Eo culture, near the coast of Angkor Borie, corresponding to the Funan dynasty (1st-6th century CE), presently recognised as the An-Giang province, which was the key cultural site in the Mekong Valley of Southern Vietnam; secondly, the Champa dynasty (2nd-13th century CE) occupying the narrow coastland of the Central and Southern Vietnam. It is notable that the Indian influence had a deep-seated influence on these two Indianised kingdoms, while the Northern parts of Vietnam remained under the sway of Chinese influence and their practices differed from the Southern and Central regions. Similar to other princely states of the early period, the historicity of both the kingdoms appear to be fragmentary and uncertain due to lack of consistent historical records as record-keeping was not a common practice prior to the introduction of

Sanskrit. Therefore, the ancient Chinese official tributaries of the Han and Tang dynasties and travelogues of Chinese monks, like – Xuanzang and Yijing, are looked upon as important ancient records for reconstruction of the past, while bringing them together with the archaeological and art historical evidence.

Based on the epigraphic and archaeological findings, sculptural vestiges and researchers of the modern day French archaeologists and scholars of this field, it has been corroborated that Buddhism was introduced in Vietnam in the later first millennium but gained a stronghold in these regions during different periods. As suggested by Le Thi Lien, 'the Buddhist icons occupied a dominant position in the Buddhist art of Southern Vietnam until about the seventh or eighth century, when a few sculptures of the bodhisattvas Maitreya, Avalokitesvara, and Lokeshvara began to appear'. (Le Thi Lien: Lost Kingdoms, New York, 119). Later, Buddhism became the state religion in the last quarter of the ninth century with the establishment of the famous monastic complex at Duong Duong, Quang Nam province, built by Indravarman II, the ruler of the Indrapura dynasty of Champa. Simultaneously, Buddhism continued to prevail in the Chinese dominated provinces of Northern Vietnam, but its philosophical affiliation reflected a Sino-centric standpoint as determined by the evolution of different sects which represented an admixture of Zen Buddhism, Taoism and Confucianism with the local belief patterns while showing trails of Indianised Mahayana sect. With regard to the basic nature, laws and philosophy of Buddhism unanimously remained the same throughout the region; indeed, the practices followed in Champa and Mekong Delta show stronger affiliation to the Gupta and Pala period as proved by the visual and inscriptional vestiges.

Indeed, the important role of China in the spread of Buddhism cannot be overlooked; however, the theories which propose that Buddhism first reached China from India, and from there it transferred to Vietnam has been ruled out by examination of the routes, through which Indian migrants reached Vietnam. (Chi, Dinh Minh, 2008: 13). Various principalities of Vietnam were extensively connected to different parts of India through overseas land-routes and oceanic routes interconnecting with river ports. For example: Indian traders from Southern India sailed on quite small boats to cross the narrow waterway between the Andaman and Nicobar Islands or one between Aceh and Nicobars a little further to the South. (Chi, Dinh Minh, 2008: 12). The traders setting off to Central India could go by Three

Pagoda Pass and sail along the Kamburi River to the Gulf of Thailand. There was another land route which connected Moulmein with Tak Rahaeng on the Mae Nam Wang, linking with the Mekong River, crossing Korat plateau. (Chi, Dinh Minh, 2008: 12) Indian monks might have come to Laos by this route and from there crossed the Troung Son ranges to Vietnam's Than Hoa or Nghe An Provinces. (Chi, Dinh Minh, 2008: 13) There was another route connecting India with Southern China, crossing Assam, Myanmar and Yunnan province in the further north. (Chi, Dinh Minh, 2008: 13)

Thereby, Vietnam witnessed the heydays of flourishing artistic traditions as a result of varied socio-political, religious and cultural milieu, embracing inhabitants of multi-ethnic groups, both autochthones and migrated, with independent and shared cultural identities, which practiced Hinduism, different sects of Buddhism – Hinayana, Mahayana, Tantric and Zen, and also local belief systems. This kind of syncretism led to the development of unique artistic style and iconographic forms of both Hindu and Buddhist deities, where the Shaivite faith had a great impact on the Buddhist rituals and practices. Indian art served as a major source of inspiration for the artistic growth and added impetus to the wave of cultural development. With the inflow of Indian religious systems and their philosophical underpinnings, the iconographic forms of the deities of Buddhist pantheon also made their way to Vietnam and became manifested in the artistic traditions of the Indianised polities of Vietnam, as stated earlier. The growing popularity of the cultic icons associated with the Saviour cults, identified with Bodhisattva Avalokitesvara and goddess Tara as the manifestations of Universal Compassion and the deified form of the foundational Mahayana text, Prajnaparamita, in form of a female divinity as embodiment of supreme wisdom, indicated the long and efflorescent tradition of Mahayana Buddhism in this region. These goddesses originated in India and their worship became extremely popular during the early medieval period when the *prajna* centric discourse gained pre-eminence in the Buddhist centres of Eastern and Western India. The same tradition was also followed in Southeast Asian spheres, where the deities of the Saviour cult were widely venerated for saving the laity from the eight great perils and for ensuring safety to the merchants and monks during their seafaring voyages; while the Prajnaparamita attained the higher rank of female Buddha, representing the Dharma, one of the Three Jewels of Buddhism.

This paper aims to shed light on the subject of Buddhist female iconography, with reference to the art of ancient Vietnam, by taking up an exploratory approach of examining the devotional imageries of Buddhist female divinities and also the depictions of female royalty, while supporting the arguments and interpretations through epigraphic, textual and parallel visual data. Firstly, in order to understand the early incoming influence of *Prajnaparamita* discourse in Vietnam, the spread of Buddhism from India to Vietnam and the flourishing Buddhist activities, beginning from the early Common Era to the early medieval period, in the vassal states of the Chinese regime in Vietnam and also Indrapura dynasty at Duong Duong and Oc Eo culture will be outlined. These ruling entities grew to power in different economic and cultural milieus, due to their distinct ethnicity, identities and local traditions, and moreover, they were political enemies, involved in power confrontations as recorded in the North Vietnamese and Chinese chronicles. An analysis of Buddhist Sanskrit inscriptions and textual sources, suggestive of the diffusion of the Mahayanic cult of Buddhist goddesses and the role of royal patronage in the promotion of the Buddhist practices will also be emphasised in the study. Secondly, a descriptive analysis of the iconographic forms of Tara and Prajnaparamita represented in the plastic art of Cham art, while tracing their cross-cultural linkages with Indian art will be shown.

Spread of Mahayana Buddhism: Early Interactions of the Ancient Vietnam with India and the Role of Patronage

The foundation of Mahayana Buddhism was laid with the introduction of the Prajnaparamita *Sutra* (Perfection of Wisdom). The Prajnaparamita discourse, written in Sanskrit, which made its appearance in South India, reached far-fetched lands of East and Southeast Asia, as its influence was enduring and wide. The Tibetan textual records state that the Prajnaparamita *sutra* was expounded and resuscitated by Nagarjuna, a renowned Buddhist scholar of South India from 2nd century CE, who is also greatly credited for professing the Madhyamika sect. The philosophical ideas of the text had a deep-seated influence on Vietnamese Buddhism, which could be seen in the belief patterns of the Chinese dominated provinces of the North and the polities of the South and Central Vietnam.

Vietnamese records accord that the Mahayana Buddhism disseminated directly from India to Vietnam and also through Champa and Indonesia by Indian monks, who left their deep impression on the society. (Chi, Dinh

Minh, 2008: 14) The *Astasahasrika Prajnaparamita Sutra*, the oldest text of the Prajnaparamita compendium, probably came to Vietnam directly from India, but not from China, long before it was translated into Chinese. There are archaeological and textual records in support of this contention. For example: Scholars have identified that at the beginning of the third century CE, the *Astasahasrika sutra* was translated by Khoung Tang Hoi and was taught in the Buddhist monasteries at Giao Chua. (Chi, Dinh Minh, 2008: 14) Though the first translation of the text was done by Lokasema during the Han dynasty by the end of the second century CE, the translation by Khoung Tang Hoi gained more importance in Vietnam, who later translated it in Chinese as well. Giao Chua became recognised as an important Buddhist site as early as second century CE, situated on the southern route to India (Chi, Dinh Minh, 2008: 19). Luy Lau, the Buddhist centre at Giao Chua was of utmost importance in Northern Vietnam, owing to its important geographical, political and economic position at that time. It was venerated as a storehouse of sutras by monks, who used to deposit the texts, garnered during their course of the journey (Chi, Dinh Minh, 2008: 14). As stated in the Vietnamese text, entitled Thien Uyen Tap Anh Ngu Luc (compiled from the late eleventh to the early thirteen century), Luy Lau flourished long ago before the establishment of Buddhism in Southern China, probably in the Zhao Tuo's reign (BC 179) (Chi, Dinh Minh, 2008: 19). This site was visited by two Indian Buddhist monks – Mahajivaka and Kalacarya, which was then under the governance of Emperor's Lingdi's reign in the Han dynasty (168-189 AD). According to another Vietnamese text, titled *Co Chau Phap Van Phat Ban Hanh Ngu Luc*, upon arrival to Giao Chua, Mahajivaka departed shortly while Kalacarya decided to stay. A number of Vietnamese and Chinese texts present interesting facts about the preaching activities and the travels of these two Indian monks. (Chi, Dinh Minh, 2008: 27)

Another text of the Perfection of Wisdom literature, known as the *Vajracchedika* (3,000) or the Diamond Sutra, which gained special importance in the Far East, marked its pre-eminence in the Vietnamese Buddhist society. The philosophical ideology was assimilated in the Zen literature of the two earliest sects, which were developed by the Zen Masters, an Indian monk of Vinitaruci of 580 CE and later by a Chinese monk Wu Yantong of 820 CE (Vo Ngon Thon in Vietnamese) (Chi, Dinh Minh, 2008: 15). With the growing interest in Buddhism, the Vietnamese monks, like the Indian Buddhist missionaries who set out on overland journeys and voyages to distant lands, also travelled to India, in search of knowledge and learning the true essence of Buddhist practices by the society who followed them in its native state.

Apart from the transmission of textual sources, it is important to note that similar to the Northern Vietnam provinces, the Indianised states of Vietnam also maintained diplomatic and trade relations with Indian and Chinese courts. The early vestiges of the Mahayana sect are traceable from the Chinese records, epigraphic sources and also from few sculptural findings that indicate that the existence of Buddhist practices in the Indianised regions as early as seventh century (Chutiwongs, Nanadana, 2008:289). While examining the Buddhist art of the Oc Eo culture of 7th-8th century, it is observed that a large number of sculptures were created at the major Buddhist archaeological sites: Go Cao Su and Long An. These imageries are clearly influenced by the art of western India in the Gupta period, Amravati school and also the Eastern Indian School of art (Lien, Thi Le. 2014: 119). In addition, several Buddhist imageries and bronzes were imported from the Han and Wei periods of China along with the trade goods (Hall, Kenneth, R, 2011: 57). The Buddhist sculptures from these regions represent mainly Buddha and Bodhisattvas and rarely any image of Tara or Prajnaparamita have been seen so far. However, the sites have yielded many images of Uma which prove the existence of the Shakta cult. This region was inhabited by settlers of Mon-Khmer speaking groups, who were trading with the merchants of the northwestern and Gangetic basin as proved by the archaeological evidence, coinages and seals, representing Bengali scripts. (Hall, Kenneth, R, 2011: 58).

Apparently, Champa was one of the most powerful Hinduised dynasties of Vietnam, colonised by the ethnic group, known as Chams, who displaced the autochthonous Mon-Khmer speaking tribes and formed the statehood in the coastal stretch of the country. Scholars have suggested that the Champs was an Austronesian (Malay speaking) linguistic group, which seem to have developed in the Taiwan region between the fifth and the third millennium BCE, and later by the beginning of first millennium BCE, they migrated to the insular and mainland regions of Southeast Asia (Tingley, Nancy, 2010: 8-9). They grew in power over the narrow coastal stretch of the central and southern region of present-day Vietnam and established their dominion from Quang Tri province in the north to Binh Thuan province in the south and the city of Phan Rang. Their administrative framework comprised of multi-centred political units or vassal states which shared allegiance to the centralised government, as commonly seen in other Southeast Asian states. Cham rulers erected brick citadels and religious sanctuaries on an upland at the river front, thereby declaring their political supremacy and religious underpinnings. The centralised power underwent continuous relocation, with the advent of each new dynasty, resulting in geographical shifting of the political and religious seats.

Based on the architectural and epigraphic evidence, recent studies have demonstrated that the Cham activity in Vietnam was centred at three principal zones, identified as hubs of commerce and exchange. Maritime trade was the chief source of income for the Cham, unlike the agrarian culture followed by other parts of Vietnam (Tingley, Nancy, 2010: 10). These were: firstly, the Quang Nam Province at the Thu Bon River Valley, where all the major Hindu and Buddhist sites are located, like – My Son, Tra Kieu and Indrapura, the later capital at Dong Doung; secondly, Nha Trang at Khanh Hoa province comprising the famous Hindu site, Po Nagar temple complex; and thirdly, Phan Rang in Nih Thuan Province. (Guy, John, 2014: 17).

Apparently, the early interactions of the Champa territory with India started during a very early period that could be gleaned from the sculptural vestiges and epigraphic records which testify the deep-seated influence of Indian tradition and its role in the formation of the Champa kingdom. The name Champa itself connotes its Indianised inclinations, as an important city of ancient Bengal also shared the same name, which is located near the city-port of Tamralipti, a major trade centre of the ancient times, which not only connected the internal land routes but it promoted oceanic trade (Guy, John, 2014: 17). Scholars have corroborated that 'one of the earliest applications of the name Champa to coastal Vietnam is in the hagiography of the Kashmiri monk Gunavarman, visiting the kingdom en route to China before 431 aboard a Hindu merchant's vessel sailing from Java' (Guy, John, 2014: 17).

Champa was founded by a Hindu King Sri Mara, alias Kui Lien, about second century CE in Annam or present-day Vietnam. Prior to the sixth century CE, the kingdom was designated as Lin-Yi, a term which invariably appears in the Chinese records until 756-77 CE, while later it was renamed as Huan Wang (Le Bonheur, A. 1998: 256). By the advent of the seventh century, the kingdom emerged a confederate state that continued to flourish as one of the mightiest political domains in the map of mainland Southeast Asia until its final dissolution in the late-fifteen century. By this time, the Hinduised appellation 'Champa' appeared for the first time in the epigraphic records inscribed in Sanskrit dating back to the seventh century, including: an inscription from My Son E6 temple at Quang Nam, dated to 658 CE, issued during the reign of Prakashadharma and another named as Kdei Ang inscription, dated to 668 CE, that was found in Cambodia make reference of the Champa kingdom for the first time (Hubert, Jean Francois. 2005: 18). This kind of transformation of the identity of a nation brings to light the idea of integration of two distinct cultural and ethnic races, the Sinicised Annamese and the Austronesian Cham people, which eventually gave way to Indianisation in Champa that became reflected in their artistic, religious and cultural practices.

One of the earliest inscriptions, the Vo Canh Rock inscription found at Khanh Hoa, the ancient Kauthara, dating between the second half of the third century CE, outline the Indianised origin of Champa (Majumdar, R.C. 2008: 77-88). It delineates the ancestry of the King Sri Mara and his filial relationship with the Indian king of the Coromandel coast (Le Bonheur, A. 1998: 257-258). In the meanwhile, by last quarter of the ninth century, Dong Doung figured in the history of Champa as the chief stronghold of Buddhism and a thriving centre of political power and cultural activities. It is located approximately twenty-two kilometres south-east of the Hindu temple sanctuary of My Son in Central Vietnam on the coast of South China. The artistic and religious developments at Dong Doung coincided with the rise of Indrapura as the capital of Champa. During this period, the newly formed dynasty, known as Bhrigu or Indrapura dynasty, reigned over the ancient province of Amravati, another name for present-day Quang Nam or Da Nang district. Buddhism existed in the Champa long before the rise of the Indrapura dynasty but remained subordinate to Shaivism. However, by this time, Buddhism attained a paramount seat in Champa, as the rulers of the Indrapura dynasty became devout followers of Mahayana Buddhism, despite their strong Shaivite deposition. They claimed their origin from the mythical personages Bhrigu and Uroja, regarded as direct descendants and earthly manifestations of Mahadeva (Majumdar, R.C.2008: 28). Besides, the kings persistently revered and made donations to the tutelary *linga* Bhadreshvara/ Shambhubhadeshvara as a part of the royal tradition and many images of Siva were also installed along with the Buddhist deities. However, these Buddhist kings also assumed titles, named after the Buddhist deities also suggestive of pervading influence of the idea of divine kingship in Champa. King Indravarman II, the founder of the Duong Duong Mahavihara, was bestowed with two titles: Paramabuddhaloka as his posthumous name and the other was Lakshmindralokeshvara, named after the patron deity of the state (Chutiwongs, Nanadana, 2008:291). Besides, their strong Buddhist affiliation could be established from their liberal patronage and benefactions made for the welfare of the Buddhist community as gleaned from the inscriptional records and archaeological findings. They established huge monastic complexes, dedicated to Avalokiteshvara or Lokanatha, commemorating Buddhism as the state religion.

The establishment of the famous monastic complex at Duong Duong, built in the vicinity of the Indrapura, by Indravarman II marked the heydays of Buddhism at Champa. The religious complex at Dong Doung stood as the state citadel, a fortified centre of massive size with bastions and protected walls, holding an influential position in the statecraft, pedagogical and artistic activities, and also the reservoir of the Buddhist faith and literature. All the major Buddhist activities were centred at Duong Duong Mahavihara, indicated by the epigraphic evidence that proclaims its celebrated position as the principal sanctuary of the Indrapura dynasty. From a stele inscription discovered at the site, it is unveiled that around 875 A.D., King Indravarman II consecrated a huge Buddhist complex or Mahavihara comprising of both *caitya* and *vihara* at Indrapura, named 'Sri Lakshmindralokeshvara founded for the usage of the Sangha and for the propagation of the Dharma' (Majumdar, R.C., 2008: 77-88). There is also a mention of installation of an image of Lokeshvara by the king in person, to propagate the idea of compassion and to bring about the deliverance of the laymen (Le Bonheur, A. 1998: 264). This tradition of the building of Buddhist monasteries was initiated by his father Bhadravarman who consecrated a monastery called Pramuditalokesvara, in honour of his advisor, a Bhikshu named Nagapushpa (Chutiwongs, Nanadana, 2008:291). Later this royal foundation was upheld by his successor, Indravarman II, who consecrated an image of Lokanatha in 902 CE as inscribed in the stele of An Thai, Quang Nam (Chutiwongs, Nanadana, 2008:291).

The later rulers were mainly supporters of Shaivite cult, but they continued to commission monasteries in the nearby regions based on the prototype of the Duong Duong Mahavihara. Structural remnants and abundant of Buddhist sculptures have been discovered at Dai-hu'u, MiÞ-duc and Thu-thu' (Chutiwongs, Nanadana, 2008:292).

The Duong Duong Mahavihara stood the test of time and continued to flourish even after the decline of Indrapura dynasty during the tenth century. It's grandiose scale and unique architectural plan, marked with imposing gateways, massive altars, large cruciform pillars and profusely decorated shrine altars and tall brick *stupas* are of remarkable artistic and historical significance. The site has yielded a plethora of stone sculptures and also bronzes, displaying narratives scenes from Buddha's life, seated and standing images of Buddha, monks and guardian figures and also various iconographic forms of Buddhist deities. The architectural and sculptural style bespeak of a distinctive artistic tradition developed from the amalgamation of indigenous and foreign influences. Besides, the dominant impact of Chinese art and Dvaravati school of Thailand, the Eastern Indian art also played a dominant role in the iconographic development of Duong Doung. The stylistic features developed during this period display typical and standardised characteristics, such as the scholars identified this artistic idiom as a school of art, which became invariably termed as Duong Duong style.

However, at present most of the archaeological sites in Vietnam are in complete ruins, decimated due to political dissension and wars in the later period. The architectural splendour of the sanctuaries has been re-conjectured based on the archaeological studies conducted by the team of archaeologists of the French organisation *Ecole Francaise d'Extreme-Orient* (EFEO) such as- Parmentier and Boisselier, Pelliot, Louis Malleret etc. These scholars conducted extensive archaeological excavations in the early twentieth century in Vietnam and other parts of Southeast Asia and reproduced archaeological findings, conjectural drawings of the plans of the monuments, including: architectural configuration, schematic and iconographic organisation of sculptures etc. Their studies have greatly contributed to unfolding the dynamic part of the Cham kingdom and the Funan period and have helped to bring to light the artistic and architectural glory of the ancient art of Vietnam.

Interestingly, the sculptures of Duong Duong reveal an important aspect which defines the early artistic interactions of Champa with Eastern India, followed by assimilation of belief patterns and cultural practices. Particularly, the presence of visual representations of Buddhist goddess, such as – Tara and Prajnaparamita, enunciate the dominant influence of Vajrayanic practices which must be borrowed from Eastern India. During the early medieval period, Eastern India became the cradle land of Tantric Buddhism from where it travelled to distant lands of South and Southeast Asia. From the textual and epigraphic records, we learn that the two Eastern Indian dynasties – Bhaumakaras (736-940 C.E.) and the Palas (750-1200 C.E.) shared strong political, religious and cultural contacts with different kingdoms of Southeast Asia. For instance, the Kalasan and Kelurak inscriptions prove the active role of Bengal in colonial enterprises and maritime activities in Southeast Asia. Also, the Old Javanese text, *Nagarakrtagama* give reference of incoming of large people from Bengal. Besides, Buddhist scholars from North and East India, like Subhakarasinha, Vajrabodhi, Amoghavajra and Atisha Dipankara travelled to China and Southeast Asia. The preeminence of Buddhism during the Indrapura dynasty is coeval with the efflorescence of Vajrayana Buddhism in Eastern India. Vajrayana Buddhism was also practiced at Duong Duong as revealed by a stele inscription of An Thai, dated to 902 CE, which shed light on the concept of the emptiness, the quintessential essence of Vajrayana, recording the concepts of *trikhala* and *trimala* developed in Java in the early 10th century CE in a text called *Sang Hyang Kamahayanikan* (Le Bonheur, A. 1998: 265). The Cam Nhan Bieu inscription of the tenth century proves that the Champa rulers were sending diplomatic missions to Java in order to learn Vajrayana Buddhism and undertook building activities on Javanese philosophical models. The same inscription records that the king built a vihara, dedicated to Vriddhalokeshvara, suggesting the name of the deity Avalokitesvara was combined with the name of the ruler's grandmother *pu lyang* Vriddhakula. This family came from Vishnupura, near the village known today as Nhan Bieu in Quang Tri province. Many dedicatory Buddhist inscriptions have found from the later period and one of the last Cham inscriptions datable to the fifteenth century indicates the culmination of the Hindu-Buddhist period in Champa (Tingley, Nancy, 2010: 192).

Imageries of Female: Divine and Royal

In Buddhism, the concept of female pantheon marked its emergence with the conceptualisation and codification of the *prajna* centric discourse (The Perfection of Wisdom) and infusion of Tantric elements. The principle of *prajna* or transcendental wisdom served as the bedrock of the genesis of female deities in the Buddhist tradition, which had markedly evolved in course of time. The role and eminence of this idea envisaged in the Mahayana and

Vajaryana phases distinguished from the realisation of the non-Mahayanist schools, the Theravadins. With the doctrinal transition, the religious practices and the philosophical framework also markedly underwent a revolutionary change. This radical shift culminated with the promotion of polytheistic belief system and advanced ritualistic practices of a higher esoteric order, involving worshipping of idols of various Buddhist deities and cosmic *mandalas*. The feminine principle became extolled as a manifestation of divine energy that played a vital role in the attainment of final emancipation. This growing eminence of female principle brought changes in the Buddhist soteriological patterns and belief patterns while promoting the development of a realm of Buddhist goddesses of variegated divine aspects. The cult of Buddhist goddesses also drew inspirations from the parallel Brahamanic Shaiva and Shakta movements by absorbing of iconographic and cultural elements. The mutual coexistence of two faiths in Eastern India largely contributed in the development of the cult and its further expansion. A similar kind of cultural and religious milieu could be sighted in most of the Southeast Asian kingdoms, including Champa, Khmer and Java, where Shaivism served as a predominant faith and Buddhism was introduced in a later period, which eventually led to religious syncretism visualised in the iconographic forms of the goddesses.

The pivotal role of Eastern Indian dynasties in the elaboration and promotion of this Buddhist female pantheon and its dispersal to different parts of South and Southeast Asia has been established on the basis of epigraphic and archaeological evidence. They largely patronized the cult of Buddhist goddesses, by putting special emphasis particularly on the worship of goddess Tara and Prajnaparamita. The same religious wave also travelled to Champa as well. Interestingly, in Eastern Indian art, manifold forms of a variety of goddesses, both peaceful and wrathful forms, are widely represented, however, in Cham art, like other Southeast Asian traditions, mainly forms of Tara and Prajnaparamita gained utmost importance in the artistic and religious practices. Both these female deities attained a distinctive rank in the political and religious spheres of both the cultural domains and had been widely illustrated in artistic and literary sources.

Prajnaparamita originated from the metaphysical concept of transcendental wisdom, manifested in the *Prajnaparamitasutras* (Perfection of Wisdom). The sacred Mahayana text was recognised as a 'cult object' and it ultimately became deified in form of a female deity called Prajnaparamita. She became the supreme embodiment of motherhood, femaleness and transcendental wisdom as propounded in the discourse. On the other hand, Tara held an exalted rank as the personification of infinite maternal compassion, deliverance and liberating wisdom. Tara absorbed the abilities of Avalokiteshvara and was featured as his female counterpart. Thereby, she became capable of instructing her devotees to achieve the salvation or the final state of Buddhahood. In Champa, unlike other Southeast Asian traditions where Prajnaparamita attained an elevated rank over Tara, here, the latter continued to retain a superior position parallel to Eastern Indian tradition. The allusion is supported by the supreme rank of Avalokiteshvara, who was the patron deity of the Duong Duong monastery. Tara became recognised as the central figure of gynocentric thoughts and ideology in Buddhist sphere, while Prajnaparamita represented the quintessential essence of Mahayana Buddhism and the Buddhist Dharma. With regard to the iconography of the goddesses, there are two important medieval period texts, the *Sadhanamala* and the *Nispannayogavali*, which present elaborated eulogies in their honour and provide elaborate iconographic descriptions of various forms of the goddesses. Interestingly, the iconographic trends followed in Cham artistic traditions derived their inspiration from Eastern Indian art and textual sources and later developed their unique artistic idiom.

From the Duong Duong period, there are only limited representations of Prajnaparamita and Tara which have been found so far. They are of prime importance while tracing the dissemination and popularity of the cult of goddesses in Southeast Asian traditions in entirety. The rendition of the sculptures displays uniformity and standardized features, typical to the Duong Duong style. The plastic treatment of the figural forms follows the defined norms of idealized feminine beauty. Despite the strict frontal pose and austere demeanour, the figures exhibit refined voluptuousness, marked by rotund breasts, thin attenuated waist and the three folds of flesh on the belly which are clearly marked by incised lines. Their appearance displays a fine blend between the profound, majestic nature and the maternal and fecund aspects of the female hood. Indeed, the bodily forms are suffused with the inherent spirituality, thus, signifying their supramundane nature. The physiognomic details are almost identical, portraying unvarying delicately carved features, such as thickly arched eyebrows delineated in a continuous line, large rhomboid shaped and slightly slanting eyes, where pupils and upper eyelids are sharply defined, representing a fixed and an inward-looking gaze. The faces are ovoid shaped, dominated by a well-defined nose with flared nostrils and fleshy chin.

The mouth with full lips is slightly parted, thereby the upturned corners of the mouth give the goddesses a benign smiling expression, adding a lively spirit to the image. The faces display a restrained and detached expression.

Interestingly, the Buddhist goddesses from this period started to be represented in an austere manner, bereft of any kind of embellishments, uncommon to the Eastern Indian art, in which the deities are bedecked with heavy ornaments and stylized headdresses. However, it is likely that the influences are drawn from the artistic specimens of the Late Anuraddha period of Sri Lanka, which belong to the tenth century. This allusion can be supported from the fact that one of the earliest representations of Prajnaparamita in Southeast Asia, which has been found at peninsular Thailand was probably transported from Sri Lanka via trade and religious missionaries, as determined by the stylistic features, corresponding to the art of Polonnaruwa period (Guy, John, 2014: 37, pl. 8) This establishes the parallel impact of Sri Lankan art information on Champa iconography. Here also the goddesses have distended and unadorned earlobes, a typical feature only seen in the Buddhist female deities of the Duong Duong period. Besides, their matted coiffures are arranged in form of a tall *jatamukuta*, with tightly combed hair knotted at the top with tresses are shown freely falling at the back. Sometimes, they are shown wearing thin diadems or fillets fastened around her forehead, such that braided locks run parallel to their temple and ears. This is a unique kind of coiffure only seen in the Duong Duong sculptures. The coiffures are generally adorned with the effigy of the spiritual sire, mostly Amitabha is depicted, whereas in certain cases the image is also absent. Besides, the goddesses are attired in a long voluminous lower garment arranged in a form of a double layered skirt, fashioned in a uniform style. This garment is marked with parallel pleats and tucked around the waist. The plastic treatment of the body is smooth and polished; the transition from bare flesh to the rich linear patterning of the garment is well-balanced.

Visual Representations of Tara

The Buddhist text *Sadhanamala* prescribes the eleven forms of Tara, which bear the *utpala* as an attribute and have been prescribed the sacred Tara-mantra (*Om Tare tuttare ture Svaha*). Sculptures from Eastern Indian art schools display a variety of forms of goddess Tara. However, from the Duong Duong phase, the images of Tara are mostly two-armed shown holding lotuses in both her extended arms, poised with *vitarkamudra* (gesture of argumentation).

Scholars have identified it as *vitarka/vyakhyanamudra* (gesture of argumentation), a gesture that was relatively popular in Dvaravati-Mon sculptures and also seen in the Sri-Lankan bronzes of the contemporaneous period (Guillon, Emmanuel, 2001: 102). Her forehead has a prominent third eye, connoting her omniscient nature. It is noteworthy that the goddess is primarily distinguished from the Hindu goddess Lakshmi, due to the presence of the effigy of her spiritual sire Amitabha, shown seated in *vajraparyanaka-asana* displaying *dhyana mudra*. Also, the Hindu goddess is never shown exhibiting the third eye, due to her Vaishnavite affiliation.

One of the most outstanding images of Tara was discovered in 1978 from the site of Duong Duong Mahavihara is presently housed in the Da Nang Museum, Vietnam (Pl. 1). This free-standing almost life-size bronze figure displays the goddess standing in a strict frontal pose with double upraised hands, displaying *katakamudra*, probably once shown clasping *utpala*. Her well-modelled fingers though now mostly effaced show traces of fragmented portion of the *utpala* stalk in both hands. Her face is angular and oblong in shape with a third eye on her broad forehead, which was once studded with jewels. Her forehead is marked with a sharp ridge of arched eyebrows delineated as a continuous curved line. Also, she wears a prominent diadem fastened around her forehead. There is an unprecedented sense of calmness and a faint smile visible on the face. She wears a long high-waist ankle length robe with parallel pleats as visible from the lower end, which has been partially swathed with a wide diaphanous robe tucked around the waist. The outer robe consists a wide plain border with incised lines, similarly, parallel lines imply a refined plastic treatment.

(A) Another standing of Tara, carved in stone, is housed in the Museìe Guimet, Paris (pl. 2). The basic iconography remains similar and the figure display features typical to Duong Duong style. The goddess is shown holding an elongated object, parts of which are now missing. Scholars have identified it as a staff, which is uncommonly seen in association with Tara, since the object connotes Vaishnavite affiliation (Guillon, Emmanuel, 2001: 85). However, a close observation reveals that the upper portion of the attribute resembles a lotus bud and the lower portion might have been representing the stalk, which also provided structural support to the stone image. This kind of rendition of objects is rare and can be traced in the early Hindu sculptures of Khmer and central Thailand. Besides, two similar types of images of Tara datable to this period have been found from different sites. One such image, though her hands are partly broken have been presently housed in the Museìe Guimet, Paris (pl. 3). Another image is presently housed in the Da Nang Museum, Vietnam, which was discovered from the south shrine of the Buddhist site of Dai Huu (Quang Binh) excavated in 1922 and 1925 (Guillon, Emmanuel, 2001: 25).

(B) Scholars have proposed that the stylistic features of these images display a fusion of Chinese and indigenous style and also influences of Dvaravati style are pronounced. But through analysis of textual sources and comparative study of images in the context of Indian art, it can be proposed that the iconography is deeply grounded in the textual sources of Eastern India and drew influences from Indian art. Similar kind of images of Tara holding lotus stalk has been very popular in the plastic art of Eastern India art from the beginning of the early medieval period. This form of Tara is generally termed Arya Tara, a green manifestation of Tara, whose right-hand displays the *varadamudra* and the left hold the *utpala*. However, here, little variation is observed in the posture of the hands. One of the best-preserved metal icons representing two-armed Arya Tara, attributable to the first half of the eighth century CE, comes from Nalanda, site no.8, which is now in the collection of the National Museum, New Delhi (pl. 4). The goddess is shown standing in *samabhanga* upon a lotus pedestal, with her extended right hand displaying the *varadamudra* and her left hand partly raised is clutching the long stem of another lotus that sinuously rises from the pedestal. The upper half of the body is draped in an upper garment *(uttariya)* that covers her breasts and falls down over her left shoulder, extending to the level of the thighs. The goddess is heavily bejewelled and her hair is knotted at the top into a sizeable bun and is decorated with an ornamental diadem. Her body is framed with an effulgent halo. The sculptor has astutely used the ornamentation in an intricate, fine and balanced manner.

(C) Besides, a standing stone image of a goddess belonging to the same period, presently housed in the Art Institute of Chicago, which is wrongly labelled as Uma, probably displays one of the green forms of Tara, known as Dhanada Tara (Pl. 5). The four-armed goddess exhibits the characteristic features of the Dhanada Tara, who is worshipped as the bestower of riches and wealth. Her lower right hand in *abhayamudra* and upper right hand holding the *akshamala*, while her upper left-hand carry the lotus stalk, while the lower left hand perhaps once held the book, indicated by the hand gesture and also the remnants of the object. She has a third eye on her head. Her matted locks, arranged in a form of *jatamukuta* are decorated with an elaborate multi-stringed diadem framing her forehead. The diaphanous lower garment worn by the deity displays exquisite foliate patterns, intricately carved on the central pleat, while the schematic folds relieve the surface of the drape. Besides, the identity of the goddess has been established based on two factors: firstly, the iconography of the Duong Duong image almost conforms to the description given in the *Sadhanamala* (*sadhana* no.107). Secondly, comparable images of Dhanada Tara have been discovered from Nalanda belonging to the Pala period, which is currently displayed at Nalanda Museum. One of the bronze icons, which is in a better state of preservation, display similar iconographic configuration of the attributes is similar and also the effigy of Amitabha on the headdress is absent in both the representations (Pl. 6). The Pala image is ascribable to the eight century, determined by the stylistic features of the figure and the typical treatment of the oval halo, which is with flames at intervals and a stick with flowers on top and is joined with the pedestal.

Visual Forms of Prajnaparamita

The *Sadhanamala* prescribes nine s*adhana* (nos. 151-59) dedicated to the procedure of the worship of Prajnaparamita, while a hymn (no. 160) is devoted to her praises (Donaldson, Thomas Eugene. Vol.1, 2001: 276). Among these, only one s*adhana* (nos. 156) describes the four-armed and golden-hued form of the goddess, while the other eight describing her two-armed form. The four-armed form also appears in other Tantric texts, recording four other iconographic prescriptions – one form appears in the *Dharamadhatuvagishvara mandala* of the *Nispannayogavali,* where is lauded as one the twelve perfection deities and another three from the *Dharmakosha-samgraha,* in which one of the explanations refer to a white-hued form of the deity (Donaldson, Thomas Eugene. Vol. 1, 2001: 277-280).

Like Tara, the images of Prajnaparamita from the Duong Duong period also display standardised iconography, such as – the goddess is two-armed, holding a lotus and a manuscript in her proper left hand and proper right hand respectively. She bears an effigy of Amitabha on her matted headdress and has a third eye or a tuft of hair marked on the forehead. The images display simplistic renditions of forms and minimal ornamentation. The attributes bear similarities with the iconographic convention followed in Khmer art, but their artistic treatment is indigenous in nature. An image of two-armed Prajnaparamita from Duong Duong site is presently housed in the Museìe Guimet, Paris (Pl.7). She is shown standing in a strict frontal posture on a rectangular pedestal, with both her pendant hands carrying attributes – a lotus in the proper right hand and probably a manuscript in the left respectively. The effigy of the spiritual sire, Amitabha, is also discernible on her crowned coiffure. She is dressed in a sarong with vertical folds; her breasts are heavy and rounded. Another image of the goddess from the same period was discovered in the village of Phu Nhan in Quang Ngai province, presently housed in the Da Nang Museum. (Pl.8)

However, in Eastern Indian sculptures, standing images of Prajnaparamita is not common, whereas she is usually shown seated cross-legged with her two principal hands in the conventional *dharmachakra mudra* symbolizing the first sermon. She holds a rosary and a manuscript in her right and left rear hands respectively. Again the sacred book is shown supported on a lotus, rising from the pedestal on her left side. (Pl.9) Besides, imageries have been also found from Odisha from the Bhaumakara region, datable between 9th to 10th century, in which the iconography is more simplified. Rather shown in a teaching gesture, the goddess is shown seated with one leg pendant and another resting on the pedestal, similar to the rendition of Tara images. However, her identity is determined by the manuscript emblem, shown resting on the lotus, which is clasped in her proper left hand, while her right hand is in the boon-bestowing pose. (Pl.10)

Visual Forms of Royal Female Personages

From the ruins of the Duong Duong monastery, two large pedestals have been discovered – first, high altar of the main shrine; and second, the pedestal of the vihara (Pls. 11, 12). These pedestals are the highest landmarks of the Duong Duong art and are presently housed in the Da Nang Museum, splendidly carved with narrative panels of carved reliefs depicting various life-episodes of the historical Buddha. In addition, the relief panels display varied images of female royal personages. According to Parmentier's drawings and studies (Inventaire), the assembly hall or vihara of the Dong Doung monastery was in a form of a large hypostyle hall centrally placed in a long courtyard preceding the central shrine. The vihara was entered by two brick *gopuras* serving as the entrance, which was flanked by two *stupas* and protected by two *dvarapalas*. The carved monumental altar was located at western end of the hall. Actually, the altars were intended to support monumental statues of Buddha represented sitting with pendant legs. The pedestals originally comprised several levels of successive substructures with sculpted mouldings and projections, which were accessed by staircases on all three sides.

The large altar of the shrine exhibit recurring depictions of the female personages in relation to the life stories of Buddha, which are identified as Queen Maya, Mahaprajapati Gautami and Yashodhara. While the narrative horizontal friezes of the *vihara* pedestal represent almost identical figural representations of princely figures and mythical figures. Royal couples engaged in a dalliance are depicted, in which the prince is shown sitting in royal ease posture on the left side and two royal females are shown seated in a relaxed pose, which is also sometimes shown holding lotus flowers or playing musical instruments.

These panels are divided by vermiculated borders into small rectangular registers carved with princely figures and are flanked by rampant lion registers. The facial expressions of the figures are pensive and poised, at times with a fleeting smile. Heavy ornaments and elaborate headdresses indicate the dignified status of the figures. They wear the common type of triple-lobed diadem decorated with lotus leaf shaped fleuron motifs, heavy dangling ear ornaments and are clad in patterned lower garment or sarong. The physiology and physiognomy are of typical Duong Duong style as the heaviness of forms and emphasis on native characteristics are conspicuous. The female figures are easily distinguished by heavy, round breasts and attenuated waist, while the male figures wear a typical kind of double belt that fastens a knee-length lower garment. In addition to the sculpted friezes of the pedestal, the staircases are also well modelled and depict the scene of a royal entourage, depicting noblewomen riding a wagon pulled by the elephant. The females are shown in three-quarters profile, seated with legs folded gracefully. All of them are heavily bejewelled with different kinds of jewellery, like-lozenge-shaped pendant earrings, necklace and bangles, which symbolize their higher rank and royalty. Except for the ornaments, their upper bodies are uncovered and are shown wearing patterned and high-waisted skirt or sarong secured by decorated belts with a loop at the centre.

Conclusion

From what has been set out above, an opinion can be put forward that the creation of visual imageries of Buddhist goddesses in ancient Vietnam not only displays artistic interaction with India but also suggests the socio-religious inclination of the region towards the learning of the sacred text and its Vajrayanic affiliation, which added impetus to the expansion and growth of the cult of Buddhist goddess. On the whole, the iconography of the goddess as discussed in this paper does give an idea about the iconographic variations, style and workmanship, which bear a relationship to Indian art, as comparisons are frequently drawn between the similarities in the art forms of the Indian prototypes. In addition, analysis of the recurrent theme of female royal personages in the Duong Duong pedestals and inscriptional evidence, add a commentary on the patronage of the ruling dynasties and their underlying belief patterns which emphasised gynocentric thoughts and practices. Also, from the study, it has been deduced that Indianised Buddhist art and practices were inherited by the Indianised sites of Vietnam, including Champa and Oc Eo cultures, but not uniformly seen throughout the region.

This paper is based on my Doctoral research titled, 'Sculptures of Buddhist Goddesses in Eastern India: An Aesthetic and Iconographic Study (8th-12th century C.E.)', carried under the supervision of Dr. Savita Kumari, Assistant Professor, Department of History of Art, National Museum Institute, New Delhi, India.

REFERENCES

Chi, Dinh Minh, Ly Kim Hoa, Ha Thuc Minh et al., *The History of Buddhism in Vietnam.* edited by Nguyen Tai Thu, Hoang Thi Tho, Washington: Institute of Philosophy, Vietnamese Academy of Social Sciences; The Council for Research in Values and Philosophy, 2008.

Chutiwongs, Nandana, *The Iconography of Avalokiteshwara in the mainland South East Asia,* Delhi: Indira Gandhi National Center for the Arts & Aryan Books International, 2002.

Donaldson, Thomas Eugene, *The Iconography of the Buddhist Sculpture of Orissa,* 2 Vols. Delhi: IGNCA, Abhinav Publications, 2001.

Guillon, Emmanuel, *Cham Art,* London: Thames and Hudson, 2001.

Guy, John, "Introducing Early Southeast Asia", in *Lost Kingdom: Hindu-Buddhist sculpture of Early Southeast Asia,* edited by John Guy, 3-13. New York: The Metropolitan Museum of Art, 2014.

Hall, Kenneth R., *A History of Early Southeast Asia: Maritime Trade and Societal Development, 100-1500,* Lanham: Rowman and Littlefield Publishers, 2011.

Hubert, Jean Francois, *The Art of Champa,* USA: Parkstone Press International, 2005.

Le Bonheur, A., "The Art of Champa", in *The Art of Southeast Asia,* edited by M. Gerad-Geslan et al., New York: Harry N. Abrams, Inc, 1998.

Lien, Thi Le, "Hindu-Buddhist Sculptures in Southern Vietnam: Evolution of Icons and Styles to the Eight Century CE", in *Lost Kingdom: Hindu-Buddhist sculpture of Early Southeast Asia*, edited by John Guy, 118-129. New York: The Metropolitan Museum of Art, 2014.

Majumdar, R.C., *Champa: History and culture of an Indian colonial kingdom*, Delhi: Gyan Books Pvt. Ltd, 2008.

Manguin, Pierre-Yves, "The Archeology of Funan in the Mekong Delta: The Oc Eo Culture of Vietnam," in *Arts of Ancient Vietnam: From River Plain to Open Sea*, edited by Nancy Tingley, 103-115, Houston: Asia Society of Fine Arts, 2010.

Noppe, Catherine and Jean Francois Hubert, *Art of Vietnam*, USA: Parkstone Press International, 2003.

"Principal Kingdoms of Early Southeast Asia", in *Lost Kingdom: Hindu-Buddhist sculpture of Early Southeast Asia*, edited by John Guy, 14-21. New York: The Metropolitan Museum of Art.

Shaw, Miranda, *Buddhist Goddesses of India*, Delhi: Munshiram Manoharlal Publishers, 2006.

Tingley, Nancy, "Introduction," in *Arts of Ancient Vietnam: From River Plain to Open Sea*, edited by Nancy Tingley, 1-15, Houston: Asia Society of Fine Arts, 2010.

____, "Champa: Riverine Polities, Port of Call," in *Arts of Ancient Vietnam: From River Plain to Open Sea*, edited by Nancy Tingley, 179-192, Houston: Asia Society of Fine Arts.

PLATES

Plate 1: Tara, ca. ninth to tenth centuries, Duong Duong Style, Champa, Vietnam, Bronze, Height-1.20m, Da Nang Museum, Vietnam, Accession No. 535. KL103 (Photo courtesy: Da Nang Museum, Vietnam)

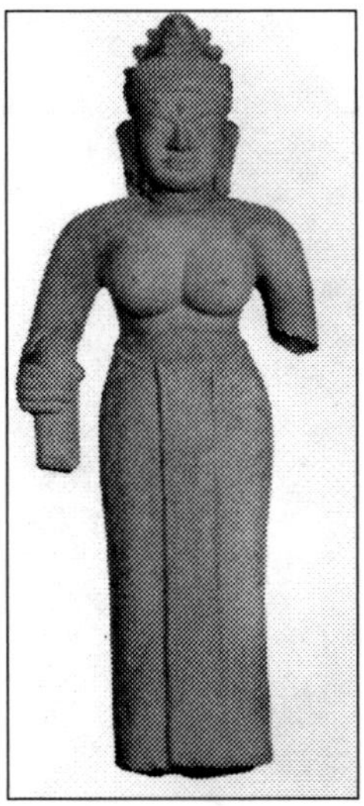

Plate 2: Tara, ca. ninth to tenth centuries, Duong Duong Style, Champa, Vietnam, Sandstone, 94 cm, Museìe Guimet, Paris (After Hubert, Jean-Francois. 2005: 39, Plate. 30.)

Plate 3: Standing *Prajnaparamita*, ca. ninth to tenth centuries, Duong Duong period, Champa, Vietnam, Sandstone, 89 cm, Musèle Guimet, Paris (After Hubert, Jean-Francois. 2005: 64, Plate. 55.)

Plate. 4: Arya Tara, ca. first half of eight century, Nalanda, Bihar, India, Pala period, Bronze, National Museum, Delhi, Accession No. 47.35 (Photo courtesy: National Museum, Delhi)

Plate 5: Standing Goddess, Probably Dhanada Tara, ca. ninth to tenth centuries, Duong Duong period, Champa, Vietnam, Stone, 74.7×23.5×23.5 cm (29 3/8 × 9 1/4 × 9 $^{1}/_{4}$ in.), Kate S. Buckingham Fund, 1999.248, Art Institute of Chicago (Photo Courtesy: Art Institute of Chicago, USA)

Plate 6: *Dhanada Tara*, ca. late seventh or early eighth century CE. Nalanda, Bihar, India, Pala period, Bronze, Nalanda Museum (Photo courtesy: Nalanda Museum, Archaeological Survey of India)

Plate 7: Standing Prajnaparamita, ca. ninth to tenth centuries, Duong Duong period, Champa, Vietnam, Sandstone, 88.5 cm, Museìe Guimet, Paris (After Hubert, Jean-Francois. 2005: 62, pl. 51.)

Plate 8: Standing Prajnaparamita, ca. ninth to tenth centuries, Duong Duong period, Champa, Vietnam, Sandstone, 96 cm, Da Nang Museum, Vietnam, (Photo courtesy: Da Nang Museum, Vietnam) (After Guillon, Emmanuel, 2001: 104, pl.57).

Plate 9: Prajnaparamita, ca. tenth century CE. Nalanda, Bihar, India, Pala period, Bronze, Nalanda Museum, Bihar, India. (Photo courtesy: Nalanda Museum, Archaeological Survey of India)

Plate 10: Prajnaparamita, ca. tenth century CE. Lalitgiri, Odisha, India, Bhaumakara period, Stone, Lalitgiri Museum, Odisha, India. (Photo courtesy: Lalitgiri Museum, Archaeological Survey of India)

Plate 11: Duong Duong Shrine Pedestal, ca. ninth to tenth centuries, Dong Duong Style, Champa, Vietnam, Stone Da Nang Museum, Vietnam (Photo courtesy: Da Nang Museum, Vietnam; Photographed by: Dr. Chedha Tingsanchali)

Plate 12: Duong Duong Vihara Pedestal, ca. ninth to tenth centuries, Dong Duong Style, Champa, Vietnam, Stone Da Nang Museum, Vietnam (Photo courtesy: Da Nang Museum, Vietnam; Photographed by: Dr. Chedha Tingsanchali)

Conclusion

Sonu Trivedi

The rhetoric of 'Look East Policy' in India, over the years has been transformed into action oriented 'Act East Policy' which reiterates focus on the extended neighbourhood in the Indo-Pacific. The 'Act East' policy was crystallised to underline the importance of East Asian neighbours of India and make them a priority in our foreign policy. It promises to inject new energy into India's engagement with Asia in the economic, political and security domains. "It has widened the canvas by drawing Australia into India's Eastern Strategy and the South Pacific back on Delhi's political radar".[1] In this most recent proposition to connect with the Southeast Asian neighbours by reiterating on historical and civilisational ties and engaging in defence and security cooperation, India has raised alarms for the rival powers in the neighbourhood. Given the history of United States' *realpolitik* of shifting alliances, priorities and commitments and its recent rebalancing strategy in the Asia-Pacific and the China's rising influence in the region, the Southeast Asian countries are welcoming greater Indian involvement in the regional architecture of Asia. In the changing architecture of world order, India's Act-East policy emerges as a significant factor shaping the 'Great Game' politics in the Asia Pacific.

Vietnam in India's Act East Policy

Given the cultural–religious linkages between the countries of India and Vietnam, based on their closer association with the historical kingdoms and the impact of Buddhist philosophy to the anti-imperialist struggle under colonial rule and foreign intervention during the Second World War and thereafter, both the countries have developed closer ties sharing a common destiny based on a shared world view. These have deepened the bond between the people of two countries. The year 2018 marks the 46th anniversary of the India–Vietnam diplomatic relations which began on 7th January 1972. Over the years, diplomatic ties between India and Vietnam have deepened, reinvigorating the age old partnership between the two countries.

Over the years, Vietnam has emerged as a significant player in India's foreign policy prescriptions – a partner in sub-regional, regional and multilateral fora. According to *Harish Parvathaneni, Indian Ambassador to Vietnam,* "Our Act East policy looks beyond the traditional paradigm and aims to forge alliances with our eastern neighbours to encompass security, strategic, political, counterterrorism, and defense collaboration in addition to economic ties. Vietnam is an integral member of ASEAN and plays an important role in our Act East policy".[2] The emerging contours of India-Vietnam relations have been guided by nuances of *realpolitik* and practice of diplomacy and geo-strategic concerns. Critical determinants guiding India-Vietnam relations could be studied from the lens of political security and strategic dimensions; trade and investment, energy cooperation; culture; commerce and connectivity.

From a strategic lens, Vietnam's geographical location in Asia pacific has added to its geo-political importance for the regional players like China, India, Australia and Japan and also for the external powers like the United States. It has become a vital element in the South China Sea dispute given the competing interests of the other claimants for the territories in this region. Vietnam's economic prosperity in recent times has added to its bargaining clout vis-à-vis the major regional powers and the United States to balance its relations with China and protecting its stakes in the South China Sea. In the background of such a geo-strategic matrix, it has been following tradeoff between China and the United States, thereby maximising strategic advantage.

Under this context of geo-strategic paradigm and the forces shaping the internal dynamics of Vietnam, its foreign policy orientations vis-à-vis the 'Great Powers' in the region and its engagement with India is a critical area of concern. In this regard, response of Vietnam in the context of emerging issues such as Belt Road Initiative (BRI) or the South China Sea (SCS) dispute becomes significant. In relation to the SCS dispute, India has demonstrated a principled stand that "states should resolve disputes through peaceful means without threat or use of force".[3] Furthermore, India's stand on BRI, the massive connectivity project initiated by China, and its official boycott for not being based on a 'consultative process' and infringing upon the sovereignty and territorial integrity of India has put Vietnam on a double edged sword.[4] On the one hand, it needs the support of India on the SCS dispute to retain its claim upon the disputed territories, and on the other, it just cannot isolate India on BRI by siding with China. Indicating his views on South China Sea dispute, the Foreign Minister of Vietnam during his visit to New Delhi in July 2017 said, "India and Vietnam share political and economic interests... As the future unfolds we have reason to be optimistic. ASEAN will benefit from India's experience of resolving maritime issues in a peaceful manner".[5] According to the Ambassador of Vietnam to India H.E. Ton Sinh Thanh, "the two countries enjoy a very good political relationship and strong security-defense cooperation... Vietnam and India are not only two reliable partners but also two brothers, willing to share almost all bilateral and multilateral issues, including the South China Sea".[6]

Given the *realpolitik* apprehensions, the Indian leadership has been more assertive about its role in the Indian Ocean region. According to Bharatiya Janata Party National General Secretary, Shri Ram Madhav,

> Geo-politics in the Indian Ocean region makes the possibility of the return of neo-Colonialism a reality with countries trying to dominate others through money, markets and military. India and Vietnam should jointly and independently work towards defeating all such tendencies and forces..... It is important for countries like India and Vietnam to come together to ensure that sovereignty, security and sentiments of all the countries are protected and maritime laws respected. Together and also by mobilising the support of other nations in the region we should strive to evolve a new Indian Ocean maritime order that ensures peace, stability, freedom of navigation and over-flights, and non-interference of outside powers in the affairs of the region.[7]

Nonetheless, there are several other areas of mutual concern for India and Vietnam – cooperation in oil and gas sector, information technology, education training, science and technology, defense and security and not to forget, the trade and commercial ties. Added to these, the already existing bilateral ties in the field of cultural, historical, non-traditional security issues and coordination in several regional and multi-lateral forums remain the core issue significantly shaping the emerging contours of India-Vietnam relations.

India–Vietnam Relations and Prime Minister Narendra Modi

Beginning from the visit of India's first Prime Minister Nehru in 1954 and Vietnam's first President Ho Chi Minh in 1958 to the September 2016 visit by the incumbent Prime Minister Narendra Modi, the two countries over the years have agreed "to contribute to regional peace, stability, cooperation and prosperity – elevating the 'Strategic Partnership' to 'Comprehensive Strategic Partnership', based on the excellent relations between the two countries".[8]

According to Prime Minister Narendra Modi,

> In India, we believe in sharing our knowledge, experiences and expertise with other developing countries. There can be no better example of this than in the success of our multifaceted bilateral cooperation with Vietnam over the last four decades..... As two partners, we must also take advantage of our synergies to jointly face emerging regional challenges, and to exploit new opportunities. It is a matter of great satisfaction that, we have now decided to upgrade our relationship to a 'Comprehensive Strategic Partnership'.... A strong India-Vietnam partnership would lead to prosperity, development, peace and stability for our people, and in the wider region. Vietnam is a strong pillar of India's Act East Policy. Our bilateral ties are based on strong mutual trust, and understanding, and convergence of views on various regional and international issues.[9]

The PM visited Vietnam in September 2016 on his way to China to attend the G-20 Summit. This visit was the first by an Indian Prime Minister in the last 15 years, apparently celebrating a decade of a strategic partnership between the two nations. This visit was a clear indication that "New Delhi was no longer hesitant to expand its presence in China's periphery", argues security expert Harsh V. Pant. According to him, "India under the Modi government has made no secret of its desire to play a more assertive role in the larger Indo-Pacific region. Modi himself has argued that India can be an anchor for peace, prosperity, and stability from Asia to Africa and from Indian Ocean to the Pacific. Therefore, a more ambitious outreach to Vietnam should not be surprising".[10]

The visit took place soon after the verdict of the tribunal at the Permanent Court of Arbitration at Hague on the dispute brought by the Philippines against China's claim on the 'Nine-Dash Line' in the South China Sea.[11] Although India is not a claimant in the South China Sea, the verdict had significant implications given India's geo-strategic and geo-economic interest in the region. In addition to its direct economic interests India is also engaged in oil exploration in the offshore waters claimed by Vietnam. It also has an interest in ensuring maritime security in the South China Sea – significant channel for India's trade with ASEAN countries as well as with Japan, Taiwan and South Korea.[12] Historically, through the South China Sea Indian civilisation had spread to the Eastern World. In this context, experts argue that "Modi's visit reaffirms India's position that it attaches importance to the protection of freedom of maritime navigation and the peaceful settlement of disputes in accordance with the United Nations Convention on the Law of the Sea (UNCLOS) and the decision of the International Tribunal Court on the South China Sea issued on 12 July 2016".[13]

During Prime Minister Modi's visit to Vietnam in 2016, altogether twelve agreements were signed between the two countries.[14] Besides boosting trade, economic and investment ties, agreements related to establishment of Software Parks and joint agreements in the field of health, defense and space cooperation were entered upon.[15] Opening up of Indian Cultural Centre at Hanoi and conservation and restoration work of the Cham monuments at My Son have been significant in deepening cultural and historical links between India and Vietnam. Prime Minister has also invited the Vietnamese companies to take advantage of the various schemes and flagship programmes of the Indian Government.[16] India has pledged to be Vietnam's 'partner and a friend' in its 'rapid development' and 'strong economic growth'.

India-Vietnam Engagements: SWOT Analysis

The elevation of the Strategic Partnership between the two countries to that of 'Comprehensive Strategic Partnership' is a clear indication of the goodwill, trust and importance the two countries place on their relationship. It is also an acknowledgment of the existing strong bilateral defense and security ties and our mutual desire to contribute to regional peace, stability, cooperation and prosperity. Moving beyond the ideological linkages, both countries have endeavoured to revamp their relations under the realities of world politics and subject to global and regional responses of the Great Powers in the Asia-Pacific.

The relationship covers a wide range of issues covering political, defense and security relations; trade and commerce; energy cooperation; science and technology; capacity building; connectivity links; health, education, culture, tourism and people to people exchange; and cooperation in international, regional and sub-regional forums. The partnership between the two countries is extremely vibrant and dynamic; however, to fully realise the potential of the Comprehensive Strategic Partnership a lot more has to be done. Both sides are committed to achieve the trade target of 15 billion USD by having greater trade and industry exchanges at the business and government levels and to remove all impediments to trade with a focus on priority areas identified by the leaders of the two countries. The two countries will benefit immensely by having direct flight and shipping connectivity. It is hoped that very soon, Vietjet would be starting direct flights to India.

Defence is an important component of India-Vietnam relationship and the PM announced a new Defence Line of Credit for Vietnam of US$500 million for facilitating deeper defense industry cooperation. The bilateral defence cooperation includes exchange of high level visits, annual high-level dialogues, service-to-service cooperation, naval ship visits, extensive training and capacity building, defence equipment procurement and related transfer of technology, and cooperation at regional fora such as ADMM-Plus. The banking and financial sector linkages are being enhanced for facilitating more intensive economic engagement. 2016 witnessed the opening of a branch of Bank of India in Ho Chi Minh City and it has also received its licence for international foreign exchange transactions. India is engaged in oil exploration in the offshore waters claimed by Vietnam.[17] The two countries have agreed to further enhance cooperation in the oil and gas sector and urged both sides to actively implement the Agreement signed in 2014 between PetroVietnam (PVN) and ONGC Videsh Limited (OVL) on cooperation in new blocks in Vietnam.[18] Vietnam has welcomed the long-standing investment and presence of OVL and its partnership with PVN for exploration of oil and gas in Vietnam. "Although the Indian company exited in 2012 by citing commercial reasons, many in Vietnam believed that Chinese pressure was behind the Indian decision". Nevertheless in its recent efforts, Prime Minister Modi has allowed Indian companies to go ahead in Vietnam "to explore oil in an area that China and Vietnam contest for sovereignty".[19] India has been actively involved in human resource development and capacity building in Vietnam in IT, English language training, entrepreneurship development, high-performance computing and other areas of Science and Technology. The two countries are also collaborating in Peaceful uses of Nuclear Technology, and a Framework Agreement on this was signed during the visit of Chairperson of National Assembly, Ms. Nguyen Thi Kim Ngan to India in December,

2016. Both countries are also collaborating on the Exploration of Outer Space for Peaceful Purposes and signed a Framework Agreement for it during the visit of Prime Minister Modi in 2016.

India and Vietnam further need to enhance people-to-people contact by promoting tourism and culture. There is a need for more cultural exchanges. The newly opened Indian Cultural Centre (ICC) in Hanoi would enable the people of Vietnam to get easy access to information on culture and tourism of India, and would also serve to showcase Indian culture and performing arts. Numerous scholarships under the Indian Technical and Economic Cooperation (ITEC) programme are offered to Vietnamese nationals. It is only with such a multi-pronged approach that we can actualise the Comprehensive Strategic Partnership between the two countries and harness the true potential for greatness of our countries and peoples.[20] Following section attempts a SWOT analysis of India-Vietnam relations based on the past, present and future engagements between the two countries (as elaborated in the previous chapters).

SWOT Analysis

Strengths	Weaknesses	Opportunities	Threats
Cultural linkages	Trade & commerce	Roads, Inland Waterways and Rail Network	Geo-strategic dimensions and maritime security related to South China Sea and the Malacca Dilemma
Historical and Religious convergences	Lack of entrepreneur-ship	Aviation Sector	Geo-political nuances in the region and the role of global and regional powers in the Indo-Pacific
Energy rich in both renewable and non-renewable sources	Limited Science & Technology exchange	Banking and Financial Sector	The China factor in India-Vietnam Relations
Natural Resources and sustainable development	Connectivity linkages	Energy Cooperation (Renewable and Non-renewable)	Both the countries face similar traditional rivalries in the maritime domain, disputed territories and the issues related to sovereignty and resource sharing.
Strategic and Comprehensive Partnership	Limited student and academic exchanges	Defence and military Engagements	Common non-traditional security threats are also being faced by both the countries – terrorism, cyber security, human trafficking, drugs, disease, climate change among others.
		Maritime Cooperation	

(*Contd.*)

Strengths	Weaknesses	Opportunities	Threats
		Humanitarian Assistance and Disaster Relief	
		Development Partnership and Capacity Building	
		Tourism and Cultural Exchange	
		Science and Technology Cooperation	
		Nuclear and Space Cooperation	
		Global and Regional Value Chains	

Strategies for Promoting International Position of India and Vietnam

The strategic contours of India-Vietnam relations in the present context have been largely shaped by the external power dynamics; role of regional powers; and the internal synergies between both the countries. Strategies for promoting international position of India and Vietnam could therefore be understood through the prism of global and regional powers and their emerging role in the Indo-Pacific.

Given the changing dynamics of World Politics, an analysis of the role of Global Powers and their responses towards the Asia-Pacific region, particularly United States (Under Trump Presidency) becomes significant. As Vietnam faces mounting pressure from China amidst its growing assertiveness in the disputed waters of South China Sea, it is looking to multiple partners in Asia and beyond. Vietnam has reached out to the United States and stepped up security cooperation with Japan, Australia and a number of its Southeast Asian neighbours.[21]

The visit of the Prime Minister of Vietnam Nguyen Xuan Phuc to White House in May 2017 has set an ambitious agenda for Vietnam–US relations. Meeting of both the leaders was in the spotlight due to the uncertainty surrounding the Trump administration's policy toward the Asia Pacific. To add further, the visit of US President Trump to attend APEC Summit at Danang in November 2017, demonstrates the Trump administration's emphasis on the importance of its relationship with Vietnam. President Trump becomes the first US President to visit to Vietnam in their first year in office and it also reiterates the message to US allies and other countries in the region that the 'United States is not pivoting away'.[22] It further signals that "Trump administration's engagement of the sub-region remains an early priority and that it continues to place an importance in cultivating Vietnam as an emerging partner in the region".[23]

While designing strategies for promoting international position of both India and Vietnam, role of regional powers, particularly in response to aggressive and assertive China also becomes significant. Vietnam shares a very significant relationship with Japan under the paradigm of 'multilateralisation and diversification' of its evolving foreign policy initiatives.[24] It is noteworthy to remember that the bilateral relationship was upgraded to an 'Extensive Strategic Partnership for Peace and Prosperity in Asia' in 2014 by the two head of the States. Japan being largest donor, an important trading partner and investor in Vietnam enjoys a strategic position in its foreign policy establishments and thereby securing its stake in the region. Japan and Vietnam have been boosting their defense ties as part of their broader extensive strategic partnership over the past few years.[25] Growing Japanese maritime security assistance to Vietnam such as naval drills, closer coast guard cooperation, as well as humanitarian assistance and disaster relief and facilitating Japanese ports have been highlights of this deepening partnership between the two countries.[26]

The bilateral links between Australia and Vietnam have developed significantly and has matured into an Enhanced Comprehensive Partnership. Key pillars of relationship between the two countries have been grounded in "shared strategic interests in maintaining peace and stability in the region; a trading relationship which has been Australia's fastest-growing among the larger ASEAN economies in recent years; enduring educational links; and Vietnam's recognition of Australia's role as a constructive and generous aid donor".[27] The relationship reflects upon diverse bilateral issues, encompassing wide ranging cooperation on political issues, trade and investment, defence and security, policing, immigration, combating transnational crime and human trafficking. Over the years, this relationship has matured into one of the most important in the region – a substantive, positive and mutually beneficial economic, political and security relationship, reinforced by warm and expanding people-to-people links.[28]

India has also been of very special strategic interest to Vietnam. Over the years, New Delhi has gradually expanded its defence and naval cooperation with Vietnam and assisted in its urgent effort at modernising the military force.[29] India's outreach to Vietnam has been a clear indication of its open challenge to China in its own backyard. "A more engaged India will also lead to a more stable balance of power in the region".[30] Fearing the growing aggression of China, Vietnam has welcomed and embraced India in this particular stance. The high-level comprehensive strategic partnership between India and Vietnam is equally important as it shares the worries about increasing Chinese presence in the region. "Vietnam regards naval activity by larger nations like India and the US in the area as a useful deterrent against China".[31] According to security experts, since China continues to increase its influence, defence and maritime cooperation and procurements from countries like India, the United States and Japan enables Vietnam to uphold its position.

Historical, religious and cultural linkages; political and economic cooperation between the two countries; and international cooperation at the sub-regional, regional and multilateral forums have also played a significant role in bringing the two countries on the same page building upon mutual trust and cooperation over the years. Given the internal synergies between India and Vietnam and external responses of the Great Powers, certain key strategies may be evolved for promoting the international position of India and Vietnam in the process regionlisation and globalisation. Vietnam has been a significant leg in augmenting India's Act East Policy. It is looked by India as its entry point for establishing presence in the South China Sea. For Vietnam, India remains a trusted and reliable partner and a balancer in the context of 'Great Power' strategy in the Indo-Pacific.

Regional Strategic partnerships are critical in the context of changing geo-politics of the Indo-Pacific. Vietnam's growing closeness with Japan can also create opportunities for a potential trilateral agreement between India, Vietnam, and Japan for shaping the power politics in the region. In the background of Vietnam's robust relationship with the United States in recent times (turnaround after the Vietnam War) and the geo-political realities in the Asia-Pacific, it calls for trilateral engagements between India, Vietnam and United States. For exploring the opportunities for greater collaboration between the United States, Japan and Vietnam, possibilities for a trilateral cooperation between the three countries have also been making rounds in various security establishments in the United States. Given the evolving comprehensive strategic ties between Vietnam and Australia and the already existing comprehensive partnership with India, to expand the relations further in a mutually beneficial way, prospects of Vietnam-Australia-India trilateral cooperation may be potentially explored. Amidst the emerging Asian geo-politics, quadrilateral partnership among India-Japan-Australia-United States is also being talked about. This emerging partnership must engage with all the Member States of ASEAN with Vietnam playing a leading role.

India's Asian strategy aims at engaging with all major Asian powers including China, at the same time not allowing it to define the limits of India's partnership with other countries like Japan and Vietnam. Economic convergences between India and Vietnam aims at enhanced trade and investment and seek collaborations in new business opportunities. Procurement of defence and military equipments by Vietnam apparently shows its desire to play a more assertive role in the larger Indo-Pacific region. Knowing the multiple stakeholders and power politics in the region, the rivalry in the Indo-pacific may aptly be summarized as 'the return of neo-Colonialism a reality'.[32] Under this assumption of twenty-first century 'neo-colonialism', both India and Vietnam must endeavour to engage at bilateral and multilateral fora with likeminded powers to expand its growing influence in the region respecting rules of international law of – territorial sovereignty, Law of the Seas, supporting regional security architecture, maintaining peace and stability in the region, promoting confidence building measures, and minimizing the risk of conflict in the region thereby keeping any possibilities of any direct confrontation and rivalry at bay.

NOTES

1. Rajamohan, *Modi's World: Expanding India's Sphere of Influence,* Harper Collins, 2015
2. *Ambassador Harish Parvathaneni*, "Vietnam a key pillar of India's Act East Policy," Interview by *Vietnam News Agency,* January 8, 2017, Online edition, http://english.vietnam net.vn/fms/government/170805/vietnam-a-key-pillar-of-india-s-act-east-policy.html. (accessed on 20 October 2017).
3. Ministry of External Affairs, "Statement on Award of Arbitral Tribunal on South China Sea Under Annexure VII of UNCLOS", *Press Release,* July 12, 2016. Online edition, http://www.mea.gov.in/pressreleases.htm?dtl/27019/Statement+on+Award+of+Arbitral+Tribunal+on+South+China+Sea+Under+Annexure+VII+of+UNCLOS. (accessed on 31 October 2017).
4. Ministry of External Affairs, "Official Spokesperson's response to a query on participation of India in OBOR/BRI Forum", *Media Briefings,* May 13, 2017. Online edition, http://mea.gov.in/mediabriefings.htm?dtl/28463/Official+Spokespersons+response+ to+ a+ query+on+participation+of+India+in+OBORBRI+Forum. (accessed on 30 October 2017).
5. "Vietnam for Greater Indian Role in SE Asia," *The Hindu,* July 4, 2017, Online edition, http://www.thehindu.com/news/national/vietnam-asks-india-to-play-security-role-in-south-china-sea/article19210720.ece. (accessed on 31 July 2017).

6. Ton Sinh Tanh. Speech at the International Conference on Emerging Horizons in India Vietnam Relations, 3-4 July, 2017.
7. Ram Madhav, Inaugural Address at the International Conference on *Emerging Horizons in India Vietnam Relations*, 3-4 July, 2017.
8. Ministry of External Affairs, "India-Vietnam Relations," 2017, Online edition, http://www.mea.gov.in/Portal/ForeignRelation/Vietnam_May_2017.pdf. (accessed on 23 October 2017).
9. Excerpts from the Prime Minister's Banquet Speech at the reception in Hanoi during his visit to Vietnam on 3rd September 2016, Online edition, http://www.narendramodi.in/text-of-banquet-speech-by-prime-minister-during-his-visit-to-vietnam-september-03-2016—522168. (accessed on 30 October 2017).
10. Harsh Pant, "India-Vietnam Relations: Beyond the Brahmos Connection," *The Diplomat*, 2017, Online edition, https://thediplomat.com/2017/08/the-india-vietnam-relationship-beyond-the-brahmos-connection/. (accessed on 31 October 2017).
11. L.T. Hang Nga, "India–Vietnam Relations since September 2016," *China Report 53*, no. 3 (2017): 400.
12. bid.
13. Rajaram Panda, *Vietnam–India: 45 Years of Diplomatic Relations and 10 Years of Strategic Partnership* (Hanoi: Ho Chi Minh National Political Publishing House, 2017), 47–48.
14. "Narendra Modi seals defence cooperation with Vietnam, signs new credit line of $500 million," *Indian Express*, September 3, 2016, Online edition, http://indianexpress.com/article/india/india-news-india/pm-narendra-modi-vietnam-visit-agreements-signed-3011170/. (accessed on 31 October 2017).
15. The following Agreements were signed in the presence of the two Prime Ministers:
    1. Framework Agreement on Cooperation in the Exploration and Uses of Outer Space for Peaceful Purposes;
    2. Protocol for Amending the Agreement on Avoiding Double Taxation;
    3. Program of Cooperation in UN Peacekeeping Matters;
    4. Protocol between the Ministry of Foreign Affairs of Vietnam and the Ministry of External Affairs of India on Celebrating 2017 as the "Year of Friendship";
    5. MOU on Health Cooperation;
    6. MOU on Cooperation in Information Technology;
    7. MOU on Cooperation between the Vietnam Academy of Social Sciences and the Indian Council of World Affairs;
    8. MOU on cooperation in Cyber Security;
    9. MOU between the Bureau of Indian Standards and Directorate for Standard, Metrology and Quality for Cooperation in the Fields of Standardization and Conformity Assessment;
    10. MOU on Establishment of the Centre of Excellence in Software Development and Training;
    11. Technical Agreement on Sharing of White Shipping Information;
    12. Contract for Offshore High-speed Patrol Boats.
16. Joint Press Statement by Prime Minister Narendra Modi at Hanoi, 3rd September 2016. Online edition. Accessed on 31 October 2017. http://www.narendramodi.in/pm-modi-at-the-joint-press-statement-in-hanoi-vietnam-522149
17. Hang Nga, "India–Vietnam Relations since September 2016," 400.
18. Joint Press Statement by Prime Minister Narendra Modi at Hanoi, 3rd September 2016.
19. Chintamani Mahapatra, "India and Shifting Power Equations in the Indo-Pacific," *Indian Foreign Affairs Journal* 12, (April-June 2017):111-118.

20. *Ambassador Harish Parvathaneni,* "Vietnam a key pillar of India's Act East Policy," http://english.vietnamnet.vn/fms/government/170805/vietnam-a-key-pillar-of-india-s-act-east-policy.html.
21. Rajamohan, *Modi's World,* 2015.
22. Prashanth Parameswaran, "US-Vietnam Ties Under Trump in the Spotlight with Premier's Visit," *The Diplomat,* May 2017. Online edition, https://thediplomat.com/2017/05/us-vietnam-ties-under-trump-in-the-spotlight-with-premiers-visit/. (accessed on 31 October 2017).
23. *Hai Hong Nguyen,* "Vietnam to pull the US back to Asia?," *East Asia Forum*, July, 2017, Online edition. http://www.eastasiaforum.org/2017/07/07/vietnam-to-pull-the-us-back-to-asia/. (accessed on 31 October 2017).
24. Sanjay Pulipaka, "India and Vietnam: Time for Trilaterals with the US and Japan," *The Diplomat,* 2016, Online edition. https://thediplomat.com/2016/09/india-and-vietnam-time-for-trilaterals-with-the-us-and-japan/. (accessed on 31 October 2017).
25. Prashanth Parameswaran, "What's Next for Japan-Vietnam Defense Ties?," *The Diplomat,* 2017. https://thediplomat.com/2017/11/whats-next-for-japan-vietnam-defense-ties/.
26. Prashanth Parameswaran, "The Future of US-Japan-Vietnam Trilateral Cooperation," *The Diplomat,* 2015, https://thediplomat.com/2015/06/the-future-of-us-japan-vietnam-trilateral-cooperation/.
27. DFAT, *Vietnam Country Brief,* Online edition, http://dfat.gov.au/geo/vietnam/Pages/vietnam-country-brief.aspx. (accessed on 25 October 2017).
28. DFAT, *A Declaration on Enhancing the Australia-Viet Nam Comprehensive Partnership*, March 18, 2015, Online edition, http://dfat.gov.au/geo/vietnam/Pages/a-declaration-on-enhancing-the-australia-viet-nam-comprehensive-partnership.aspx. (accessed on 31 October 2017).
29. Rajamohan, *Modi's World,* 2015.
30. Harsh Pant, "India-Vietnam Relations: Beyond the Brahmos Connection," 2017.
31. Helen Clark, "Vietnam and India: Shared interests in the South China Sea," 2017, Online edition, https://www.lowyinstitute.org/the-interpreter/vietnam-and-india-s-shared-interests-south-china-sea. (accessed on 31 October 2017).
32. Ram Madhav, Inaugural Address at the International Conference on *Emerging Horizons in India Vietnam Relations*, 3-4 July, 2017.

Index